D1171345

TAKING CONTROL

POLITICS IN THE INFORMATION AGE

**MORLEY WINOGRAD
AND DUDLEY BUFFA**

☆ ☆ ☆ ☆ ☆ ☆ ☆ ☆ ☆ ☆ ☆ ☆

A JOHN MACRAE BOOK

HENRY HOLT AND COMPANY ▪ NEW YORK

Henry Holt and Company, Inc.
Publishers since 1866
115 West 18th Street
New York, New York 10011

Henry Holt® is a registered trademark of
Henry Holt and Company, Inc.

Library of Congress Cataloging-in-Publication Data
Winograd, Morley.
Taking control: Politics in the information age /
Morley Winograd and Dudley Buffa.
"A John Macrae book."
Includes bibliographical references and index.
1. United States—politics and government—1993–
2. Information society—United States.   3. United States—
Social policy—1993–   4. United States—Economic policy—
1993–   I. Buffa, Dudley W.   II. Title.
JK271.W656   1996   95-46891
320.973′09′049—dc20   CIP

ISBN 0-8050-4489-2

Henry Holt books are available for special promotions and
premiums. For details contact: Director, Special Markets.

First Edition—1996

Designed by Victoria Hartman

Printed in the United States of America
All first editions are printed on acid-free paper. ∞
10 9 8 7 6 5 4 3 2 1

In memory of Bernie Ryan, John Dewan,
and Sam Fishman—their Irish doubt
and Jewish skepticism educated us both.

· CONTENTS ·

TAKING CONTROL

POLITICS IN THE INFORMATION AGE

When the twentieth century began, most Americans worked as either farmers or domestic servants. As the century comes to a close, less than 3 percent of the population is engaged in those occupations. By mid-century the assembly line had replaced the home and the farm as the principle place of employment: in 1950, nearly three out of every four workers were engaged in manufacturing or production enterprises. The most rapid transformation of a nation's workforce in history made America the leading industrial power in the world. Forty-five years later, the United States is in the midst of another transformation, this one even more rapid and more profound than the last. Less than 15 percent of Americans now work in factories; far more work in offices creating ideas and knowledge. By the year 2000, 44 percent of all workers will be gathering, processing, retrieving, or analyzing information, as new technology once again transforms the workforce.[1]

This new information age is not only changing the way we work and the way we live, it will soon change the way we are governed. In the industrial age, the emergence of large concentrations of private power brought about a new political imperative. The enormous monopolies created were, in Woodrow Wilson's words, run by a "few dominant men," whose greed and power made it necessary to protect others who could no longer protect themselves. Once a majority of Americans believed that government had to regulate business in the public interest, a new social contract for the industrial age was born. Labor and capital became not only the two components of economic wealth, but the two major constituencies that divided American politics.

The industrial age, built on the technology of the internal combustion engine, is now being replaced by an age built on the technologies of the computer and other devices for encoding and analyzing information. Members of the old class of industrial workers who earned their livelihood doing repetitive physical labor that often seemed to make them appendages to the machines they worked were drawn to FDR's New Deal; they became the cornerstone of the Democratic coalition that dominated American politics for more than a half century. Today there is an emerging class, known as knowledge workers, who earn their living by sharing information and solving problems, usually within an organizational setting.[2] Team members and groups of teams focus on achieving specific outcomes in what appear to be spontaneous ways, frequently with no more instruction from outside authority than a clear statement of the goals to be accomplished and the process to be followed.[3] These self-governing teams of knowledge workers serve as the organizational model of the information age, creating values and metaphors for Americans that are light-years removed from Henry Ford's assembly line and the pyramidal organization Alfred Sloan created at General Motors. This new constituency has not yet promised its loyalties to any political party. Instead, it is waiting for political leaders who will offer a new direction for a new age.

In the information age, it is neither labor nor capital, nor their combination, that is crucial to economic success; knowledge is the key ingredient. In the public and private sectors, the measure of efficiency is no longer the size of the organization, but the speed with which information is transferred from those who have it to those who need it. Learning and innovation determine the success of the enterprise. New information technologies have virtually eliminated time and distance and, in the process, have almost abolished national boundaries as barriers to the movement of goods and ideas. Old-style institutions dependent upon the assumptions of the industrial age are struggling to survive, while well-managed, nonhierarchic organizations designed to thrive in the new environment are already achieving astonishing rates of growth.

The original ENIAC computer, built in 1944, occupied more space than an eighteen-wheeler tractor trailer, weighed more than seventeen cars, consumed 140,000 watts of electricity, and executed 5,000 basic arithmetic operations per second.[4] Advances in computing technology—most notably IBM's 360 series, introduced in the mid-sixties—rapidly improved performance levels, but each mainframe still had to be housed in a specially constructed air-conditioned facility whose access was restricted to highly trained personnel. After the invention of the microchip in 1971, the economic game began to change. Today, the video camera, for example, has more processing power than the IBM 360 mainframe did,[5] while a digital wristwatch contains more computing power than existed in the entire world before 1961.[6] An Intel 486 microprocessor, the size of a dime, uses fewer than two watts of electricity and can execute up to 54 million instructions per second.[7] Computers are ahead of the curve; had the same rate of progress occurred in automobile technology, "Today," as Randy Tobias, former vice chairman of AT&T, observed, "you could buy a Lexus for about $2. It would travel at the speed of sound and go about 600 miles on a thimble of gas."[8]

In 1990, 875 million fax messages were sent from the United States to foreign countries. By late 1995 that volume had increased to over 2.2 billion. Since 1987, 26 million people have obtained an E-mail address; 800 million people worldwide are expected to have one by the year 2000.[9] Bill Clinton receives 20,000 messages a day, compared to only

8,000 sent daily to George Bush. Ten percent of these arrive via an electronic format.[10] It is just the beginning. Though information and speed of delivery are not the same as judgment and knowledge, they enhance the process of creating ideas.

By the year 2000, fiber optic transmission systems will be able to send one terabit of information per second; medical decisions will be made by video consultation between patient, doctor, specialist, and technicians, no matter what city, state, or country any or all of them may be in. Teachers will communicate across an entire school system, or even across the world, on video monitors that will become the student desk. The lecture will be only one part of the lesson; the rest will be customized to the level of learning of the individual student and presented on his or her monitor.[11]

Despite the promise of the information age, a great unease grips the country; the problems of middle-income Americans often seem insurmountable. In the early 1990s Kevin Phillips noted that "for America's two or three hundred thousand somewhat rich or genuinely rich families, combined taxes as a share of income were probably at their lowest point in more than sixty years, whereas for middle-class families, combined federal, state and local taxes took a higher portion of income than ever before and were rising steadily."[12] The middle class was paying more and more for a government that did less and less, and it wasn't as if they could afford it. Unless they were among the fortunate few in the top 1 percent of the population, Americans were working longer hours and making less than they had ten years earlier. And the trend continued to worsen. Between March 1994 and March 1995, median family income fell a precipitous 2.3 percent, the largest decline since 1987.[13] Job security became a thing of the past. The number of temporary, self-employed, part-time, and consultant workers in the United States soared by 57 percent over what it had been in 1980. In 1991, nearly one in three Americans had been working for his or her current employer less than a year; two in three had done so for less than five years. Continuous learning may be the key to continuing employment in the information age, but many people have found that the only way to learn and to earn was to change jobs or even careers.[14]

The use of information age technologies in the private sector had reversed the industrial age assumption that quality always costs more. On the other hand, the continued reliance on enormous public bureaucracies only accelerated the decline in public services. Government could no longer pretend it was capable of adequately protecting the health and safety of the public. Between 33 and 39 million Americans had no health insurance coverage of any sort, and those who did were paying between eight and nine times what the same coverage had cost in 1980.[15] Americans were also at greater risk of falling victim to physical violence than ever before. In 1948 there were 3.32 police officers for every crime committed; by 1989 the ratio was reversed, with 3.1 violent crimes committed for every police officer.[16] Not only was crime—especially violent crime—increasing nationwide, but America was becoming two different nations in terms of the protection offered its citizens. In the mid-seventies, nearly $30 billion were spent by government at every level for police—twice that expended on private security. By the early 1990s, that ratio was reversed as well; for every tax dollar spent on police protection, citizens spent two dollars to protect themselves.[17] In a growing number of American neighborhoods, no one felt safe.

The problems that confront America as it moves into the information age cannot be solved with solutions formulated during the industrial age, a lesson that has yet to be learned by the two major political parties. Race and gender have become the dominant considerations in policy decisions within the Democratic party. Because African Americans are the most reliable voting bloc, issues such as affirmative action and quotas are decided on the basis of their effect on the black vote regardless of economic implications. Though more women are motivated to vote based on economic concerns than on the issue of reproductive rights, the involvement of pro-choice activists within the party means that the abortion issue will be used to maintain the supposedly favorable "gender gap." Without any clear vision of the information age to sustain them, Democrats are left with an economic policy that is little more than a hollow echo of industrial age class warfare.

Despite its victory in the 1994 election, the Republican party has a similar problem. The pro-life movement, with its base among conservative Roman Catholic and evangelical Christians, has been successful in making abortion a litmus test for aspiring presidential candidates. The religious right's unity and narrow focus, which have mobilized grass-roots activists in numbers disproportionate to its power to elect candidates, continues to hold most Republican politicians hostage to positions of the right. The closest vote on the Republicans' Contract with America, for example, occurred when religious groups threatened to withhold support for the welfare reform bill, jeopardizing "thirty or more votes" in the House. Speaker Newt Gingrich had to promise that the proposed 1995 $500 tax credit would apply to almost all families before the Christian Coalition would agree to leave school prayer, abortion, and other "powerfully divisive issues" out of the Contract. Despite the size of the budget cuts required to keep the commitment and still balance the budget, Gingrich kept his word. He knew that if he did not, it would cost him the support of a powerful group whose only voting allegiance was to its religious constituencies.[18]

Both sides, right and left, demonstrate less understanding of the new economy than do those who work in it daily. The belief that tax cuts and balanced budgets will bring economic prosperity to America has been repeated over and over again, like some New Age chant, ever since it was first enunciated by Ronald Reagan during the 1980 presidential campaign. It has never convinced the majority of those who are now actively engaged in the knowledge economy; nor have they been persuaded by the Democratic claim that increased government spending and the redistribution of income will achieve both fairness and prosperity. What knowledge workers do believe is that the information age requires nothing so much as a renewed dedication to the fundamental importance of learning.

While Democrats and Republicans wait for a return of the clarity that once marked the political divisions of the industrial age, a growing majority of Americans wait impatiently for political leadership capable of coming to grips with the age *they* have already entered. This new age, like the industrial age before it, is driven by a technology that creates new sources of wealth and thus new sources of power. Though the microprocessor creates fresh opportunities for citizens to take control over their own lives, it challenges America to create a democratic system of governance capable of adapting to a rapidly changing world. The country's success in responding to this challenge will not be determined by any computer, no matter how well programmed. It will be decided by the political choices Americans make in the next decade. If technology is to be put in the service of the public interest, and not the other way around, a new set of public policies is needed that will be nothing less than a social contract for the information age.

1

THE DEATH OF
INDUSTRIAL AGE POLITICS

N o one had ever seen anything like it before: just above a palm-lined street in Baghdad a cruise missile suddenly appeared, made an abrupt turn to the left, and then vanished from view. Where it would strike, and when it would strike, was left to the imagination. The Gulf War was being waged in front of everyone who owned a television and chose to watch. And they could watch it in a way that no one, not even a combatant, had ever been able to do. The missiles that were raining down on Baghdad broadcast pictures of their own. All over the world, in the security of their homes and offices, men and women looked on, awestruck, as one missile after another closed in on its target until, just a few yards before detonation, the screen went blank. Some of those who watched were reminded of video games; others were reminded of the movie *Star Wars*. War, which had once been considered an art, even if the most brutal one, appeared now to be a science.

War had also become a strange new form of entertainment. CNN, which carried the war from the first moments of the attack on Baghdad, almost monopolized the television audience—no one seemed to watch anything else. Americans had been exposed to devastating pictures of the war in Vietnam, but those scenes had always been of events that had already taken place. The Gulf War was completely different. It was *now*. The same technology that had revolutionized communications had changed the face of war. The news had become instantaneous and, for the first time, available on every TV in the world.

It was over almost as soon as it began. The Iraqi army, the third largest in the world, was a relic of the industrial age, organized under a strict hierarchy of control. The generals at the top were the only ones who knew what to do and how to do it, so orders had to be transmitted from the top down through each level of the military organization. When the United States and its allies launched the first strike, it was directed not at the 4,500 tanks waiting in the desert for orders from Baghdad, but at the communications systems connecting the Iraqi command structure with its troops in the field.[1] Once their fiber optic cables were severed, the Iraqi army became a headless hulk wandering aimlessly in the desert.

The Gulf War demonstrated, as perhaps nothing else could have, the enormous transformation that was beginning to take place as the industrial age came to an end. The Iraqi army, which had fought Iran to a standstill in years of conventional warfare, capitulated in a matter of days. There had not been anything quite like it since the Polish cavalry began its famous charge against a German Panzer division at the beginning of the Second World War. In each case defeat and disaster had been the fate of those in command who failed to understand that a significant new technology had changed the rules.

The political consequences of the war were almost as dramatic as the war itself. Three months earlier, just a week before the midterm elections of 1990, a *New York Times*/CBS poll had disclosed the worst possible news for an incumbent administration—two thirds of the American people thought the economy was in serious trouble. Nearly three fifths claimed it was difficult to make ends meet. This discontent, however, was not limited to economics. Fifty-nine percent of those polled were convinced the country was heading in the wrong direction, for which nearly all blamed Washington. An astonishing 77 percent insisted that government was run for the benefit of a privileged few.[2]

Days after his triumph in the Gulf, George Bush received an approval rating of 91 percent; suddenly he seemed invincible. Two months later, his approval rating was 78 percent, and his reelection to another four-year term was considered a foregone conclusion on its way to becoming a mere formality.[3] Every Democrat who had been considered a serious candidate for the party's nomination found an excuse not to run. Bill Clinton confided privately that the only real advantage in becoming a candidate in 1992 was to have a better chance of winning in 1996.

Whatever Clinton thought about his own chances after the Gulf War ended, he had learned the basic political lessons of the information age long before it ever began. Al From, a longtime Washington insider, had organized the Democratic Leadership Council after the 1984 rout of Walter Mondale for the express purpose of moving the Democratic party away from the discredited liberal policies of the past. On November 3, 1989, he wrote a memo to his key senatorial supporters outlining a plan to run a different kind of Democrat for president in 1992, along with a new set of ideals and a new commitment to middle-class values. Phase one of the plan was completed when Governor Clinton and other Democratic leaders gathered in New Orleans for their annual meeting and signed the DLC's declaration of values and beliefs. Now the DLC needed a platform and a candidate. On December 6, 1990, along with a hundred elected officials, lobbyists, and contributors to the DLC, Clinton listened as four speakers analyzed the recent election results and tried to explain to the DLC what Democrats would have to do to win the next presidential campaign.[4]

Democrats had been repeatedly denied the White House, they were told, because the party spent too much time talking about the problems of the poor and the disenfranchised.

Democrats had become so preoccupied with the removal of every conceivable form of inequality that they had destroyed their identification with the aspirations of working Americans. Nor could Democrats hope to win by trying to convince the country that government would be more effective if power were no longer divided between the parties. For thirty years voters had consistently sent Democratic majorities to Congress and, for the last twenty-two years, elected as president either Republicans or, in the case of Jimmy Carter, someone who promised fiscal responsibility and swore hostility to Washington. Voters persisted in doing what politicians of both parties dismissed in public as unfortunate and derided in private as the fickle and obtuse nature of the American populace.

What politicians thought irrational, however, was just the opposite. "What voters get by having Democrats control Congress and Republicans control the White House," one of the speakers explained, "is government programs without increases in bureaucracy. They get effective control over increases in taxes without any decrease in entitlement benefits. In effect, they get the kind of service from government that they want, at the price they want to pay." The electorate was not schizophrenic; it had, in fact, "been speaking very clearly and rationally for some time."

Still caught in the categories that defined and divided liberal and conservative, politicians were mystified by an electorate that no longer felt a strong allegiance to either. Moreover, the electorate itself, dissatisfied with the whole "tenor and tone of politics and politicians,"[5] as pollster Peter Hart had found, was changing in fundamental ways. Nothing like it had happened in America since the steam engine began the process by which the agrarian was replaced by the industrial age. New technologies based on the principles of quantum mechanics—principles that in turn had made possible the understanding of atomic physics—had transformed the economic and social structure of the country. More than any other discovery or invention, the microchip changed not only America, but the world. Computers, fax machines, high-speed communication—indeed, the whole bewildering array of new technologies—had altered the way America worked and, more important, the way Americans thought. It had also created a new class of voters.

One of the speakers told Clinton and the other members of the DLC that this new class was unlike any other. It had no clear economic or social interests that could be arranged neatly along the old left–right continuum. It fit none of the time-worn categories of the industrial age. Membership in the new class was made up, in the words of Peter Drucker, of "knowledge workers"—"neither farmer nor labor nor business." Instead, these people were "employees of organizations" that might be corporate structures but could just as easily be public bureaucracies or religious or charitable institutions. They were not like blue-collar workers, who had once formed unions and supported government programs of redistribution. They were not like white-collar workers, who identified with management and tended to vote Republican. Information age employees "have no specific economic or social culture, and very little identification by way of issues."[6]

There was something else about this new class that immediately caught the attention of everyone in the room: this new class of knowledge workers, according to Drucker, would become the *new majority*.[7] "Even where outnumbered by other groups, knowledge workers will give the emerging knowledge society its character, its leadership, its social profile."[8] Middle class in economic status, the class nevertheless differed from the rest of the middle class in values and beliefs. This emerging new majority in American politics was just waiting for someone with the intelligence, or at least the cunning, to recognize its existence and attract its support.

▪ ▪ ▪

There weeks after he announced his presidential candidacy, Bill Clinton delivered a speech at Georgetown University that was portrayed as an attempt to explain the plight of the entire middle class and bring it back to the Democratic party. Forgotten by Washington, members of the middle class had "watched their economic interests ignored and their values run into the ground." It was not in Washington, but "in your hometown and mine" that "people have lost faith in the ability of government to change their lives for the better. Out there, you can hear the quiet, troubled voice of the forgotten middle class, lamenting that government no longer looks out for their interests or honors their values—like individual responsibility, hard work, family, community."[9]

Those who blamed the special interests or the bureaucracy alone were, according to Clinton, simply playing the old political game. Out there in America, everyone knew what was occurring. Bureaucracy was taking tax dollars from the middle class, while special interests were not paying their fair share. "They think their government takes more from them than it gives back and looks the other way when special interests only take from this country and give nothing back," Clinton continued, his speech sounding in tone remarkably like the sort of populist attack on special privileges and government for the few that southern Democrats had made for generations. Clinton, however, did not want to restrict government; he wanted to reinvent it. He promised a "New Covenant" that would change not just what government *did* but, more importantly, the way government *worked.* "People don't want some top-down bureaucracy telling them what to do anymore," he said. Government would become more efficient, " . . . and more effective, [by] giving people more choices in the services they get, [and by] empowering them to make those choices."[10]

Clinton had become the first candidate with an information age message. It was no longer about choosing between more government and less, between more bureaucracy and more freedom, or between government regulation and lower taxes. Government could be redesigned to obtain better results at less cost—government, in other words, could begin to do more with less. Clinton did not mention that the private sector was already doing this. He didn't have to. Every employee who had worked in a company that had survived the downsizing of the late 1980s and early 1990s understood that the old bureaucratic structures had to be replaced with new information networks. Every consumer who had paid even passing attention to goings-on in the marketplace had learned that the relationship between quality and price had been turned on its head. From automobiles to computers, price was going down as quality was going up.

His New Covenant speech gave Clinton the start he needed. Between November 1991, just weeks after the Georgetown speech, and January 1992, support in New Hampshire for his candidacy almost quintupled, moving from barely 5 to more than 23 percent.[11] Suddenly Clinton was in the lead, and not only in New Hampshire. A national poll released by the Yankelovich organization on January 16 showed Clinton running better against George Bush than any other Democrat. Though Bush led, 47 to 31 percent, only 46 percent of those polled said he should be reelected.[12] The president's fortunes were on the decline, while those of Clinton were on the rise. *Time* magazine devoted its January 27 cover story to answering the question "Is Bill Clinton for Real?" in an effort to explain his meteoric rise. Clinton's information age message had clearly struck a chord with the public.

With barely a month to go before the August Democratic national convention, the nomination of Bill Clinton had become inevitable and George Bush had become anything but unbeatable. The *Los Angeles Times* reported that Clinton led Bush by a single percentage point in California[13] while the *Washington Post* announced that Bush's lead nationally was down to only two percentage points.[14] Despite this, after months of promising to reinvent government to make it both more efficient and more responsive, to end welfare as we know it, and to restore respect for the values of the middle class, Clinton was running third in what was supposed to be a two-way race. Any possibility that a new message for the information age would be articulated with clarity and force was all but eliminated, as the public turned its attention to the surprising—some might say bizarre—candidacy of a man who claimed that the solutions to the country's problems were so simple anyone *except* an elected politician could understand them.

Though his company, Electronic Data Systems (EDS), was in the computer business, H. Ross Perot was firmly and permanently fixed in the industrial age. Like IBM, the company where Perot had gotten his start, EDS was organized in a strict, almost military, hierarchy. Absolute loyalty and the prompt, unquestioning execution of orders were prized above all else. It was only an apparent irony that Perot, often called the first billionaire of the computer age, kept suggesting that everyone needed to "look under the hood" to see what was wrong with America. Had anyone bothered to look, he or she would have found not the kind of engine a 1950s high school mechanic could tinker with, but rather, more computing power than existed in the first lunar landing module. But no one bothered. Instead, the electorate—especially that part of it that clung most tenaciously to the industrial age—listened intently as Ross Perot assured them that as "their servant" he would restore the American dream by helping them to reclaim their rightful ownership of the country.

Clinton had to do something to win back the attention of that portion of the white middle class attracted to the message of Ross Perot. His DLC advisors wanted him to do everything necessary to distinguish himself from the old Democratic party and suggested the candidate publicly distance himself from Jesse Jackson while privately notifying Jackson that he would not be considered for vice president—advice Clinton followed. While addressing Jackson's Rainbow Coalition, Clinton declared that Sister Souljah (a rap performer who had recently declared that if a gang member were going to kill someone anyway, he might as well kill a white person) was nothing more than a black version of a white Nazi. "If you took the words *white* and *black* and reversed them," he said, "you might think David Duke was giving that speech." Jackson was furious, the white middle class was delighted, and Clinton jumped seven points in the polls.[15]

Bill Clinton's concentration on this Perot segment of the middle class was almost compulsive. Clinton might have been fascinated with the new information age technologies, and he may have been intrigued by the possibility of the new class that Peter Drucker and a few others thought was fast becoming a new information age majority, but even for Clinton political reality, including the nature of the middle class, was still defined by the lessons of the past.

Those lessons were conveyed in their most persuasive form by the modern techniques of survey research. The opinions of the public could be measured with remarkable precision, but there could only be answers where there were questions. No one who did political polling had asked so much as one question that would identify the growing number of people who worked in the information sector of the American economy. For pollsters, knowledge workers did not exist as a separate class with a set of interests and opinions that distinguished them from the rest of the population. Instead, they measured the American electorate according to sex, race, age, income, and education. Their conclusions were inevitably the same— the election would depend on whether the white middle class decided that the economy was the most important issue. It was all Clinton needed to know.

Mario Cuomo nominated Clinton with a speech that spoke of the politics of inclusion as if they were the only politics that mattered. Everyone, ". . . from wherever, no matter how recently, of whatever color, of whatever creed, of whatever sex, of whatever sexual orientation, all of them equal members of the American family, and the neediest of them, the neediest of them," he repeated, "deserving the most help from the rest of us. That is the fundamental Democratic predicate."[16]

Clinton accepted the nomination with a speech that ignored everything Cuomo had said. "The New Covenant," he explained, "is a solemn agreement between the people and their government based not simply on what each of us can take but what all of us must give to our nation. We offer opportunity. We demand responsibility. We will build an American community again." He was more specific. "One sentence in the platform we built says it all. The most important family policy, labor policy, minority policy and foreign policy America can have is an expanding entrepreneurial economy of high-pay, high-skilled jobs." And it was all to be done, not for a new class of knowledge workers who would dominate the American future, but for the middle class, or rather that part of the middle class that had been deserting the Democratic party for years. "And so," Clinton said, "in the name of all those who do the work and pay the taxes, raise the kids and play by the rules, in the name of the hardworking Americans who make up our forgotten middle class, I proudly accept your nomination for president of the United States."[17] It was a line that could have been—and indeed was—delivered by Richard Nixon and Ronald Reagan.[18]

By the time the Republicans began their own national convention, Perot had dropped out and Clinton was leading Bush by an astonishing margin of 23 points.[19] The Republicans wasted no time in responding to the Clinton surge, immediately opening the same line of attack they had used to win the middle class to their side in every presidential election since 1968. Pat Buchanan denounced Clinton and Clinton (Bill and Hillary) for having an "agenda" they planned to "impose on America." It was comprised of "abortions on demand, a litmus test for the Supreme Court, homosexual rights, discrimination against religious schools, women in combat units."[20] Vice President Dan Quayle added his own, now famous, formulation. "When family values are undermined, our country suffers. All too often, parents struggle to instill character in their sons and daughters only to see their values belittled and their beliefs mocked by those who look down on America. The gap between us and our opponents is a cultural divide. It is not just a difference between conservative and liberal. It is a difference between fighting for what is right and refusing to see what is wrong."[21]

The Republicans had staked the entire campaign on the hope that nothing was more important to Americans, or to at least a majority of them, than the threat to the traditional American way of life. Not a single word was uttered about the forces that were silently and remorselessly changing the world around them. The information age was dawning, and the party that had dominated the country when the industrial revolution changed the face of America found itself struggling to recapture the close-knit ties of the small towns and small farms that same revolution had destroyed.

Trying to revive his lagging fortunes, George Bush began a whistle-stop tour of the rural villages of the South and the Midwest. But as his train wound through the green hills of Wisconsin, the president agonized through an interview he had not wanted to do. It was with a young television reporter from the hottest television network news show, watched almost exclusively by a generation raised on the technology of the new information age. George Bush answered the questions asked by the MTV reporter, never once looking into the camera.[22]

Meanwhile, as the Republicans were arguing for a return to an earlier, mythical age in which government did next to nothing and everyone shared the values of smalltown America, Ross Perot, returning to the race he had abandoned, invoked an image of a more recent past—a time when government provided security for the middle class and the United States' industrial power made it the leader of the free world. It was a powerful message for those whose job security had been destroyed by the new information age technologies, and it produced a phenomenon not seen since the election of

1912—a third-party movement that gained support as the election grew nearer.[23]

When it was finally over, almost two thirds of the electorate had voted to demonstrate dissatisfaction with what might be called the old industrial age social contract. Those who voted for George Bush believed government should enforce community values and protect the citizenry from enemies abroad and criminals at home. Content with the existing arrangements, they saw no reason to change the established ways of government. Perot voters, on the other hand, whose real hourly wages had suffered a greater rate of decline over the last twenty years than those of Clinton voters, felt threatened by the economic changes transforming the country.[24] They disliked government and despised what they perceived as the political establishment. Many of them had become "Reagan Democrats" when their own party began to move too far to the left and subsequently turned to Perot and third-party politics when the Republicans, faced with staggering job losses in the industrial sector, refused to change at all.

If the 57 percent of the electorate who did not vote for Clinton were divided over the kind of social contract the country should have, so were the 43 percent who did vote for him. Clinton had advertised himself as a "New Democrat" and had campaigned during the primaries on a platform of "opportunity, responsibility, and community." After the convention, however, he adopted a strategy summed up in the notorious motto that read, "Change versus more of the same. It's the economy, stupid. Don't forget health care."[25] The strategy worked. He won the support not only of those who had first been attracted to him by the information age message of the New Covenant speech but also those who still believed in the industrial age answers of the New Deal. Bill Clinton had become president; no one could be quite sure what that would mean.

■ ■ ■

What it seemed to mean at the beginning was a return to 1970s liberalism. Suddenly insisting that his administration would "look like America," Clinton proceeded to pick a cabinet as if race and sex were the only important qualifications. One of the first casualties was James Blanchard, former governor of Michigan and one of Clinton's closest political allies. He was notified by Warren Christopher, transition head, to interrupt his family's Christmas plans and fly to Washington to be "vetted" before being announced as secretary of transportation. Assured he had been selected after a thorough review, Blanchard was stunned to hear CNN proclaim two days later that Federico Peña had been chosen for the post. It was not until the next morning that Christopher called to explain. "I am sorry we had to make some last minute changes," he explained to a disappointed Blanchard. "We had chosen Congressman Bill Richardson to be Secretary of the Interior in order to give us two Hispanics in the Cabinet. But the environmentalists just wouldn't stand for it. So we had to go with Bruce Babbit. And there was no way we could have only one Hispanic Secretary (Cisneros) with four Blacks already chosen. So we have decided to make Peña the Secretary of Transportation."[26]

There was no room left for a white male. Months later, James Blanchard was appointed ambassador to Canada.

What happened to Blanchard was a private embarrassment. What occurred when Clinton proposed to lift the ban on gays in the military was the beginning of a public controversy that ended in a feeble compromise. Instead of having a New Democrat pledged to the same values as mainstream America, the country found itself with a new president espousing the thoroughly discredited policies of the old-style McGovern liberalism. Within six months of taking office, Clinton's popularity fell from a postinaugural high of 58 percent to less than 40 percent, and even that hid more ominous numbers. Only 27 percent of the American public thought the country was moving in the right direction, 10 points lower than just two months earlier and 20 points lower than in the 1993 postelection period. The numbers were even worse in the South. Only 29 percent of the southern electorate now considered themselves core supporters of the president. But because four out of every ten African Americans described themselves as core supporters, the percentage of white southerners who supported Clinton was even less.[27] The issue of gays in the military, which had cost the administration support nationwide, had almost completely wiped out Clinton's base among white southerners.

The congressional battle over the North American Free Trade Agreement gave Clinton the chance to win back public support. He argued that the future growth of the American economy depended on the creation of larger markets and insisted that NAFTA was a necessary first step. Organized labor, fearful of anything that might cost jobs in the short run, wanted to maintain the protectionist policies that screened some of the country's most inefficient industries from the rigors of competition. The Democratic congressional leadership, including the new majority leader, Richard Gephardt of Missouri, abandoned the president for the unions. For the first time in living memory, the offices of the minority whip were organized to oppose the policy of a president of the same party. David Bonior, representing Michigan's Macomb county, one of the most heavily unionized districts in the country, used every weapon at the whip's disposal and wielded his power with more energy and passion than he had ever expended opposing any policy of either George Bush or Ronald Reagan. It was more than a simple disagreement over a matter of principle. It became all-out war.

Clinton won, but only because he finally refused to follow the congressional leadership of his own party when it insisted on defending the industrial age status quo. He defeated the last remnants of the New Deal coalition by fashioning a new coalition of those Democrats and Republicans who believed that America had to become competitive in the new world economy. With victory on the NAFTA vote, Clinton's approval ratings shot back up, and by January 1994 they had almost reached their postinaugural high. More people now thought of him as a New Democrat, as distinguished from the kind of "tax-and-spend" liberal traditionally associated with the Democratic leadership in Congress.[28] Americans were split almost evenly on the direction they felt the country was taking.[29]

Below the surface of the simple percentages, which tracked the way the country as a whole viewed the president, something important was happening. Even as his overall approval ratings were rising, Clinton's support among both blue-collar workers and people over the age of fifty was actually declining. These two groups were disappointed in Clinton and discouraged about where they thought the country was headed. Perot voters were even more disenchanted. After watching Al Gore embarrass their former candidate during the NAFTA debate on *Larry King Live*, only 21 percent of them expressed a willingness to vote for Clinton in the next presidential election.[30]

But these losses were more than offset by the gains Clinton registered among members of the new constituency. The improvement in Clinton's approval rating was attributable in large part to his increased support among working women who earned between $20,000 and $50,000 annually, many of whom were employed in the new information sector of the economy and who were among those most attracted to the new economic ideas Clinton had advocated both during the campaign and during the fight over NAFTA.[31] They were eager to support a president willing to fight for the future against anyone—regardless of party—who wanted to turn back the clock.

Clinton seemed to know there was a new constituency, but he never appeared ready to accept it. The New Covenant speech and the argument he made for NAFTA were both clear signs that he recognized there had been a fundamental break with the past. But as often as he spoke about the need to adopt new assumptions and policies for the information age, he acted as if his primary objective were to complete the liberal agenda for the industrial age. Bill Clinton had become the Mikhail Gorbachev of the Democratic party, issuing calls for renewal and change while appealing for support from those most interested in the preservation of the status quo. He promised universal health care and offered to provide it through bureaucracies designed to control and regulate private business. The Democratic leaders of Congress, for whom the New Deal was still a work in progress, were nothing short of ecstatic; the rest of the country, including the new constituency, began to look around for someone else.

They did not have to look far. Republicans in Congress— especially Republicans in the House—had begun to realize that they had nothing to lose, and perhaps a great deal to gain, by opposing the president on legislation that increased or that seemed to increase the size and power of the federal government. They attacked the Clinton health care proposal as a bureaucratic nightmare that not only would raise taxes but would destroy what many of them claimed was the greatest health care system in the world. Their success was overwhelming. In July 1994, while the debate over health care was at the center of public attention, the president's approval rating fell from its January high of 53 percent to a dismal 43 percent.[32]

The failure of Clinton's health care proposal was the direct result of his inability to understand the nature of the new constituency that had elected him. Indeed, neither the existence nor the importance of the new constituency could be doubted any longer. On September 21, 1994, the Times Mirror Center for the People and the Press published a comprehensive survey of the American electorate demonstrating just how fundamentally and rapidly public opinion had changed.[33] In 1987, the most reliable adherents of the Democratic party were divided among three groups: those who were labeled older FDR *loyalists*, upper-middle-class *social liberals*, and heavily minority *partisan poor*. Those three groups together had made up 41 percent of all likely voters. Seven years later, in 1994, there was a fourth group, which the survey labeled *New Democrats* because of its more favorable attitude toward business. This group consisted mostly of female knowledge workers in health care, education, and social services. The four groups combined, however, now comprised only 34 percent of the voting population.

Republicans had concurrently experienced changes of their own, but with a much different result. In 1987, core Republicans accounted for 30 percent of the electorate and were divided among only two groups, socially conservative *moralists* and economically conservative *enterprisers.* In 1994 a third group, New Republican *libertarians,* had been added, and the core Republican vote had reached 36 percent. For the first time since the beginning of the New Deal, Republicans outnumbered Democrats. But neither group represented a majority; independent voters had become nearly as numerous as the loyalists to either of the two parties.

Self-identified independents fell into three different categories. One group, labeled *bystanders* by Times/Mirror analysts, disdaining both parties and politics, simply did not vote. The second group, designated *embittered,* comprised 7 percent of the electorate and 25 percent of the independent vote, and was characterized by low incomes and low levels of education. They were the most likely of the independent voters to be attracted by the message of a Ross Perot. The third, and by far most significant, group was the *New Economy Independents.* These were younger voters, often working women, whose attitude on issues was close to that of the New Democrats, but who were not willing to align themselves with either party. They comprised almost one fifth of the entire electorate.

Any Democratic strategist with even a minimal understanding of the new age and the new constituency could have seen that there was a new coalition ready for the taking. A combination of the "new economy" Independents, the New Democrats, and what remained of the Democratic core support could defeat anything the Republicans could muster. Even if the Republicans held all of their core vote, and even if the Democrats won none of the "embittered" vote, the Democratic majority would still be at least 53 percent. It was a strategy guaranteed to win, and it was a strategy no one in the Clinton White House even thought to follow.

One week after the Times-Mirror survey provided the last decisive piece of evidence proving the existence of the new information age constituency, three hundred Republican candidates for the U.S. House of Representatives gathered together on the steps of the Capitol and signed their names to a ten-point program, the "Contract with America." Under the watchful eye of Newt Gingrich they pledged to act on it within the first hundred days of the new Congress. The Contract was the first Republican attempt to formulate a public policy for the information age. Gingrich said all legislation passed by a Republican-controlled Congress would have to further the goals of propelling America into Alvin Toffler's vision of a third wave information society.[34] It was hoped that the Contract, which appealed to a growing American distrust of government, would aid in the effort to combine the three elements of the Republican party with the "embittered" and the "new economy" Independents into a majority powerful enough to capture, for the first time since 1952, control of both the House and the Senate.

The Contract with America was the antagonist the White House was searching for. Clinton had turned to Tony Coelho, a former California congressman, to give the Democratic National Committee a coherent strategy and a clear message. Like the Democratic congressional leadership, of which he had been a part, Coelho believed that the principles of the New Deal provided the solution to most problems and that the electorate was still divided by a line between right and left, rich and poor. He was not alone. Everything he did was based on polling information supplied by Stan Greenberg, who, during the first two years of the Clinton administration, had convinced the president that the way to win the middle class was to unite its members in a class-conscious crusade against the wealthy.[35]

Coelho and Greenberg attacked the Contract with America as a "contract *on* America." Democratic incumbents, following their lead, claimed it was nothing more than a call for a return to the dangerous excesses and fiscal irresponsibility of the 1980s. As the campaign battle entered its final phase, the Democrats rolled out their ultimate weapon. The cuts in federal spending called for in the Republican contract, they warned, could only be made by reducing social security benefits. Voters were left to choose between the preservation of industrial age entitlements and a different, more limited, role for government in the information age. And when they made that choice, five years to the day that the Berlin Wall came down, politics in America was changed forever.

2

THE BIRTH OF A NEW CONSTITUENCY

There was a strange symmetry about it: in 1930, as the Great Depression worsened, fifty-three Democrats were elected to the U.S. House of Representatives from districts that, two years earlier, had elected Republicans. In 1994, in the midst of an economic recovery during which 200,000 new jobs were being created every month, fifty-two Republicans were elected to the House from districts that, two years earlier, had elected Democrats. For the first time in forty years Republicans had a majority in the House, and for only the second time since Dwight D. Eisenhower was first elected president, they had a majority in the Senate as well.

Almost before the last vote had been counted, Democrats began to point out that the Republican victory was based on a paper-thin margin. Only 51 percent of those who voted for one of the two major party candidates for Congress had voted Republican; 49 percent had cast their ballots for Democrats. Party leaders, including what was left of the Democratic congressional leadership, made no secret of their belief that the election outcome was the result of the public's frustration with the Clinton administration's apparent inability to decide what to do and how to do it. Republican control, in their judgment, was a temporary phenomenon that would last only until the president became more persuasive, or until the Republican party actually attempted to carry out their agenda—now that they had the power to do so.

The narrow margin, however, only served to conceal the depths of discontent that had come to dominate the public mood. Americans were worried, not nearly so much about the present as about the future. Just days before the election, 55 percent thought the economy was in "good" shape, but 42 percent thought things would be worse, rather than the same or better, in five years. This marked the highest degree of short-term pessimism since 1980, the year Ronald Reagan was elected to the presidency. The outlook for the long term was even more ominous: 57 percent were convinced that the next generation would be worse off than they themselves now were.[1] The American Dream, the belief that each generation will be better off than the generation preceding it, was dying a slow death.

Restoring the dream required rekindling faith in America as a land of economic opportunity and close communities. Republicans, none of them more vociferously than the seventy-three freshman members of the House, argued this would happen only if traditional American values became the basis for making fundamental changes in what the federal government did and the way it did it. Newt Gingrich, who was about to become the first Republican Speaker of the House since the long-forgotten Joe Martin of Massachusetts stepped down in 1955, called himself a revolutionary and promised that the new Republican majority would not stop working until each of the ten proposals in the Contract with America had been passed by the House and sent to the Senate.

Whatever enthusiasm the new Republican House leadership might have for it, the Contract with America was anything but a revolutionary program for a new age. Clearly success in the information age requires nothing so much as a radical revision in the way we train our workforce and educate the next generation. Yet the Contract with America mentioned education but once, and then only to support the Christian Coalition's call for home schooling. The chairman of the Republican National Committee, Haley Barbour, later admitted that the Contract was nothing more than the same demands for less government and lower taxes that Reagan had first used to gain the presidency.[2] Gingrich talked about fiber optics and microchips, but the program his supporters offered spoke more about their hope of reinforcing the divisions of a dying industrial age than about their desire to offer a new vision.

If the proposals contained in the Contract with America had their origin in a reaction to the growth of the size and power of the federal government from the New Deal to the Great Society, they still struck a chord with an electorate that had come to fear the future and blamed government for their fears. At the same time they were giving control of Congress to the Republicans, 77 percent of the American people did not trust government to do what was right even some of the time, and 68 percent were convinced they had no impact whatsoever on government actions.[3] Americans felt ignored by a government that was too concerned with other people—too concerned, to put it bluntly, with the poor. Immediately after the 1994 election three out of four people agreed with the statement "It's the middle class, not the poor, who really get a raw deal today."[4]

Large numbers of Americans sensed that the future of the country was at risk and that government was at least part of the problem. Public frustration was based on a more accurate view of reality than was possessed by either elected Democrats—who were suddenly reduced to defending the social programs of the past—or Republicans—who seemed to think the role of government had been defined once and forever by the laissez-faire policies of the nineteenth century. Americans understood that their country had evolved and that politicians were the only ones who had not yet figured that out. George Bush spoke of a "new world order" and thought he was describing the future of foreign policy in the post-Soviet era.

Anyone who had lived through the organizational transformation of corporate America, however, believed that the new world order had already arrived and that it was based on economic, rather than political principles.

▪ ▪ ▪

Success in the private sector had come to depend on a quick, nonbureaucratic response to the changing needs and desires of one's customers. Success depended on one's ability to offer services and products that were not only better, but cheaper. It also necessitated becoming the best at what you did, not just in your own domestic market but in the world. For those who understood the new information age economy, the rewards were unprecedented. For those who failed to understand it, the only question was whether their business—which perhaps had even once dominated the competition—would undergo a slow and painful death or a quick and merciless end. Private enterprise was reshaped by the new technological and organizational imperatives of the information age.

These changes have not yet affected either what government does or the way it does it, but they will. The same thing happened during the last major transformation in America, when the industrial age replaced the agricultural era. The internal combustion engine was invented in 1870; the automobile was introduced at the turn of the century. Some twenty years later Henry Ford created the assembly line, and Alfred Sloan centralized policy and financial control at General Motors, creating the bureaucracy needed to run the line with maximum efficiency. It was thirty years from the time new technology was embedded in a product before manufacturers finally understood the kind of organization they needed to produce it profitably. That new organization then became so commonplace that it is still difficult to envision a world without the American-style corporation. It was only after that new form of organization, with its armies of blue- and white-collar workers, began to determine the way most people worked and lived that the way they thought about the world began to change.

The great political realignment dividing the electorate between a Democratic party that emphasized social welfare and a Republican party that defended laissez-faire economics occurred only after the overwhelming majority of Americans had begun to identify themselves as either labor or management. Without the economic transformation brought about by industrialization, the political division between parties of the left and right would have been impossible.

Today that same pattern is repeating itself. At the turn of the century, while the first automobiles were being produced, physicists began to understand the principles of quantum mechanics. It was not until 1960, however, that this understanding was embodied in a new technology with which to process and encode information. Ten years later the microchip was invented and through the subsequent invention of the personal computer became universally available. The information age was born.

By 1990, the percentage of blue-collar workers, which had risen to as much as 40 percent of the working population at the height of the industrial age, had fallen to less than half that high-water mark.[5] By then, most Americans were working in jobs that had been restructured to provide them greater decision-making freedom. Many were self-employed or working in small businesses. There were no bosses to keep the assembly line moving with commands and threats and the success of each member of the enterprise depended on everyone working as a team to accomplish common objectives. No one instructed these newly empowered employees how to do their jobs, nor did they conduct frequent inspections to make certain they were doing them correctly. Instead, employees worked in *reengineered* organizations with *flat structures* linked together with electronic mail and decentralized databases that provided the information to guide their decisions.

Unlike this new world of work, politics continued to be governed by the intellectual assumptions of an earlier age. The anxiety of living in a new age, while those who govern still debate the issues of the past, will continue until there is a new alignment between the way we live and the way we think.[6] That alignment, however, first requires that we understand both the nature of the technological change that has transformed the way we work and the new ways in which work has been organized. Engines, the fundamental technology of the industrial age, substituted mechanics for muscle power and made it possible to do more cheaply and more reliably the work that animals and human beings had always performed. What the engine—whether steam or gas—did for human muscle, the microchip does for the human brain:[7] it provides the ability to process encoded information faster, cheaper, and more reliably.

Information also changes—and changes radically—the assumptions of economics in three ways. First, information is more valuable when it is shared than when it is hoarded. Second, it places a premium not on size or mass, but on speed. Finally, information makes geographic distances less relevant by shrinking time and space.[8] These three new assumptions, each of them fundamentally at variance with the working assumptions of industrial age economics, explain both the meteoric rise of the wealthiest people in America and the sudden decline of the country's most successful corporations.

The first computers were built for the military in the 1940s by scientists, most notably George Stiblitz, on loan from Bell Laboratories.[9] Tom Watson, founder of International Business Machines, next used computers to automate large corporations' bookkeeping and payrolls. Ironically, then, IBM used the first wave of information age technology to automate tasks created by the rise of the industrial age corporation. The organizational structure of IBM was also based on industrial age principles first implemented by Alfred Sloan at GM: though operationally decentralized, all policy was made at the very top of a gigantic pyramid in which the myriad levels of the hierarchy descended from Tom Watson and his staff. It was a bureaucracy that was both enlightened and modern; nevertheless, it was bureaucratic to the core. Any attempt to trim or reduce it was always undercut by the central role it held in planning and strategic decision making.

The theory of its business was also rooted in the industrial age. With the introduction of the 360 mainframe computer, IBM required that all its customers invest in a proprietary operating system. Corporations could use IBM mainframes to automate their businesses, but only if they used the programs IBM had written to control the basic functions of the machines. This operating system could not be purchased from anyone else and its secrets were jealously guarded; indeed, IBM brought suit against anyone who tried to imitate or copy its software. "Big Blue" knew that once a customer had contracted for the use of its machines, it could charge whatever it wanted for the right to also use the operating system.[10] With a guaranteed stream of rental payments, there was never any economic necessity to consider making changes in the way IBM did business. As late as 1985 IBM could—with complete confidence—predict a future of uninterrupted growth, all of it centrally planned and coordinated from headquarters in the IBM Tower in downtown Manhattan.[11]

IBM attempted to build similar market dominance in personal computers based on its manufacturing prowess. The company had written and rented the operating systems for the mainframe computers. Personal computers, however, were a different matter. The real money, IBM believed, was to be made in efficiently manufacturing these relatively low-cost pieces of hardware or terminals, rather than in creating the software for operating them. Instead of developing the software itself, IBM struck a deal with a young entrepreneur from Seattle, agreeing to license the operating system that Bill Gates had developed, without bothering to ask that the license be theirs exclusively. IBM used the Microsoft Disk Operating System in their new line of personal computers; Gates, who believed that economic value was to be found not in the machine or the hardware, but in the software, sold it to all who wanted to buy it.[12]

Gates shared his operating system with companies writing software for personal computers. By making available the information about his software, he attracted thousands of people to write programs to run on MS-DOS machines, without having to pay any of them to do so. They earned their money when PC users bought their software; Gates made money every time an IBM computer (or any computer that used his operating system) was manufactured. Any company could copy IBM's manufacturing designs and, using more efficient techniques or cheaper labor, or both, then sell personal computers at lower prices. All the public wanted to know was whether they were "IBM compatible." The single greatest shift of economic power in America during the last twenty years happened for no reason other than that IBM continued to believe in hoarding its secrets and Bill Gates believed in sharing information.

Industrial age economic laws suggest that larger enterprises are more efficient than smaller ones—with proper economies of scale, the cost of an enterprise can be spread over a greater number of individual sales. Success depends on the ability to sell more than the competition and, using the leverage that comes with lower unit costs, gain more profit per dollar of sale than the competition. No corporation ever did this better than General Motors. GM had done it so well, in fact, that by the late 1950s it began to focus on what it called "the sixties," referring not to the next decade, but to the share of the automobile market it fully expected to own in the future. By 1972 it was almost there, but twenty years later no one at General Motors contemplated the sixties—they were all too busy trying to keep their share of the market from falling below 30 percent.[13]

In 1973, one year after General Motors had come closest to

the 60 percent share it had been striving for, the Organization of Petroleum Exporting Countries (OPEC) began to curtail the worldwide supply of oil. The embargo drove the price of oil from three dollars to ten dollars per barrel. Over the next ten years the price would jump to nearly thirty dollars per barrel. As the price of gasoline at the pump doubled and then tripled, consumers began to search for more fuel-efficient cars. General Motors was unable to respond quickly. Each step in its product development cycle, which lasted five years, was performed by a separate functional department with its own bureaucracy and its own decision-making process.[14] Every department concentrated on doing its own work more efficiently, without considering the requirements of others. As a result, the marketing department could ask for more fuel-efficient cars in 1973, but until all the other departments agreed that this should be the objective and changed their plans accordingly, nothing would happen.

Meanwhile, the Japanese, with no market share to protect, had responded more quickly. Honda Motors had organized itself to adapt almost immediately to the changing mood of the customers to whom they sold motorcycles. As soon as their salesmen heard about a new idea from a consumer, they began simultaneously to design the new model and retool the assembly line. Their development cycle was measured not in years but in months or even weeks, and the same organizational model that had worked so well with motorcycles was applied with equal effect to the production of automobiles.[15] While General Motors would have to wait five years after a decision was finally made before introducing to the market more fuel-efficient cars, Honda responded almost instantly to the new market that first began to emerge with the Arab oil embargo. And what Honda could do, so could Nissan and Toyota. The Japanese were able to steal a march on the Americans, and once they had the advantage, they defended their position ferociously. Ten years after the oil embargo of 1973, the only way that General Motors hoped to survive was to ask the government, whose anti-trust laws it had once opposed, to protect it against competition by imposing a limit on the number of Japanese cars that could be brought into the country.

Size, which for years had been the prerequisite of success, had become the enemy: bigger, instead of being better, meant it was that much harder for a company to change. The conventional wisdom of the industrial age had been turned on its head by the new economics of the information age. Japanese automobile companies learned how to get information quickly from the marketplace to everyone in the company who needed it. Information did not have to travel up one chain of command and back down another to reach the appropriate person. The process of researching the market was integrated with the process of designing the car, which in turn was integrated with the process of manufacturing it.

The organizational model that made this possible was not a pyramid of the sort designed by Alfred Sloan; it was a network of relationships and communication built on a fortuitous combination of culture and information technology. It was, in the lexicon of corporate consultants, a *flat* organization, an organization in which the largest numbers of people possible were connected with one another in a web or network that provided more information to more people more quickly so that each individual could make more informed decisions.[16] As a result, it was an organization better able to make rapid decisions than any command and control bureaucracy, no matter how well run, could ever hope to do.

The great distance that separates Japan from the American market and the time difference between Asia and North America—barriers that had once made it almost impossible for a business to stay in touch with its overseas customers— had simply become two more historical facts, prized by antiquaries and ignored by nearly everyone else. Undersea fiber optic cables and satellites delivered information worldwide instantaneously. No one, not even the Japanese, understood this better than Sam Walton.

In the 1950s and 1960s, while General Motors and the other large industrial organizations that dominated the American market concentrated their collective attention on the nation's heavily populated urban areas, Walton began to build a business in what was derisively dismissed as the "boonies." Rural, small town America simply wasn't a focus of most corporations. New consumer products were marketed in cities, where the majority of Americans lived. The cost of reaching consumers who were spread along the vast reaches of rural America was simply too expensive, the necessary economies of scale unavailable.

Wal-Mart took the opposite tack: it opened stores where there was no major competition. Consequently, its operations were dispersed over a large geographical area. Initially, Walton visited each store regularly by flying between them. Eventually, through the use of state-of-the-art technology, he did not have to travel at all. As each purchase was made at any given location, pertinent information was scanned into a computer and transmitted over high-speed communication links to corporate headquarters. Not only were these data analyzed immediately by Wal-Mart's buyers, the same information was communicated to the company's major suppliers, who were empowered to ship the best-selling items directly to each store as sales were recorded.[17] Time and distance, the oldest enemies of rural America's prosperity, had been shrunk to nothing.[18]

While the old economic assumptions have been shattered, the new ones are not yet widely understood. In many corporations, where the transition from the industrial to the information age took the painful form of what has come to be called "downsizing," the processing power of computers replaced the people who used to do management work. Middle managers, occupying a place on the chain of command between worker and owner, collected and analyzed data from the company's operations and then passed the results of their work to a decision maker farther up the chain. The computer changed this forever.

These data were initially captured on large mainframe computers that eliminated the middle manager's collection function. Then the processing power was moved into departments where the analysis, too, could be performed by midsized computers. In the last stage, the personal computer provided the decision maker all the support he or she needed to act on the analysis and send the appropriate instructions as needed. In less than three decades computers, with their immensely efficient processing capacities, eliminated the need for all but a few middle managers to run the daily work of corporate America.

The people who lost these jobs made up a substantial part of the middle class. Some of them found new work and new levels of success using the nonlogical, or intuitive, capacities that distinguish the human brain from the computer. They became entrepreneurs, which, many of them joked, was really just a euphemism for "recently unemployed." Those who succeeded learned what it was like to take risks and what it meant to be accountable for their own decisions. But not everyone succeeded, and many found themselves reduced to menial work, which paid less than they had ever earned before. The absence of an office, with its comforting amenities, became, for them, a mark of failure. Their frustration, coupled with the decline in blue-collar work, produced what Labor Secretary Robert Reich termed the "anxious class."[19]

In new corporations that either have transformed themselves to align their structure with the realities of information age economics or were created from the beginning by those who grew up with the new technology, the old chain of command has virtually disappeared. The organization is no longer a *machine* designed to turn out a uniform product; it is now a *system* designed to satisfy the unique needs of each customer. The purpose of information age enterprises is to maximize the learning of those doing the work so the company can adapt quickly to the rapidly changing marketplace.

The value each employee brings to a job is his or her own creativity. All of them earn their salaries by processing information and combining it in new ways to solve problems. Though their creativity may still be stifled, because they have not yet been sufficiently empowered to make all the decisions they could, they enjoy more authority than the middle managers of industrial age organizations ever dreamed of. Indeed, nearly everything about the organization has changed. The strict hierarchy, in which every worker reported to a superior and in turn gave orders to his or her subordinates, has been replaced. Managers are now expected to coach employees, to bust barriers that stand in the way of customer satisfaction, and to provide vision and values to improve the context of the work for those they support rather than supervise. Mr. Sloan's pyramid has been turned upside down and then flattened.

The world of the knowledge worker is not limited, however, to the middle management of corporations. It includes, for example, workers on an assembly line who monitor automated equipment and have the power and the authority to stop the line whenever they discover a quality defect, and those who work in health care or education and are paid for what they know and how well they can communicate it to others. The information age divides the workforce between those who are paid for the value of their intelligence, what might be called their unique *software*, and those who are paid for the value of their muscles, or the *hardware* they bring to the job. Every day the number and value of the former grow larger, while the number and worth of the latter decline.

Daily life has also been radically transformed. Shopping, which once required moving from one place to another, may now be done through television, over the telephone, or on the Internet. Eating can be done quickly and cheaply at fast food restaurants or with the convenience of home delivery. Entertainment, whether movies, sporting events, or music, can be personalized by means of an increasing variety of cable channels or by turning on a PC and plugging in a given CD-ROM. Formal education, once the province of schools and libraries, can now be provided on computer programs replete with color graphics and interactive options. In almost every walk of life we are suddenly confronted with a sometimes bewildering variety of choices.

▪ ▪ ▪

Even in politics, where the choices have remained rooted in the industrial age dichotomy of Democrats and Republicans, different approaches to public policy have finally begun to surface. The new constituency of knowledge workers, the emerging new majority in American politics, has already begun to make its influence felt. With the largest and most diverse set of human and natural resources in the nation, 20 percent of the electoral votes needed to carry a presidential election, the seventh largest economy in the world, and a greater percentage of knowledge workers than any other state, California frequently provides a preview of what will occur in the rest of the country. The 1994 contests for governor and senator provided an opportunity for the new class to respond to four distinct attempts to win its support. What happened in these two statewide races shows clearly that the politics of the information age has arrived and that the new constituency of knowledge workers now determines the difference between victory and defeat.

Not since John Adams and his son John Quincy Adams both held the presidency has any family in America exercised more power over more people than the Brown family of California. Edmund G. "Pat" Brown served as governor for eight years, until he was defeated by Ronald Reagan in 1966. In that time, Brown virtually created the physical and educational infrastructure that led to the state's explosive growth. In 1974, after Reagan had served two terms, Pat Brown's son was elected governor. Ridiculed by his opponents as "Governor

Moonbeam," Jerry Brown was the first politician to see beyond the rapidly eroding constraints of the industrial age.[20] Twenty years later, his sister ran for governor as if she had never met her brother and could remember only the accomplishments of her father.

On the night she won the primary, Kathleen Brown gave three reasons why she should be elected governor: she was a Brown, a Democrat, and a woman. Lest anyone doubt what kind of Democrat she was, she proceeded to invoke the memory of Franklin Delano Roosevelt. But having begun the primary campaign with a more than twenty-point lead against the incumbent Republican, by the night of the primary, as she confirmed her credentials as a New Deal liberal, her lead had evaporated.[21]

Brown's opponent, Governor Pete Wilson, had been a Democrat's dream. An experienced politician who had served first as mayor of San Diego and then as a member of the United States Senate, Wilson had presided over the worst spectacle of governmental gridlock in the state's history. With the end of the cold war, the aerospace industry was in serious trouble, sending the California economy into a tailspin. As state revenues plummeted, Wilson proposed in 1993 to cut welfare payments, reduce state support for higher education, and decrease the allocation for public education below the increase in inflation. Led by Democrat Willie Brown, Speaker of the State Assembly, the legislature refused to agree.

As the stalemate dragged on through the summer, the state was reduced to the embarrassing extremity of paying employees with worthless scrip. Eventually a settlement was reached and, though it was closer to what the governor had wanted than to what the Democrats had demanded, the damage had been done. In the public eye, the Wilson administration had become the very model of ineptitude. By early 1994 a majority of Californians disapproved of the Republican governor.[22] It seemed Pete Wilson had no chance of being reelected.

It was almost shameless. While Democrats everywhere were

distancing themselves as much as possible from Bill Clinton, the Republican governor ran for reelection the way Clinton had run for the presidency: Wilson campaigned on behalf of the middle class, "the ones who play by the rules and go to work and try to make a better life for their family."[23] The line might have been written by Al From. The difference was that in California in 1994, it became a line drawn to divide the middle class, "who play by the rules," from all those who broke the law. The enemies were criminals and illegal aliens. The issues were crime and immigration.

Brown took the bait. She argued that she was tougher on crime than Wilson but in fact, like both her father and her brother before her, she opposed the death penalty. She tried to make immigration an issue of fairness by decrying the threatened denial of education and health care services, but she failed to make any distinction between legal and illegal immigrants. As she fell farther behind, Brown tried to direct attention to a different set of issues. She began to speak about creating a new California, offering a detailed plan of economic and educational investments that would make it come true.[24]

Unfortunately, Brown's vision of the future was rooted squarely in the past. Instead of talking about the newly emerging middle class of minority entrepreneurs, high-tech employees, and knowledge workers, she spoke to the immediate concerns of those whose economic status was most threatened by the transition to an information age economy. Brown, who had switched her position on NAFTA to win labor support and head off a primary challenge, seemed convinced that nothing had changed and that the New Deal coalition of labor, liberals, and minorities remained the key to victory.

The election was not even close. Wilson won, 55 percent to 41 percent, with Republicans riding his coattails to new levels of power in the state legislature. Brown's attempt to make jobs and the economy the central issue in the campaign persuaded 29 percent of the electorate to cite that as at least one of the most important issues, but only half of those voted for her. She did much better among the 22 percent for whom education was a critical issue, receiving 70 percent of their vote. Wilson, however, defeated her by the staggering margin of three to one among both the 28 percent who cited crime and the 27 percent who cited immigration as one of the two most important issues.[25]

While Kathleen Brown was running and losing as a New Deal liberal, Dianne Feinstein, seeking reelection to the Senate, was running and winning as a New Democrat. During her first two years in the Senate, Feinstein had worked diligently on legislation that addressed the very issues Wilson had seized upon. She introduced a ban on assault weapons and then lobbied not only the Senate but the House to include it in the final version of the crime bill. She secured increased funding to provide more effective law enforcement on the border with Mexico and during the last few months of the campaign could point to at least some reduction in the flow of illegal aliens. She also negotiated passage of the most important conservation act of the last ten years. In its final official act before adjournment, the Senate approved the designation of California's deserts as national parks and preservation lands. Feinstein's belief in a pragmatic, activist government that used sensible, fiscally sound policies to deal with community problems was precisely the kind of message California's new constituency wanted to hear.

If Feinstein wanted to change the way government worked, her opponent, Michael Huffington, seemed to want to abolish government—at least the federal government—altogether. After spending $5 million to win a congressional district primary against a Republican incumbent, Huffington waited only a year before announcing his candidacy for a Senate race in which he would eventually spend more than $30 million of his own money. He hired the best help money could buy: Ed Rollins, who had tried to give some coherence to the Perot campaign, was brought in to direct overall strategy. Larry

McCarthy, who had produced the famous—or infamous—
Willie Horton ads in 1988 not only developed a new generation of attack ads for Huffington, but put together a team that
was able to respond to any news event with a brand new television commercial within twenty-four hours.[26] There never was
a campaign, in California or anywhere else, that was able to
buy more television time or engage in more radio and news-
paper advertising. It would have been hard to find a single
Californian who did not know by the end of the campaign
that Michael Huffington thought that the best government
was the least government.

Huffington's answer to the problem of welfare was simply to
eliminate it completely. The poor could be taken care of
through private charities and, to show that he was really serious about it, he proposed an increase in the allowable tax deduction for charitable contributions. California's economy
had been devastated by the reduction in the defense budget,
but Huffington pledged never to vote for more expenditures
of any kind, including defense. Like Pete Wilson, Huffington
also supported the elimination of government benefits of any
kind for illegal immigrants. When it was reported by the *Wall
Street Journal* that, during his short career in the House,
Huffington had actually voted for more increased appropriations than cuts, he dismissed it as an irrelevancy. When his
hometown Santa Barbara paper revealed that he had employed an illegal alien in his household, he blamed his wife.[27]

In a choice between a traditional Democratic approach to
government and a Republican governor who promised to use
government to defend the interests and values of the middle
class, Californians voted overwhelmingly in favor of the latter.
In a choice between a Republican candidate who viewed government as the enemy and a Democratic senator who thought
government should be used on behalf of the whole community, Californians voted for the latter. In rejecting Kathleen
Brown voters rejected the traditional liberalism of the Democratic party. In rejecting Michael Huffington they rejected

what was, in effect, the logical extension of Newt Gingrich's Contract with America. Californians were looking for something different than either the welfare state of the New Deal or the narrow selfishness of Michael Huffington's version of New Age radicalism.

If California represents America's political future, Silicon Valley represents the leading edge of the information age economy in America. The nation's personal computer and high-tech industries have largely grown up in this center of technical know-how located in Santa Clara County, just southeast of San Francisco.[28] The people who live there, in communities like Sunnyvale and San Jose, chose among these four varied political choices. In recent elections, Santa Clara County residents cast about 53 percent of their vote for the Democratic candidate. But when it came to the race for governor in 1994, they split their vote, giving a slight edge to Republican Pete Wilson, the champion of middle-class values. Dianne Feinstein's showing was even more impressive: she ran twenty points ahead of Michael Huffington.[29]

The same pattern repeated itself throughout the state among other categories of voters with disproportionate numbers of knowledge workers. College graduates gave Feinstein a 51 percent to 41 percent edge, while Wilson defeated Brown by a virtually identical margin, 53 percent to 43 percent. Among those who professed to see an improvement in the economy, 53 percent voted for Feinstein, while only 49 percent voted for Brown.[30]

Perhaps the most clearly identifiable participants in the older, industrial age economy are those classified as members of union households. They now comprise only 25 percent of the California electorate, compared to the 29 percent who are self-employed or work for firms employing fewer than ten people.[31] Union households virtually split their vote between Brown and Wilson, 48 percent to 47 percent. Feinstein, running on a centrist, New Democrat record, received 60 percent of their vote, while Huffington, whose message was so far removed from the daily concerns of wage earners as to be from another planet, received only 40 percent.[32]

Brown lost and Feinstein won for the same reasons. The old industrial base of the Democratic party is now too small to offer victory to defenders of the New Deal. The new information age constituency will only vote for a candidate who knows how to use government efficiently to build a better community. When Newt Gingrich and his "third wave" political allies proclaimed that the new Republican majorities in the House and Senate signaled the end of New Deal liberalism and the dawning of a new age in American politics, they told the truth—but not quite the whole truth. The old liberalism was dead, but it was by no means clear that this was quite the advantage Republicans believed it to be. Shortly after the election, Americans were asked in a poll to choose between a traditional Democrat, "who believes government can solve problems and protect people from adversity," and a New Democrat, "who believes government should help people equip themselves to solve their own problems." Seventy-one percent chose the New Democrat, while only 16 percent picked the traditional Democratic approach. They were then asked to select either the New Democratic approach or Republicans "who believe government should leave people alone to solve their own problems." Fifty-two percent chose the New Democrats, while only 34 percent preferred the Republican message in that party's Contract with America.[33] Republicans had won the election of 1994, but the race to attract the allegiance of the new class of knowledge workers, the emerging information age majority, had barely begun.

3

REINVENTING AMERICAN GOVERNMENT

Al Gore wanted to know what had happened: Democratic losses in the midterm elections had been worse than anyone had expected. Republican gains were 10 to 15 percent better than polls taken the weekend before the election had predicted. It was now December 5, 1994, almost a month since the Republican sweep had restored their senatorial majority and ended forty years of Democratic control in the House. Everyone the vice president had invited to this private meeting had now had plenty of time to think about it.[1] "What," he asked, "was the reason for the Republican victory?"

Richard Neustadt, who had authored the book on which John F. Kennedy had relied in organizing the White House in 1961, thought he knew. The election of 1994, he explained, was, in reality, a continuation of the election of 1992. The country was still looking for change. With the exception of the South, which had become implacably hostile not only to Clinton but to Democrats in general, the country remained anxious about the future and uncertain about which party to trust. People continued to seek answers to the problems that were created by the transition to an information age economy. The voters seemed to agree with *what* Clinton had been trying to do, several others present at the meeting suggested, but they were very concerned about *how* he was trying to do it. After experiencing two years with a Democratic president and a Democratic Congress, Americans had decided that the only way to control government expenditures and encourage efficiency was to once again have a president of one party and a Congress of the other.

Doug Ross could not have agreed more. Now an assistant secretary of labor, Ross had been one of the principal political theorists of the Democratic Leadership Council. No one had been more insistent than he on the need to move the Democratic party away from its traditional reliance on the constituent groups of the New Deal coalition. Ross knew there was a new constituency and that the only way to gain its support was to develop public policies to replace bureaucracies with programs that allow individuals to choose the services they need. The electorate, Ross insisted, had turned on Clinton when health care reform, which they supported, became just another bureaucratic program of big government, which they opposed.

If the first question was what had happened, the more pressing second question was what to do about it. Republicans were in control of both houses of Congress and the presidential election hovered less than two years away. It was, Neustadt reminded them, the same situation in which Harry Truman had found himself after the Republican victory in the congressional election of 1946. There were a number of reasons for Truman's remarkable victory over Dewey in 1948, including the state of the economy and the arrogance of the Republican candidate, but the fact that Truman had managed to unite the country behind a bipartisan foreign policy should not be overlooked.

What Neustadt seemed to suggest was that a president who managed to lead the country in a direction in which even the opposition was willing to go was a president the opposition might not be able to defeat. Truman, of course, had the cold war and Joseph Stalin to help unite the country behind a single course of action. But Stalin was long dead, and the cold war was over—foreign policy would never work. Clinton would have to concentrate instead on domestic policy. It was suggested that the public would certainly support a bipartisan effort to make government more efficient, to which everyone agreed; hardly anyone thought it was the type of issue that would generate excitement or large-scale enthusiasm.

The vice president, however, was willing to listen. He was, after all, the administration's point man on what had come to be called "reinventing government." Now he was being told that *reinventing* had to encompass *reengineering*, that it was necessary to be dramatic and bold. Gore had heard Gingrich talk about selling a federal office building, which he agreed was "great symbolism." Gore also seemed to agree that the administration should take the lead in proposing a bipartisan approach to government reorganization where that was possible, but should go beyond that to frame its own set of proposals for a radical revision of what government did and how.

Whether or not Al Gore would be able to convince the rest of the administration that the key to Clinton's reelection was the complete restructuring of American government, such a restructuring was bound to happen. As the industrial age gave way to the information age, the changes that were taking place throughout the country would inevitably transform the American government. The only question was, how long before politics caught up with the new reality? Indeed, it was something of a surprise that it had taken this long; this was not, after all, the first time that an economic revolution had required a radical revision in the organization of government.

■ ■ ■

Thomas Jefferson had thought it would last forever. There was, he insisted, enough land for the "thousandth generation" of Americans. The yeoman farmer, self-sufficient and independent, forming his own opinions without concern for what anyone else thought, would protect the American democracy from any attempt to impose either a despotism of the state or the more subtle and dangerous tyranny of the mind.

What Jefferson thought would take a thousand generations took only two. The technology of the steam engine changed everything and by the end of the Civil War the railroad had created the transportation system necessary for a national market. Farmers began to specialize in whichever crops would bring the highest price—self-sufficiency yielded to dependence on a market mechanism that provided cash for what they grew and let them buy what they could no longer supply themselves. Cities, which had once been dominated by small tradesmen, now became the scene of enormous factories in which specialization and the division of labor were taken to the extreme. America had become industrialized, and industry was rapidly coming under the control of a steadily diminishing number of powerful corporations.

The American republic had been organized to set finite limits on the power of government, but no one had ever thought to guard against the possibility of private economic power. Within twenty years of the Civil War's resolution, few thought of anything else. In 1887, responding to an agrarian protest that swept over the prairie states, Congress passed the Interstate Commerce Act. The railroads would no longer be free to charge what they wanted to ship farm goods to market. Three years later, in 1890, Congress passed the Sherman Anti-Trust Act, outlawing monopolies and restraint of trade. The invisible hand of Adam Smith was now replaced with the very visible hand of government. Where competition was impossible and monopoly inevitable, government would regulate in the public interest. Where competition was possible, but monopoly had emerged to destroy it, government would act to restore the free workings of a competitive market.

The Interstate Commerce Commission could regulate railroad rates, but it could do nothing to halt the way the railroads expanded or the way in which increasing numbers of people became dependent on them. The Sherman Anti-Trust

Act could be used to break up the Standard Oil Company, but it could do nothing to stop each of its component parts from becoming almost as large and powerful as Standard Oil had been. Industrialization proceeded according to a ruthless logic of its own, and there seemed to be nothing to stop its remorseless march toward an oligopoly in which a few capitalists would own the wealth of the country and dispose as they saw fit of the lives of all its citizens. The question of how to preserve individual liberty and economic opportunity in the face of this continuing consolidation of economic power became the dominant issue after the end of the Civil War.

With the exception of Lincoln's election in the three-way contest of 1860, no presidential campaign in American history has done more to define the future of the nation than that of 1912. William Howard Taft, the Republican incumbent, was matched against not only Woodrow Wilson, the Democratic candidate, but former President Theodore Roosevelt, the candidate of the new Progressive Party. While Taft was content to let the economy take its course, Roosevelt and Wilson engaged in a far-reaching debate about what should be done to diminish the concentrations of private power that dominated the economy and threatened to control the government. It was, as they both described it, the "industrial question," and their respective answers would eventually become the basis of a new social contract for the industrial age.

For Roosevelt, the only solution to the power of private business was to regulate it in the public interest. "Again and again while I was President," he insisted, "I pointed out that under the anti-trust law alone it was neither possible to stop business abuses nor possible to secure the highest efficiency in the service rendered by business to the general public." To the degree to which the anti-trust law prevented business from reaching the size needed to produce the greatest efficiencies, it was actually harmful. It was now necessary "to compete with other nations in the markets of the world as well as to develop our own material civilization at home," and that meant using "those forms of industrial organization that are indispensable to the highest industrial productivity and efficiency."[2]

To ascertain that these large industrial organizations were operated in the public interest, Roosevelt proposed a method of regulation broader and more extensive than anything ever seen. He asked for "a National industrial commission . . . which should have complete power to regulate and control all the great industrial concerns engaged in inter-State business— which practically means all of them in this country. This commission should exercise over these industrial concerns like powers to those exercised over the railways by the Inter-State Commerce Commission . . . and additional powers if found necessary."[3]

Woodrow Wilson was opposed to the regulation of monopolies because that would permit their continued existence, stating that "private monopoly is indefensible and intolerable."[4] It was not only—contrary to what Roosevelt believed— inefficient, but monopoly threatened an end to the American way of government. In a speech delivered during the campaign, Wilson described a country that had undergone one of the most radical transformations in history.

> We are at the parting of the ways. We have, not one or two or three, but many, established and formidable monopolies in the United States. We have, not one or two, but many, fields of endeavor into which it is difficult, if not impossible, for the independent man to enter. We have restricted credit, we have restricted opportunity, we have controlled development, and we have come to be one of the worst ruled, one of the most completely controlled and dominated, governments in the civilized world—no longer a government by free opinion, no longer a government by conviction and the vote of the majority, but a government by the opinion and the duress of small groups of dominant men.

Wilson resisted the call for regulation on the ground that those who were to be regulated would "capture the government, in order not to be restrained too much by it,"[5] and proposed instead a federal trade commission to investigate and publicize the misdeeds of big business. The anti-trust law was to be strengthened and vigorously enforced so that monopoly could be destroyed and the competitive market restored. The labor laws were to be changed so employees, helpless as individuals against the power of the corporation, could organize themselves into unions, which, with a monopoly over labor, could negotiate on an equal basis with those who held a monopoly over capital. The same sort of checks and balances that had kept government under control could be used to limit the power of business.

Wilson won the election and proceeded to do not only everything he had promised, but some of what Roosevelt had promised as well. The Clayton Act strengthened the anti-trust law and, by declaring that labor was not an article of commerce, removed the threat of court injunctions for restraint of trade from labor's attempt to organize. The Federal Trade Commission Act established a commission with the power to investigate and publicize the abuses of big business and to more vigorously enforce the anti-trust laws. The banking system was reorganized and put under tighter federal regulation. Pure food and drug laws and laws to protect the health and safety of employees were passed, all for the purpose of providing protection to those who, on their own, no longer had the power to protect themselves.

But all this was not enough. For twenty years, from the election of 1912 until the campaign of 1932, the process of industrialization continued. The internal combustion engine fully freed people from the limits of their agrarian existence. Huge cities rose up around the centers of industry, creating a new type of urban constituency. More and more power was held by fewer and fewer people until, finally, two thirds of American industry was controlled by no more than 600 corporations (the other third was divided among ten million small businesses). If the rate were to continue, Franklin Roosevelt warned in a speech to the Commonwealth Club of San Francisco, "at the end of another century we shall have all American industry controlled by a dozen corporations and run by perhaps a hundred men. Put plainly, we are steering a steady course toward economic oligarchy, if we are not here already."[6]

The Great Depression was in its third year and Roosevelt called for "a reappraisal of values." The new task was "not discovery or exploitation of natural resources or necessarily producing more goods. It is the soberer, less dramatic business of administering resources and plants already in hand ... of meeting the problem of under-consumption, of adjusting production to consumption, of distributing wealth and products more equitably, of adapting existing economic organizations to the service of the people. The day of enlightened administration has come."[7]

Building on the principles debated in the campaign of 1912 without any thought that he had to choose among them, Roosevelt launched the New Deal and established a new social contract for the industrial age. The original contract, formulated by John Locke and followed by the American founders, had been based on the proposition that the only legitimate object of government was the protection of life, liberty, and the property without which neither life nor liberty could be secure. For Roosevelt, industrialization made it necessary for government "to assist the development of an economic declaration of rights, an economic constitutional order." That declaration, like the original Declaration of Independence, includes the rights to life, property, and liberty, but their original meaning has been amended by the transition from an agrarian to an industrial economy. The right to life now means "a right to make a comfortable living," and the right to property "a right to be assured, to the fullest extent attainable, in the safety of his savings."

The remaining right, what Roosevelt called the "final term of the high contract," was "for liberty and the pursuit of happiness." Much had changed in the past century, and much had been learned about both liberty and the pursuit of happiness. "We know that individual liberty and individual happiness mean nothing unless both are ordered in the sense that one man's meat is not another man's poison." The rights, which had in the original contract seemed so absolute, were now, in the new contract, subject to certain conditions. No one was self-sufficient; all were dependent on one another. Government was now required to maintain "a balance within which every individual may have a place if he will take it, in which every individual may find safety if he wishes it, in which every individual may attain such power as his ability permits, consistent with his assuming the accompanying responsibility. . . ."[8]

Under the New Deal the "day of enlightened administration" arrived with a vengeance. The Clayton Act had permitted the organization of labor; the Wagner Act encouraged it and established the National Labor Relations Board to regulate it. Theodore Roosevelt had suggested a national commission to regulate all of industry; Franklin Roosevelt proposed, and Congress passed, the National Recovery Act, under which each field of industry was invited to draft a voluntary code by which to regulate production and government was empowered to impose one for those who did not. Agencies like the WPA and CCC were invented to put people back to work, and for the first time government became the employer of last resort. Social security was adopted and government was in the business of forcing people to save for retirement. The enormous concentrations of power that had developed in the private sector were now matched by huge bureaucracies in the public sector.

The country in which democracy was to rest on the shoulders of yeoman farmers scattered across a continent was now the most heavily industrialized society in the world and power—once dispersed among individual citizens—was now concentrated in the centralized, hierarchical organizations of big business, big labor, and big government. The original contract had guaranteed liberty by limiting the powers of government. The new social contract was a *new deal* between government and the governed in which at least some part of each citizen's liberty was given up in exchange for economic security against the hazards of an economic system on which everyone depended. In his fireside chats, FDR became the father figure for a nation increasingly dependent on government to protect and preserve it.

▪ ▪ ▪

The large, centralized hierarchical organizations of the industrial age led to large, centralized government bureaucracies. As information age technology changes the structure of the economy, dispersing people and power to the edges of the system, it will dramatically change the way the American government works. The crucial question becomes what kind of change Americans want. While the new class watches with increasing frustration—even anger—as Republicans and Democrats struggle to fashion responses to this new world, the outline of the next social contract is being written not in the public but in the private sector.

At the turn of the century quality and price were often determined by the producer. Henry Ford's famous remark in 1912, "Any customer can have a car painted any color he wants so long as it is black,"[9] typified the attitude of corporations whose market dominance allowed them to decide what the consumer would get. The pattern in which the oil companies all raised their prices for a gallon of gas by exactly the same amount within a twenty-four-hour period at the beginning of the Arab oil embargo typified the way oligopolies could share a market and set a price. Today all that has changed. By creating a single world market and introducing new products in rapid succession, information technology has eroded the power of any one company or any group of companies to set price or quality standards—companies are now forced to give the customer what the customer wants at a price the customer is prepared to pay.

Successful information age companies have adopted quality management techniques that use new technologies to produce products and services that not only cost less but provide greater value. Beginning with the success of the Japanese automobile industry in the 1970s and continuing through the transformation of American manufacturing in the 1980s to present-day trends in retailing such as warehouse stores and customized blue jeans, these techniques have changed the buying habits of America. Companies that have absorbed the lessons of the quality revolution have learned how to do the right thing and, equally important, they have learned how to do it the right way.

Quality has two components: doing the right thing, or being effective, and doing it the right way, or being efficient. When an outcome is produced in the most effective and efficient way possible, the ultimate level of quality has been reached. The upper limits of both effectiveness and efficiency change as technology advances and techniques improve. Success in the marketplace, whether with cars or computers, goes to the company that has taught its workforce how best to use these quality principles.

On the flip side, there are three sure methods of failure. The first and most obvious is doing the wrong thing the wrong way. Many companies, including the American automobile companies in the 1970s, did precisely that. Somewhat less obvious, but equally damaging, is doing the right thing the wrong way or doing the wrong thing the right way. If a competitor has grasped how to do the right thing the right way, companies who have solved only half the problem will begin to fall farther and farther behind.

The same right thing/right way matrix that spells the difference between success and failure in the private sector can be applied to the public sector. If the quality approach in business *begins* with the premise that what the customer wants is always right, the quality approach in politics and government *ends* with the conclusion that the judgment of the electorate is always final and irrevocable. Just as a business may succeed for a while in convincing the public to buy what it knows how to make, parties and politicians may continue to advocate policies and programs that worked in the past, but that no one is interested in any longer. In both cases, failure is inevitable. The business goes into bankruptcy, the parties go into opposition, and the politicians who thought things would never change find themselves out of office.

American corporations that reengineered themselves through the painful process of eliminating both middle management and routine work are once again able to compete in the world market. Similarly drastic measures need to be applied to the bureaucracies of government if the United States is to remain the leading economic power in the world. Moreover, only the creation of a government that does the right thing the right way will provide the basis for a social contract for the information age. But what consumers have found in the marketplace, and what knowledge workers have discovered in the workplace, has yet to be heard by the voter in the public debate. Republicans attack Democrats as "tax and spend liberals" who insist on raising taxes to pay for government services. Democrats attack Republicans as "cut and slash conservatives" who insist on spending less on the poor to reduce taxes on the rich.

A growing number of voters believe there are other choices. As one independent voter from Riverside, California, told her focus group after the 1994 election, "I think that government should be run more like a business. . . . If you are running a business you are trying to satisfy your customer, you are trying to look and see what their needs are because you are trying to meet their needs and you have to do it in the most efficient manner in order to stay competitive."[10] Information age voters, especially the new constituency of knowledge workers, want to know why government cannot—like business—spend less and do more.

▪ ▪ ▪

It was a question that, for a while, Bill Clinton seemed to address. The Clinton presidential campaign had taken considerable pride in its use of information technologies to measure public reaction, often through focus groups, and to then air a television commercial within twenty-four hours designed to take advantage of that reaction. On election day Clinton's campaign director James Carville was seen wearing a T-shirt that read, "Speed killed—George Bush!"[11] It was a technique that worked so well during the campaign there seemed to be no reason not to keep right on using it. When Clinton gave his first state of the union speech, the White House had every tool it needed to measure the immediate reaction, not simply to the speech as a whole, but to each of the specific policies Clinton would announce.

While the cabinet, the justices of the Supreme Court, the members of Congress, the Diplomatic Corps, and millions of Americans watched the president deliver the state of the union message, a select group sat together in a darkened room, peering at a television set, each of them clutching a dial. Whenever the president said something they liked, they immediately turned the dial up; whenever he said something they didn't like, they turned it down. The group liked three things in particular: first and foremost, Clinton's proposal for a "three strikes and you're out" sentencing program for repeat offenders. The second most popular line of the speech was his promise to change the "unemployment system to a re-employment system." The third most favorable promise was the president's announcement that one hundred programs would be cut as part of the process of "reinventing the federal government."[12]

On a Wednesday in early March, less than three weeks after the state of the union address, the president was scheduled to give a speech providing more details to take advantage of the popular new idea of reinventing government. On the preceding Monday evening, Clinton met with Gore. There was a slight problem. Although he had announced that one hundred programs were to be cut from the federal government, no one, including the president, had the slightest idea which programs these might be or just how government was going to be "reinvented." The vice president was asked to implement a policy that consisted of little more than the original line of the president's speech. Al Gore was suddenly in charge of reinventing the American government.

Gore moved quickly. On Wednesday, the same day the president gave his speech, Gore informed Elaine Kamarck, his senior advisor for domestic policy, that she would be in charge of the administration's task force on reinventing government.[13] Gore was convinced that much could be learned from both the reengineering efforts and the quality management programs by which corporate America had reorganized itself to compete in the new world economy, one of the keys to which had been to involve the workers in discussions of how to operate more efficiently. Several hundred federal employees joined the Reinventing Government Task Force (REGO), the first time anyone had ever asked them for their ideas on how they could better do their jobs. Gore visited every major federal agency and department, inviting everyone who worked there to submit ideas to the task force. The leadership of the federal employee unions, who were also involved in the work of the task force, agreed to support its recommendations because all of the workforce reductions were to be achieved through attrition and early retirement.[14]

The National Performance Review (NPR) phase of REGO's work was complete by mid-summer. It identified a number of specific improvements that would allow government to "work better and cost less,"[15] many of which involved the processes of purchasing goods and services or hiring new workers. Only the Pentagon bureaucrats could oppose changes in a procurement system that had managed to produce two-hundred-dollar wrenches and five-hundred-dollar toilet seats. The chairman of the Post Office Committee, Clay Shaw, might object to civil service reform, but most people would support a proposal to streamline the system by which new personnel were selected. Gore's task force pointed out the 140 steps outlined in a manual for hiring federal workers, noting that it frequently took longer to follow these than to complete the actual task for which the person was being hired. Facts like these tended to overcome bureaucratic resistance. The task force's draft report recommended specific reductions in the federal workforce that would reduce the number of federal employees to a level not seen since the administration of John F. Kennedy.

The chairmen of the congressional committees that had oversight responsibility for the agencies affected held the key to the future of these recommendations. The Democratic leaders of the most powerful committees were all well entrenched, and every one of them had close links to the special interests regulated by the agencies they controlled. It was just as Woodrow Wilson had feared—those government was supposed to regulate all too often decided what government was going to do. The committee chairmen had been in Congress for decades; they were confident they knew more about the public policy questions they dealt with every day than anyone else. They were also certain that Clinton, who had been elected with only 43 percent of the vote, could do nothing without them.

The president's own tendencies toward conciliation and compromise had been massively reinforced by George Stephanopoulos, who had joined the Clinton campaign as communications director only after he had become convinced that his boss, Congressman Richard Gephardt, was not going to make a second successive attempt at the Democratic nomination. Stephanopoulos saw every political issue in terms of the effect it would have on public opinion, and every legislative issue in terms of the effect it would have on the Democratic leadership of Congress. The relative importance of committee chairmen was determined by the size of the agencies and departments for which they had jurisdiction. Downsizing might be good for General Motors or Ford, and efficiency in government might be a good thing to talk about in the next election, but a reduction or elimination of any part of the federal government a chairman oversaw meant less influence and power for members of that committee. And that, for Stephanopoulos, meant more trouble for the White House.

Together with Howard Paster, chief lobbyist for the administration and former lobbyist for the United Auto Workers, Stephanopoulos reviewed every major NPR proposal that either changed what government did or how it did it. When they were done, the two had gutted one proposal after another, more afraid of offending the Democratic congressional leadership than interested in any serious attempt to eliminate bureaucracy or reinvent government. Vice President Gore, a former senator who understood better than anyone else in the administration the need to accommodate the legitimate desires of Congress, was nevertheless appalled. He insisted that the report continue to state that no fewer than 250,000 federal jobs were to be eliminated, that it continue to specify how much money would be saved, and that it identify the elimination of a sufficient number of federal programs to meet the president's commitment.

Stephanopoulos would not agree; the issue had to be decided by the president himself. Stephanopoulos argued that if the actual amount of savings was given in the report, Republicans would have an advantage when the budget reconciliation bill was debated in Congress. They would insist on using the savings to reduce the expenditure caps, which would leave no discretionary money to invest in programs such as health care or welfare reform. But Gore pointed out that a report claiming to streamline government would lose all credibility if it did not say how much money was to be saved or how many federal jobs were to be cut. Every major corporation in America that had embarked on a serious attempt to downsize had announced precisely those two things and government must do likewise. After listening to the debate and weighing the comments of several others among the twenty or so people who attended the discussion, Clinton agreed with Gore.

It did not matter who Clinton sided with—the power to decide was still in the hands of Congress, and Congress, or at least the House, was still in the hands of Tom Foley. The Speaker hated every line of the report. When Congressman Dave McCurdy, Democrat of Oklahoma and chairman of a congressional caucus sympathetic to the ideas of the DLC, requested it be combined into a single bill and then voted up or down in the House, Foley made clear his intent, telling McCurdy, "I know too many fine federal government employees who have worked all their lives to properly serve the Congress and the people to have them subjected to such a vote."[16] The Gore report was subsequently divided, each part assigned to the congressional committee that had jurisdiction over the agencies potentially affected. Only about half of the $108 billion in savings Gore's task force had identified survived the appropriations process. Had it not been for the need to cut something to meet the deficit reduction targets established in Clinton's budget, not even that much would have been done.

Before the congressional election of 1994, Al Gore had been compelled to give up much of what he wanted out of deference to the Democratic majorities in the House and Senate. After November 8 he was suddenly forced to think about just how far he was willing to go toward eliminating much of the federal government altogether. What had begun as an effort to make government "less expensive and more efficient"[17] had now become a serious struggle over just what the role of government in America should be.

4

☆☆☆

PRESERVING THE AMERICAN COMMONS

The only surprising thing about the results of the 1994 election was how long the country waited before throwing congressional Democrats out of power. After sixty years New Deal liberalism was delivering the wrong set of government services and spending more to pay for them. Higher taxes were imposed, not to supply more services, but to pay the salaries of the large number of bureaucrats needed to provide them. For more than thirty years, while the productivity of American manufacturing increased sixfold, the productivity of public employees had actually declined.[1] The discipline of the marketplace had compelled private business to increase revenues and decrease costs, but Lyndon Johnson's Great Society had dissolved the link between public revenues and public expenditures.

New Deal programs such as social security had become so much a part of government that it was difficult for anyone, especially the most senior Democratic members of Congress, to believe that the public really wanted to change the way they worked. Without the discipline of market alternatives to compel the kind of radical transformation private enterprise had undergone, the established political leadership of the country went about its business, oblivious to the fact that its support was dwindling daily. By the 1994 election, 74 percent of the

American people were convinced that government was simply not interested in what they wanted.[2]

The New Deal was over, and while everyone talked about what the Republicans were going to do with their new congressional majority, scarcely anyone stopped to ask what the country wanted them to do. It would not have been difficult to find out. Two thirds of the public want various elements of what has become known as the American Dream: They want to have good incomes and to be able to afford to send their children to college. They want to own their own homes. They want their children's futures to be brighter than their own.[3] What they want, in other words, is economic opportunity. But voters are motivated by more than material goods—they also want to feel secure in their personal lives. They want safer streets, better schools, and friendlier neighborhoods, and they believe government can help provide them.[4]

If Americans want economic opportunity and better communities, they also have an abiding interest in the kinds of values that are taught at home, in school, at work, and through religion. Americans look to the intermediary civic organizations of church, school, and voluntary associations for the quality of their lives and the values that shape the civic culture of their country.[5] They do not expect, nor do they want, government to impose those values, but they do want public policies that reinforce, rather than work at cross-purposes with, their fundamental beliefs.

If doing the right thing means providing physical safety, creating economic opportunity, and building better communities, doing it the right way means doing it as efficiently as possible. The private sector has employed information age technology to reduce unnecessary costs by eliminating the levels of middle management that were the core of the corporate bureaucracy. Front line workers, who once followed a strict set of regulations enforced by an immediate supervisor, now work directly with the customer. Computers, rather than human employees, now count and keep track of what has been and what remains to be done. The twin forces of competition and new technology have not only restructured the American economy, they have reinvented it. Government services, however, are still delivered through the same hierarchical structures that have been in place for more than half a century.

The price of government keeps rising, though American citizens' willingness to pay for it continues to decline. The result has been an enormous increase in the deficit since 1981. When Clinton tried to lower it by raising taxes and reducing the size of at least some government programs, Republicans countered with demands for a tax cut and reduced spending. The public agreed, but not because they wanted government to do less. According to the University of Chicago's comprehensive annual social issues survey, "for most problems, most people see additional government spending as needed. But they want that spending to be effective, to actually ameliorate the problems that they are designed to address. What the public wants is not less spending but spending that works."[6]

The public wants a government that offers the same efficiencies as the marketplace. They want bureaucracy to disappear so they can choose the services they need when they need them. What they seem to get instead are government monopolies that force the public to take the services offered in the way the government wants to provide them at a price the government wants to charge.

Elimination of bureaucracy is one aspect of doing things the right way; choice is another. At the end of World War II, millions of returning servicemen created a sudden and unprecedented demand for education and housing. Instead of creating a government monopoly to educate and house them all at once, the GI bill let each eligible person choose the type and amount of government services he wanted. Government money would pay for a college education, and each individual could still choose the college or university he wanted to attend. Rather than build huge tracts of federal housing, the

Federal Housing Authority provided a guarantee for home mortgages. Families could finance their homes based on future earning potential, and a market developed to supply the homes they wanted. These are old examples of the types of new choices Americans now demand.

Doing the right *thing* produces effective government that concentrates on what people want. Doing it the right *way* produces an efficient government that delivers services the way the public wants to receive them. The party or candidate that first formulates a program that meets these two requirements will win the confidence and votes of the American public. Effectiveness and efficiency have become the new criteria of American politics, and they will form the basis of the new social contract for the information age.

▪ ▪ ▪

In Haley Barbour's view, the best government was no government at all. The Republican national chairman had done perhaps more than anyone else to bring about the Republican victory of 1994, born not of any systematic analysis of the political imperatives of the new information age, but in the grim reality of Republican defeat. In 1992 George Bush received the lowest percentage of votes of any Republican candidate for president since 1912. The lesson, Barbour believed, was that "you need to stand for something";[7] he had no doubt what that something was. The public—especially the part of it that had voted for Ross Perot—still wanted the same things it had in 1980, when Ronald Reagan was first elected: lower taxes, smaller government, fewer regulations, and less government spending.

H. Ross Perot's votes came principally from people whose real income had suffered the greatest reductions from the dislocations occasioned by the transition from an industrial to an information economy. Those who had experienced wage losses extending beyond a decade were far more likely to have voted for Perot than for Clinton. Indeed, the greater the wage

loss and the longer it had lasted, the higher the correlation.[8]
Following the advice of his pollster, Stan Greenberg, Clinton
had tried to capitalize on this resentment by claiming he was
the candidate of those "who do the work and pay the taxes,
raise the kids and play by the rules."[9] He tried to appeal to
those constituents by promising cuts in the bureaucracy to
make government more effective and more efficient,[10] but he
had failed to win them over. When they considered Clinton,
according to Greenberg's analysis, "they dwell on the question
of trust and promise, not specific policy differences."[11] But
while they may have had doubts about the new Democratic
president, they were certain about the Democratic-controlled
Congress. The Perot voters, according to From and Marshall's
analysis, reserved "their deepest and richest criticism for the
Congress of the United States."[12]

The Contract with America was specifically designed to take
advantage of the skepticism with which Perot voters viewed
Clinton and the resentment they felt toward Congress. The
president was attacked for not keeping his promise to enact a
middle-class tax cut while he raised taxes in general, for campaigning as a "New Democrat" and then calling for an end to
the ban on gays in the military, and for promising to make
health care simple and affordable and then calling for the creation of a massive new health care bureaucracy. Congress was
attacked as a bastion of power and privilege dominated by
Democrats who collected money and favors from the special
interest lobbyists who really ran government.

It was more than an attack on Clinton and the Congress; it
was also, as Haley Barbour had said it would be, a statement
of what the Republicans stood for. Or, rather, it was a statement of what the Perot voters wanted to hear. Perot's pollster,
Frank Luntz, had been hired by Gingrich to hone the language used by the signers of the Contract during their 1994
campaigns for Congress.[13] Luntz convinced Barbour that the
Republicans would win the 1994 elections if they captured the
votes of two thirds of those who had voted for Perot and main-

tained the allegiance of the Republican faithful. Greenberg had test-marketed everything Clinton said during the presidential campaign by asking questions of focus groups. Luntz, in turn, carefully measured the responses of focus groups to each part of the message the Republicans would offer during the congressional elections.[14] The ten-part program for the Contract with America was thus written in the simple slogans that tested best with Perot voters.

This political strategy explained what was otherwise a strange paradox. While Newt Gingrich talked incessantly about Alvin Toffler's "third wave" and the need to prepare for the new information age, the Contract with America was a document that looked more to the past than it did to the future. There was nothing in it to appeal to the new class of knowledge workers because everything in it had been designed to appeal to those who refused to believe that the industrial age was over. As Luntz put it, "Perot voters are more afraid of the future, more apprehensive about the quality of life and whether it will improve in the future."[15]

The Perot voters were convinced that what their candidate had told them was true—in this case, that there was nothing wrong with the machine a new mechanic and a little tinkering couldn't fix. They were also convinced that the reason for their declining incomes was because too much of their money was being wasted by government. The Republican promise to "cut the deficit and cut taxes" echoed the demands of this third-candidate constituency. Gingrich undercut his own rhetoric about the possibilities of the future by adopting a political program designed to appeal to those focused on the past. In what was almost a mirror image of Clinton's fascination with Greenberg's middle-class populism, Gingrich was seduced by his own pollster into offering a Contract that had little to do with the requirements of an information age and everything to do with his becoming the first Republican Speaker in forty years.

Frank Luntz's prediction that Republicans would take control of Congress if two thirds of those who had voted for Perot in 1992 voted for Republican candidates in 1994 was precisely correct.[16] The anger of Perot voters had not subsided during the two years since the presidential election; they still wanted to see Washington turned inside out. Two thirds of them voted Republican as the only way to get rid of the Democratic establishment they blamed for the bulk of America's ills. Flushed with victory, Republicans reaffirmed their promise to enact the specific proposals contained in the Contract with America during their first hundred days in office. Gingrich, suddenly famous, declared himself a revolutionary and assumed the leadership of the most powerful reactionary force to hit Capitol Hill in this century.

The Contract with America, designed to appeal to precisely that part of the population most anxious to return to the past, was only the first step in a full-scale assault on the federal government, an attack that took several forms. The new Republicans used the popularity of their demand for a balanced budget amendment to insist, not simply on cuts in spending, but on wholesale reductions in the size of government. While the Clinton administration talked about the need to abolish specific programs, Republicans advocated the elimination of entire departments. The departments of Education, Energy, Housing and Urban Development—even the Department of Commerce, originally created to advance the interests of American business—were all scheduled for extinction.[17] With the lone exception of the Department of Defense every federal agency was viewed by the new Republican majority as a potential target. By adding huge tax cuts to an already enormous deficit, the achievement of a balanced budget would require, and would excuse, the kind of reductions that could only be accomplished by limiting the role of the federal government to national defense and not a great deal more.

The sudden emphasis on devolution was part of the same pattern. Republican governors argued that states could do a better job of delivering government services to their residents than a bureaucracy thousands of miles away from the people it was supposed to serve. Whether welfare or food stamps, school lunch programs or education, better solutions, they said, could always be found at the state and local levels. But while the GOP governors wanted to have the power and authority to decide how things should be done, they were perfectly content to let the federal government continue to pay for them. Power was to be devolved to the states; the responsibility for taxation was not. The introduction of the idea of block grants to the states, never mentioned in the Contract with America, was a work of pure political expediency: programs would be run by the states while revenues would continue to be supplied by the federal government and, because the size of each grant would necessarily be limited by the requirements of a balanced budget, the programs themselves would gradually be restricted to ever smaller numbers. While the public was looking for a government that did more with less, Republicans sought a government that did increasingly less—period.

▪ ▪ ▪

Adopting a provision of the Contract with America, the new Congress passed, and Clinton signed into law, a procedure by which to limit—if not end—unfunded mandates.[18] It was an attempt to stop the federal government's practice of imposing obligations on the states without providing the financial wherewithal to meet them. But if a state or a municipality could now choose to ignore any regulation regarding clean air or water, for instance, that cost them money, why should it be expected to treat private citizens or businesses any differently? Republicans were ready with an answer designed to appeal not only to the widespread disenchantment with the regulatory policies of the federal government, but to the specific demands of Western ranchers.

The "sagebrush rebellion" had swept through the Rocky Mountain states in the late 1970s. The policies of Reagan's first secretary of the interior, James Watt, were designed to address the complaints this group of intermountain-state land-owners had about what they considered to be the unwarranted intrusion of the federal government in their lives. It was organized and led by ranchers who found nothing inconsistent in their use of publicly owned lands to graze their cattle with their demand that government leave them alone to use their private property as they saw fit. In their judgment, regulations to protect the environment were at best misguided and at worst part of a federal conspiracy to put them out of business. When the spotted owl was declared an endangered species and federal courts began to prohibit logging on large tracts of national forestland, the Pacific Northwest joined the Rocky Mountain states as a battleground between those who favored federal regulation to protect the environment and those who opposed it as a threat—not simply to their economic interests, but to their whole way of life.

What had begun as the sagebrush rebellion ultimately reached a point of almost outright secession. In a singular interpretation of the Constitution, the leaders of what was now called the West's "property rights movement" insisted that the federal government had no authority to regulate anything that happened on either public land or private property.[19] Beginning with Yellowstone in 1872 (in that case for Montana and Wyoming), national park or forest lands had been set aside as a condition of statehood. Property rights advocates argue that the mountain states did not have the authority to agree to such provisions and that the land is still owned by the counties, who never authorized the state grants. Supporters of the property rights movement thus insisted that the only valid legal authority on what were called federal lands was not the forest service or the bureau of land management but the county's sheriff.[20]

The federal government had even less right to regulate private property; the Tenth Amendment reserves to the states all power not expressly delegated to the federal government and certainly no provision of the Constitution expressly delegated authority concerning private property. To the ranchers this seemed straightforward; only someone connected with the federal government, they felt, would deny their logic. Every attempt by a federal agency to regulate what took place on private property was an unconstitutional usurpation of authority and, it was openly asserted, should be resisted by every means possible.

All the tendencies of the Western property rights movement were brought together in the person of one of its leaders, Nevada rancher Wayne Hage.[21] On the one hand Hage alleged in a lawsuit that the federal government owed him money because its fish and game agencies had failed to prevent elk from drinking water and eating grass on his property. On the other hand he, along with several other like-minded ranchers, alleged in a second lawsuit that the U.S. Forest Service and the Bureau of Land Management had acted improperly in trying to restrict grazing for their cattle on public lands. It was no longer a case of "what is mine is mine, and what is yours is negotiable," but rather, "what is mine is mine, and so is whatever else I think I need."

The freshman House Republicans were determined to make this concept—originally embraced by the Reagan administration—the law of the land. In 1988 Reagan had signed an executive order requiring government agencies to evaluate the private property takings implications of any regulatory actions they might initiate.[22] Under the Contract with America, the provision of the Fifth Amendment prohibiting government from taking private property for a public purpose without due compensation was now to be applied to any government action or regulation that caused the value of property to decline by more than 10 percent. In an attempt to gain some bipartisan support for one of the most radical attempts ever devised to limit the ability of government to protect the public interest, the new Republican majority in the House ignored the express language of their Contract and

limited the compensation requirement to regulations affecting wetlands, endangered species, and water use. If the new
Republicans had their way, the U.S. government would no
longer be able to require private individuals or businesses, let
alone state governments, to take steps to protect the environment, unless it was willing to pay them for their troubles.

A Democratic administration might have been expected to
resist these radical reductions in the power and authority of
government by insisting on the need for such essentials as
clean air and water, and protection for species threatened with
extinction. Clinton, however, had never been a committed en-
vironmentalist and had always been able to see both sides of
an argument. He asked Vice President Gore, a recognized en-
vironmentalist, to try to find some middle ground.

There was no middle ground. Republicans were threatening
to make federal agencies the new endangered species. But
even among those most threatened, Gore's aide, Elaine
Kamarck, had a hard time finding anyone willing to embrace
any major changes in how their agency functioned. Representatives of both the EPA and the FDA eventually agreed to minor reductions in the paperwork requirements connected
with regulations they had been passing without restraint.[23]
These bureaucrats seemed certain they were the only ones
who understood how to protect the nation from Republicans'
zeal to turn over her most important resources, and the
health and safety of her citizens, to the rapacious desires of
the marketplace.

If many Democrats, and a great many federal bureaucrats,
thought the takings bill was extreme, most freshman House
Republicans thought it only logical. Most economists believed
that the market was the most efficient way to allocate scarce
resources, so it followed that any attempt by government to
regulate the market, no matter how well intentioned, could
only make it less efficient. Gingrich Republicans, like nine-
teenth-century liberals, believed that in the long run, at least,
the market, left to its own devices, would always produce the

best outcome for everyone. Government regulation was the last refuge of misty-eyed reformers who were unable, or unwilling, to face reality.

It was a classic case of ignoring what is called the "tragedy of the commons."[24] While markets are the most efficient way to allocate resources, by themselves they can do nothing to determine which resources, particularly scarce ones, need to be preserved for future generations or whose use has a harmful effect on the community. Unless informed by public purpose, they have no values. In the agrarian age, when uncontrolled grazing was allowed on public lands, the grass eventually disappeared altogether. Had grazing on the commons been banned, damage to the land would have been minimized, but there would have been no economic benefit. The problem was that the land was a free good whose use had no economic penalty until suddenly the land itself became worthless. That was the tragedy of the commons, and the only way to avoid it would have been to encourage limited grazing to produce an economic benefit without destroying the resource itself.

■   ■   ■

This kind of solution continues to elude the newest wave of free market Republicans. The Contract with America promised "to renew the American Dream by promoting individual liberty, economic opportunity, and personal responsibility, through limited and effective government, high standards of performance, and an America strong enough to defend all her citizens against violence at home and abroad." The Contract, which purports to describe the new Republican "basic philosophy of American civilization,"[25] never even mentions community, and never so much as suggests that there could be a conflict between the immediate self-interest of the individual and the long-term best interests of the country.

The Contract with America was written from a libertarian perspective in which the only legitimate end of government is to provide protection for private property and defense against aggression, whether foreign or domestic. This is what was known in the nineteenth century as the "night watchman theory of the state,"[26] used at the beginning of the industrial age to justify using children for factory labor and both economic and legal servitude for women. It is a theory now being used at the beginning of the information age to justify the abandonment of everything that preserves the American commons.

The Food and Drug Administration was created early in this century in response to the exposure by the muckraking press of major health hazards in the new food and drug processing industries in America. The FDA's power was broadened over the years by Democrats in Congress who favored the command and control model for protecting the community's interest in the workings of the marketplace. Gingrich and his supporters went after the agency with more than their standard hostility to regulation. One of the bones of contention was the FDA's refusal to acknowledge the potential benefits of megadoses of vitamins or other "natural" remedies. In keeping with its original responsibility, the FDA acted to restrict the medicinal claims that today's home remedy manufacturers made for their products.[27] When it became known that the owners of one of these companies, Amway's Rich De Vos and Jay Van Andel, were also the largest contributors to a Republican congressional fund-raising dinner, the personal involvement of the Speaker in issues of this kind appeared to be less a function of belief than a question of politics as usual.[28]

These suspicions were hardly dispelled when lobbyists for individual corporations and industry associations were seen helping the new Republicans write the legislation designed to free them from regulation. But the indifference of the new Republicans to the needs of the community reached its extreme when they demanded that government not issue any regulations designed to enforce laws protecting health, safety, and the environment until they were first subjected to a cost-benefit analysis. Even if it were possible to quantify the benefit of saving a life, preventing the outbreak of a disease, or preserving the sheer beauty of a forest or a wilderness, it would be only the beginning of an impossible social calculus. A determination of the effect on consumers of a decision to make regulation less stringent would still be necessary. If consumers were less willing to buy a product they could no longer trust, then less of that product would be made, fewer people would be employed, and the economy as a whole would suffer. The attempt to replace human judgment with a mechanical application of mathematics would lead only to endless questions.

That was precisely what the new Republicans were hoping for. Compliance with cost-benefit requirements would become so difficult that agencies would find it almost impossible to issue any regulations at all. When they did, those regulations would be subject to judicial review whenever anyone affected by them chose to challenge them in court. Ultimately the greed of those lobbying for such changes exceeded their reach, and after a long debate during which Democrats found common ground with moderate Republicans, the bill was pulled from the Senate calendar. That did not stop the House from trying to use the power of the purse, however, to restrict the operations of any government agency whose regulatory responsibility interfered with the unrestricted operation of the marketplace. But when freshman Republicans attached riders that gutted numerous environmental regulations to the appropriation bills, Gingrich lost the support of Republican moderates whose loyalties were to their constituencies and their own convictions rather than to the principles of the Contract with America. These moderates joined with House Democrats to force the conferees to agree to the Senate's efforts to strip such language from the budget reconciliation legislation.

▪ ▪ ▪

The current regulatory debate fails to consider the difficulty inherent in any attempt to quantify the public benefit from safe food and drugs or national parks or forests untouched by commercial exploitation. More important, new free market conservatives generally fail to understand the fundamental changes that have been caused by information technology. In the industrial age oil and gas and all other resources essential to the economic engine were valuable precisely because demand kept growing while supply kept shrinking. The oil embargo of 1973, by which OPEC drove up the price of oil, threatening in the process the economic stability of the West, showed as nothing else could the power of those who control a scarce resource. But in the information age, the availability of what were only recently considered scarce resources can actually be increased.

The list of examples is endless: programmed thermostats reduce the energy needed to produce goods or services. With its sophisticated system of sensors and computers, a Boeing 757 burns nearly 30 percent less fuel per passenger mile than the previous generation of jet aircraft.[29] The amount of energy saved through the use of information technology is measured in what have come to be called "Negawatts." They supply 28 percent of America's energy, almost as much as the country gets from petroleum.[30] The oil pumped out of the deserts of the Middle East has become less important than the desert sand—oil runs machinery, but sand provides the silicon for the microprocessors that have altered forever both the economy and all our economic assumptions.

The ability to preserve natural resources occurs with materials other than oil. "Immaterials," measured and described in the same manner as "Negawatts,"[31] are materials created through more efficient means made possible by information technology. During the last twenty years, the application of this technology to the use of iron ore has produced efficiencies that have had the net effect of adding three hundred years to the available supply.[32] During the same period, the consumption of metal in one thousand soda cans has fallen from 164 pounds to approximately 35 pounds.[33] According to one estimate, these "immaterials" now make up almost one third of the total material usage in the United States.[34]

While the new conservatives rush toward their goal of a limited government and an unregulated market, the community they ignore is looking in a completely different direction. Thus, only 4 percent of the public agrees with the idea that we have the right to take from the earth the resources we need no matter the long-term consequences for the environment, while 72 percent believe government has a responsibility to help preserve it.[35] That does not mean, however, that the public wants the kind of regulation in which some faceless policy maker in Washington decides what is best for everyone.

Not only has the technology of the information age come to dominate American life, so has the perspective of the new class of knowledge workers. While Republicans and Democrats in Congress fight over how much government to get rid of, a majority of both Republicans and Democrats in the country believe that the role of government should be to do whatever is necessary to help "people help themselves." They do not want government to walk away from the problem, but neither do they want it "fixed" with more rules and regulation. By overwhelming margins, both conservatives and liberals want government to provide the community with the tools with which to do the job itself.[36]

This is precisely what government in the information age is able to do: it can disseminate to each individual what he or she needs to know about activities or behavior that affect the community as a whole. It can further provide an incentive for all to learn the consequences of their failure to conform to the requirements of the community. And instead of the old command and control method of ensuring compliance by threatening punishment, it can establish a marketplace with boundary conditions to protect the public interest, thereby preserving the commons for the continuing benefit of the entire community.

▪ ▪ ▪

Consider again the problem of the commons, but in a more contemporary guise—the roadside litter caused by bottles and cans. Along with a number of other states, California and Michigan passed laws by which consumers were given an economic incentive to reduce litter by returning empty beverage containers for recycling. The California law became an administrative nightmare while the Michigan law eliminated the need for bureaucracy altogether.

The California law, like that of every other state enacting so-called "bottle bills," was predicated on the assumption it would not be completely effective. If it was, then each person buying a beverage in a can or bottle with a deposit would return every such empty container for the full value of the deposit and no money would be available to pay the handlers of the containers for recycling the returned materials. But only California's legislature, under the influence of the most powerful interests affected by such a law, attempted to manage a market by governmental fiat. To save grocery stores the logistical problems involved with accepting containers for recycling, the 1986 law sought to encourage the development of stand-alone recycling "convenience centers." A circle was drawn within a half-mile radius of every major grocery store, based on retail sales tax receipts; only if there was no convenience center within that radius did the store have to accept containers from their customers. If there was a center, the store had only to post a sign informing customers where to return the bottles and cans they were buying in that particular store. But of course the single "convenience" center was not as convenient as the store itself, so many stores gave in to their customers' requests and began accepting all containers. This inevitably led to complaints from the centers, which depended on the law's 1.7 cent handling fee from the containers.

Responsibility for administering this complex set of interactions rests with the Department of Conservation. Of the $364 million raised each year, the department spends $20 million per year on program administration alone. Even so, the fund of unredeemed money grew over the years to over $80 million. The state's municipalities thought they knew how to spend it. The original law provided that any government establishing curbside pickup, the ultimate in consumer convenience, would be entitled to keep the 2.5 cents that would otherwise go back to the purchaser of the container. But curbside pickup is by far the most costly method of recycling. To help subsidize this inefficiency, the latest amendments to California's law now provide $5 million to help cover each city's costs in providing such services. This is considered only right by the cities since a separate piece of legislation passed by the same legislature mandates that by the year 2000 each city collect half of its total wastes for recycling or face daily fines—presumably to be paid by taxpayers who fail to recycle their trash curbside and thus lose the money they paid in deposits. Now cities are passing legislation making it a crime for any unauthorized person to take recyclable trash from a curbside container and return it directly to a recycling center. The legislature has managed to create a system so complex and rife with inherent inconsistencies between administrative rules that it is the subject of intense negotiations in Sacramento almost every year.[37] But that outcome also works to the benefit of those who passed the law because it provides ample opportunities to solicit campaign contributions from whichever side of the negotiations each legislator happens to favor.

Michigan, on the other hand, passed a referendum establishing a recycling policy that requires no interference by the legislature and no bureaucracy to administer it. By redefining the market with two simple rules and enough information, the state created a system that, in ten years, achieved the highest recycling rates of any state—93 percent of cans and 97 percent of bottles.[38] The first rule is that the Michigan deposit is ten cents on each container, four times that of California and twice that of any other state with a bottle bill. This relatively high "tax rate" has created a law that requires only the mechanisms of the marketplace to achieve its goals. At the end of each major sporting event, for instance, an army of kids scurries up and down the aisles of the venue carrying large garbage bags and grabbing every can and bottle they can find for redemption. The law, which expresses the interest of the community in a litter-free environment, created a private market to accomplish a public purpose. The second rule is that every private enterprise—no matter what its size—that sells beverages in cans or bottles must redeem such containers whether or not it sold them in the first place. This makes returning bottles at least as convenient as buying them.

Michigan created a market in used beverage containers by the simple expedient of making the reward for collecting them greater than the cost of handling them. Rather than seizing upon the community's interest in a clean environment as an excuse for governmental restraints on personal behavior, the Michigan law actually expanded individual freedom. It says, in effect, "you can litter if you want to, but it will cost you ten cents each time you do it. Better yet, even if you decide to ignore the wishes of the community, there is a market mechanism in place that will repair the effects of your bad behavior without forcing the community to pay for it."

By establishing the rules within which a market functions, government in the information age can create systems capable of regulating themselves. The California electorate did precisely that when it passed Proposition 65 by a two-thirds vote in 1986. Because of Proposition 65, patrons of California restaurants are greeted with perhaps the least inviting sign ever hung on a barroom door: "Warning: Drinking Distilled Spirits, Beer, Coolers, Wine and Other Alcoholic Beverages May Increase Cancer Risk, and During Pregnancy Can Cause Birth Defects." The statement, which may seem obvious and obtrusive, has, in fact, produced remarkable reductions in the production and sale of potential toxins. It has done so without a bureaucracy and without costly enforcement mechanisms at a more rapid rate than anything ever accomplished under the command and control approach of industrial age regulation.

The Environmental Protection Agency, which has become one of the favorite targets of Gingrich Republicans, determines, on the basis of scientific evidence, safe levels of exposure to particular chemicals and promulgates rules to enforce them. Because it can take years to make a scientifically accurate assessment of the risk at various levels of exposure, those who produce any chemical under review have no incentive to hasten the time at which they have to comply with a rule that could cost them a great deal of money. Proposition 65 reengineered the process by shifting responsibility for determining safe levels of exposure from the government to the producers. It dealt with this threat to the "commons" by giving the functions of investigation and enforcement to the marketplace.

The governor of California is required to regularly compile a list of chemicals known to the scientific community to cause cancer or birth defects. Any business that a year after publication of a list is still using any of the listed chemicals must either warn the public or pay a fine of $2,500 for each person exposed. The potentially enormous fine, combined with a provision allowing anyone to sue on behalf of the public, created the kind of risk every business wanted to avoid. The only way to avert the penalties is to either have clear agreements on what levels are safe or not use the substance at all. The burden is on industry to conduct its own tests to determine what, if any, levels of exposure will meet a legal challenge, creating a rather unusual situation in which business requests that government give its approval to their research and conclusions.

More than 280 chemicals have been limited in their use through the procedures created by Proposition 65; only two dozen have been limited by the federal EPA.[39] The governmental action identifying a substance as carcinogenic has caused industry to eliminate chemicals as diverse as lead in crystal wine decanters and trichloroethylene in liquid paper.[40] The budget for the entire program is less than 1 percent of the money spent by the state EPA. Like the bottle bill in Mich-

igan, Proposition 65 in California combined the spread of information with the power of government to establish rules
that redefine markets in ways that build a better community.
Whether litter, carcinogens, or any other threat to the commons, government can protect the public interest by imposing
a cost that will either eliminate the problem or pay for its effects. Contrary to the ideology of new Republicans, this does
in fact require the full participation of government. Contrary
to the desire of old Democrats, the shifting of costs of compliance to business and the private citizen will eliminate the
need for certain bureaucracies.

The finite nature of our natural resources creates a sense of
urgency for finding the right government policy to efficiently
and effectively preserve our environment. One study done by
Global Futures estimated that, if current policies are not
changed, in the United States by the end of the next century
fossil fuel consumption will be four times greater than it is today, carbon emissions will triple, and the standard of living
will be approximately half of what is today defined as the poverty level. If, on the other hand, environmental policies are
changed to reflect the information age approaches embodied
in Michigan's bottle bill and California's Proposition 65, an alternative future is possible. Shifting taxes from income to consumption, improving our education system, and providing
equal opportunity and reasonable security are policy changes
that, combined with land stewardship, will make it possible to
triple the standard of living during the same period.[41] But all
of these changes must begin with an understanding of the
fundamental principle of the commons. Whenever the actions
of some members of a society adversely affect the well-being of
the entire community, government must set rules for the
marketplace that put the interests of the commons ahead of
the avarice of private interests.

5

REENGINEERING AMERICAN GOVERNMENT

The results of the 1994 election had convinced Al Gore. It was not enough, the vice president decided, to make government "less expensive and more efficient"; the administration needed to make government more effective. The National Performance Review, led by Elaine Kamarck, had "focused on how government should work, not on what it should do."[1] Now it was time to examine each agency and program of the federal government in light of the four strategies of corporate reengineering. First, should the activity be eliminated altogether? Second, should it be moved to a different division, in this case, the states? Third, should it be "outsourced" to private business? And fourth, should the activity be reengineered to create a new and better way by which to accomplish its objective?[2] Gore wanted government to "work better and not just cost less, but do less."[3] The Republicans were way ahead of him.

At first Kamarck thought it might be possible to eliminate three entire departments: Energy, Transportation, and Housing and Urban Development. Yet all of them survived. Energy was saved because control over nuclear energy would have gone to the Department of Defense. Civilian control had been a fundamental principle of nuclear policy since it was first established by President Eisenhower, and the Clinton administration was unwilling to change it. HUD and Transportation avoided extinction by eagerly embracing the cause of reinvention: HUD offered to abolish the command and control bureaucracies that had turned public housing into a public disaster and replace them with block grants to the states and housing vouchers for the poor. Transportation agreed both to consolidate and streamline block grant programs of its own and to transfer the air traffic control system to a semi-private corporation.

While the Clinton administration discussed the details of reinventing three cabinet-level departments, the new Republican majority in Congress called for the abolition of four: Energy, HUD, Commerce, and Education.[4] The Department of Commerce was viewed as an ideological fifth column. The financial support it gave to industry for basic research and dealings with foreign governments was much too close to the notion of economic planning for the new Republicans, who believed devoutly in the beneficent workings of old-style laissez-faire capitalism. The elimination of government grants to business would, of course, also end a major incentive for business to make political contributions to a Democratic president.

If they viewed Commerce with suspicion, new Republicans looked at the Department of Education with something close to hatred. Nearly all of the gains Republicans had made in the House had come from the South, where the party had become increasingly dominated by religious fundamentalists convinced the federal government had no business telling local schools what they could teach and to whom. The Christian Coalition wanted to eliminate the Department of Education as the first step toward the creation of an educational system in which parents had nearly complete authority to decide what their children learned and where they learned it. In lieu of public education that taught the lessons of a common citizenship, the religious right was determined to install a system of private education that taught the faith of a community of true believers.

■ ■ ■

While the Democratic administration could not move beyond its reinvention recommendations and the Republican Congress could think of government only in terms of reduction, few at either end of Pennsylvania Avenue gave any serious thought to reengineering. Instead, the debate over how much government to cut was driven by how much money each side needed to fund the tax cuts for the constituencies they wanted to attract. Clinton and Gore decided their best response to the 1994 election was to make good on the middle-class tax cut they had promised during the 1992 campaign. The Contract with America promised a $500 tax credit to families with incomes up to $200,000 a year for each child under the age of eighteen.[5] As with everything else in the Contract, Frank Luntz had thoroughly tested this idea in focus groups. The Republicans found that the higher they raised the income level for eligibility, the more popular it became. By excluding only families that made more than $200,000, the cost had become an extraordinary $117.5 billion.

Clinton offered both less and more than the Republicans. He offered less in that the $500 tax credit he proposed would be limited to families earning under $75,000 a year and would be available only for each child under the age of thirteen, rather than eighteen.[6] He offered more in his broad "Middle Class Bill of Rights."[7] In calling for a tax deduction for college tuition, Clinton went further than any proposals in the Contract with America, focusing attention on the connection between knowledge, future income, and what government should do to encourage the kind of education necessary to compete in the information age.

For all his third wave rhetoric, the new House Speaker greeted with silence the proposal to use the tax system to encourage the acquisition of information age skills. While the Republicans—or at least the ideologues who now dominated discussion in the House—said they were in favor of reinventing or even reengineering government, their collective approach in fact had nothing to do with the new imperative of the information age. What they really were interested in was reversing the whole tendency of the twentieth century toward a larger, more powerful federal government. The most effective and permanent way to do that was to combine drastic tax cuts with a balanced budget amendment.

Despite all claims to the contrary, Republican tax cuts were not designed to make life easier for the middle class, and the balanced budget amendment was not the only way to force government to live within its means. Tax cuts would decrease revenue and make it more difficult for the federal government to spend money on anything but the bare essentials, which meant "security, at home and abroad."[8] The balanced budget amendment was not needed to balance the budget; Congress could do that whenever it chose to. The amendment was necessary, however, if a balanced budget was going to become something that could only be overturned by a two-thirds majority. Republicans could not be sure just how long they would have control of both the House and the Senate but, given their ability to elect at least one third of the Congress even in their most difficult years, they were certain this "supermajority" requirement would protect their ideas for generations.

Having lost the battle for a balanced budget by a single vote in the Senate, Republicans did the next best thing to secure a permanent reduction in the size of government: they cut taxes as if raising revenues were the only serious sin. They had promised the Christian Coalition that their $500 per child tax credit would extend to virtually every family in America, and would therefore help defray the costs of private education for those families wanting to send their children to religious schools.[9] This proposal, as expensive as it was, represented only half of the most costly tax giveaways ever proposed. Cap-ital gains taxes were to be cut by 50 percent, and depreciation schedules would be changed to restore the generous write-offs the Reagan administration had provided for the purchase of capital equipment.[10]

The cost of these write-offs was so great that the Reagan ad-ministration had almost immediately been forced to rescind the change. What made no sense in 1981 had become lu-dicrous by 1995. While capital investment was the key to economic growth in the industrial age, the continuing devel-opment and deployment of microprocessor technology en-abling innovation and learning to take place was the source of growth in the information age. Yet none of those in Congress so eager to give unprecedented tax breaks to business had fo-cused on how to encourage investments in learning and new technology rather than rewarding investments in real estate and machinery, the symbols of America's economic past.

The Republicans did not stop there. They reduced the so-called "marriage penalty," repealed the increased income tax imposed on social security payments to the most affluent se-nior citizens, and eliminated the alternative tax requirements for corporations that earned no income. When they were fin-ished, House Republicans had proposed tax cuts worth $365 billion.[11] Republicans in the Senate thought the package fiscally irresponsible, but Newt Gingrich didn't care. Following the lead of Haley Barbour and Frank Luntz, he was deter-mined to enact what he himself called the "crown jewels"[12] of the Contract with America and to show everyone that Repub-licans, at least those who followed him, kept their promises. Even more important, this huge tax cut, combined with the promise to balance the budget even without a constitutional amendment to require it, would give new Republicans all the leverage and protection they needed to pass and defend the most dramatic reductions in domestic spending since the New Deal was established.

Clinton and Gingrich were engaged in a debate designed to

attract the one constituency that, more than any other, was resistant to the changes necessitated by the transition from the industrial to the information age. Perot voters blamed government for all that had gone wrong and believed that if someone just had sense enough to somehow make things right again factories would reopen, corporations would rehire, and wages would end their twenty-year downward spiral. The Republican strategy was nothing more than Reaganism redux; the Democratic strategy nothing more than another attempt to attract the middle class by denouncing policies they claimed were designed to benefit the rich alone. Neither strategy appealed to the new constituency, which wanted to balance the budget without either raising taxes or curtailing government services.

The first step toward this new policy is the reduction or elimination of the tax breaks and subsidies given to private businesses during the industrial age. After an extensive analysis the Progressive Policy Institute, a Washington think tank associated with the Democratic Leadership Council, discovered that $256 billion could be saved over five years by cutting what was quickly dubbed "corporate welfare."[13] Nearly half this money would come from the agricultural, mining, timber, energy, and construction sectors of the economy. Instead of encouraging the formation and expansion of new enterprises to lead the country into the information age, the tax system was being used, in effect, to subsidize declining industries. The government was not only losing the tax dollars from one source but hindering the growth of precisely those new businesses that would generate even greater revenues.

An industry protected by a tariff or a tax break does not have to work as hard to increase its productivity nor must it respond as quickly to the demands of its customers as one without such government largesse, because defeat in the marketplace is no longer an immediate threat. Thus the tax system was being used to do precisely what it should not—rather than encourage the formation and expansion of new enterprises that will lead the country into the information age, it was being used to prop up some of the least competitive concerns of the industrial age in a way that flew in the face of every conceivable form of fairness. No less than $16 billion of the net benefits from these subsidies and tax breaks went to the wealthiest 5 percent of Americans, while nearly $7 billion a year of their cost was borne by the bottom 80 percent.[14]

Reducing or eliminating corporate welfare as a means to balance the budget received support across the entire political spectrum. Bob Greenstein, executive director of the liberal Center on Budget and Policy Priorities, agreed with the Progressive Policy Institute that these subsidies should be cut. He also agreed that at least some of the savings should be used for public investments to further economic growth. Stephen Moore, on behalf of the libertarian Cato Institute, was willing to make a commitment to "end corporate welfare as we know it." He disagreed with Greenstein's investment suggestions but identified a list of $100 billion in cuts—$15 billion of them tax breaks—that would help achieve this objective. David Frum, author of *Dead Right*, was perhaps the most emphatic of all. What "these kind of subsidies convey to the American public," he said, was "that its government is for sale." Insisting that it would be a test of the seriousness of the Republican party to its stated commitment to cut all kinds of spending in its proposed balanced budget resolution, Frum laid down what he termed a "moral and political challenge" to his party.[15]

It was a challenge that neither Republicans nor Democrats were willing to accept. When Robert Reich, the prolific Harvard scholar who had been named Clinton's secretary of labor, publicly endorsed the "cut and invest" strategy of the Progressive Policy Institute, he was privately reprimanded by the president, who wanted no cuts proposed until the Republicans did so first.[16] The Republicans' failure was even more dramatic. Ohio's John Kasich, the new Republican chairman of the House Budget Committee, had announced confidently that corporate lobbyists who had obtained and then fought to keep their tax subsidies would find life more difficult. "We are going to focus on those who struck gold at Gucci Gulch," he declared,[17] and then suggested that Congress should recover $25 billion in lost revenue through the elimination of a few of the same tax subsidies the Cato Institute had identified as unwarranted.

Kasich, however, was not in charge of tax policy in the House. Texan Bill Archer was, and the new Republican chairman of the Ways and Means Committee made it plain that, during his watch, "this will not be the tax-raising committee of the United States,"[18] with respect to eliminating tax breaks for corporations. Archer was not, however, referring to removing the tax breaks for the poor. Archer endorsed Kasich's proposal to cut the earned income tax credit, by which the federal government subsidizes those who work for a living but whose earnings fall below the poverty line. With the enthusiastic support of Newt Gingrich, Kasich and Archer helped construct a budget-balancing resolution that raised taxes on the working poor by curtailing their tax subsidies and retaining every industrial and agrarian age subsidy that was supported by campaign contributions to the Republican party. There was still gold in Gucci Gulch.

The Democratic response did not address any of the questions concerning economic growth that were implicit in the Republican budget. House minority leader Richard Gephardt refused to be drawn into a debate about the best way to use the taxing and spending powers of government to stimulate economic activity. Instead, he and the rest of the Democratic congressional leadership assumed that little—if any—growth would take place and attacked Republicans for taking from the poor to give to the rich. The endless barrage of criticism was a part—in Democrats' judgment the crucial part—of their strategy for recapturing control of Congress. The working poor, the Perot voters, even some blue-collar members of the middle class who were now voting Republican almost habitually could be convinced to vote Democratic again, once their resentment and anger were turned on the wealthy few for whom life seemed to be perpetually improving while the rest of the country struggled to make ends meet.

It was the classic strategy Democrats had practiced for sixty years, and it had little chance of success. Gephardt did not even offer an alternative budget. The debate, to the extent there was one, was between the faithful Republican followers of the Reagan revolution who still insisted that supply-side economics alone made sense, and those who believed the Laffer curve was, as its name suggested, something that should not be taken too seriously. House Republicans had never given up their commitment to the idea that dramatic cuts in the income tax would free up the investments necessary for economic growth, and they now had the power to do something about it. Democrats continued to argue that it was, in George Bush's famous phrase, "voodoo economics." The difference between the two sides, however, was not nearly so great as it seemed. Neither Republicans nor Democrats had yet come to grips with the changing nature of economics in the information age.

■ ■ ■

As Sir Isaac Newton viewed the universe, so did industrial age economists view the system by which wealth was generated and distributed as a machine. When Ross Perot suggested that the cure for a recession was to lift up the hood and tinker with the engine, he was simply using an accepted metaphor for the economy. From the 1930s, when Keynesian economics first acquired intellectual supremacy, government economists concentrated on trying to create a stable equilibrium between a nation's demand for goods and services and the supply or production required to meet the demand. Keynes emphasized the use of government expenditures to raise demand and consequently stimulate production. Supply-side economics, embraced by Ronald Reagan and his followers in the 1980s, claimed that by increasing the supply of investment capital, tax cuts would raise both demand and production and achieve the necessary stable equilibrium.

Both Keynesian and supply-side economics were concerned with the most efficient way to produce the savings by which to invest in new plant and equipment, based on the belief that increases in both productivity and real wages were dependent on increasing the amount of machinery applied to each hour of labor. What was true in the industrial age, however, is no longer valid. The information age economy is more comparable to an ecosystem than to a machine.[19] Not only have time and distance become irrelevant, but the system thrives by sharing information among all those who participate in it. Like a rain forest, its proper maintenance has more to do with the principles of biology than with the simple mechanical dynamics of classical economics.[20]

The new economy requires not just elimination of government support for outdated industrial age enterprises but a completely new system of taxation. Among the many tax proposals discussed in the Republican-led Congress, only a handful have addressed the requirements of the information age. Democratic Senator Sam Nunn of Georgia joined with Republican Senator Pete Domenici of New Mexico, chairman of the Senate Budget Committee, to propose a graduated consumption income tax designed to penalize those who spend their money and reward those who save it. All income, including interest and dividends, would be subject to what the senators called the Uniform Savings Act (USA TAX).[21] Income either invested or saved would entitle one to a tax deduction. The incentive for home ownership, provided at present by the mortgage interest deduction, would be retained—even increased—by establishing the purchase as an investment and the purchase price therefore a deduction. All investments would become fully depreciated in the year in which they were acquired, thereby creating a boom in real estate, machinery, and equipment, the likes of which has never been seen in the United States.

This proposal would favor capital investment over human

investment. The application of labor to more advanced machinery, however, no longer guarantees economic success. Knowledge is now the most important economic asset, rather than capital or labor. Having the latest technology to work with is no guarantee of improved economic opportunity, and the tax proposal offered by Nunn and Domenici, constructed from the working assumptions of the industrial age, does nothing to encourage this kind of human investment.

The same could be said of the flat tax proposal from House Majority Leader Dick Armey. Jerry Brown had suggested a flat tax during the 1992 presidential primaries, only to have candidate Clinton remark that perhaps the former governor of California would also like to join the flat-earth society. What was considered too radical when Brown proposed it was suddenly taken seriously when the second-ranking House Republican became its principal advocate. The difference between simplicity and simplemindedness seemed to depend on who was doing the talking.

A flat tax appealed to those for whom the income tax had become an unintelligible mass of bureaucratic rules and regulations that trapped the hardworking while offering loopholes to the wealthy. Everyone applauded as Armey stood in front of crowds of taxpayers and claimed that with a flat tax anyone, from richest to poorest, could complete his or her tax return just by mailing a postcard stating amount of income and, multiplying that by 17 percent, the amount of tax owed to the IRS.

If a flat tax could be free of exceptions and exemptions, the system of taxation would undoubtedly become more efficient. The administrative overhead of the IRS would be reduced dramatically, and the legions of tax lawyers and tax accountants would have to find other employment. Personal computers, which can already calculate taxes, would make compliance not only simpler, but a good deal quicker than Armey's handwritten postcard.

The idea is too simple. It may be more efficient but it is not effective, failing as it does to meet the basic requirements of taxation in the information age. The proponents of a flat tax argue that not taxing income from interest or dividends creates incentives for savings and investment.[22] No incentive, however, is provided for investment in what are the new prerequisites for success. Armey and other advocates of the flat tax refuse to countenance the inclusion of exemptions and, as a result, offer no incentives for education, training, or any other means by which to create and expand knowledge. Those who have made enough money to save and invest will pay less in taxes, while those who are trying to learn to best help themselves and raise their families—whether through job training, academics, or otherwise—will pay more. Designed to reduce government and liberate economic activity, the flat tax prevents government from promoting either learning or economic opportunity.

Nothing is so difficult to escape as the prison of the way we think. If investment in new machinery was the key to success in the industrial age then—most everyone assumes—investment in the latest technology must be the key to success in the information age. Technology, however, is not knowledge, a lesson General Motors learned the hard way in the 1980s. A typical GM plant in 1986 required thirty-one hours of work to make a car, while Toyota, using the latest in lean production techniques, required only sixteen.[23] GM's chairman, Roger B. Smith, decided the way to catch up was to build the most automated assembly line in the world. Brand new robots of every description were lined up, ready to dance, programmed by the software writers of GM's latest acquisition, Ross Perot's EDS, the leading systems integration company in America. The result was a disaster. The robots began tearing one another apart, smashing cars, and spraying paint everywhere. The automatic guided vehicles designed to move parts around often appeared to be on strike—refusing to move for anyone. The production line was stopped continuously while technicians tried to get the bugs out of the software. GM had succeeded in creating the most costly, least successful automation experiment in automotive history.[24]

On the other side of Detroit, in Dearborn, Ford's CEO, Don Petersen, had come to a different conclusion about the reasons for Japan's success: it had less to do with technology than with knowledge. Japanese automakers, Petersen had noted, involved each assembly line worker in discussions on how to improve production. The Japanese, in other words, had abolished the old distinction between managers, who gave orders, and workers, who blindly did as they were told. Instead, each employee learned from what he or she did, using that knowledge to suggest ways in which the system could work even better.[25]

Petersen gained the support of not only Pete Pestillo, Ford's vice president for human resources, but also Steve Yokich, head of the UAW's Ford bargaining unit, for a new investment strategy focused on employee involvement. The first results of this joint effort were the Ford Taurus and the Mercury Sable, both built in Atlanta, Georgia, by newly trained workers using only a minimal amount of new plant and equipment.[26] It was enough to save the company in the 1980s and to transform the entire American automobile industry. Knowledge was everything.

The introduction of the microprocessor in 1971 and its subsequent improvements have decreased the cost of encoding and processing information to almost nothing. The key to economic growth is no longer new machinery or new technology; it is the elimination of structural barriers that limit the spread of knowledge. In the information age, the entire economy must become one vast learning organization that can rapidly adapt to the changes created by its own momentum. Japanese automakers taught their American counterparts that the way to make near perfect cars was to let the worker on the line detect and prevent defects in quality. They engaged the minds of the workers while gaining their commitment by giving them the training they needed and the authority to stop the line whenever they discovered a problem.[27] All barriers of rank and privilege were eliminated, and knowledge was withheld from no one.[28] The Japanese created a learning organization that was able to make any necessary adjustments whenever the requirements of the marketplace changed. Thus Toyota used what it had learned about making a quality low-priced car to enter the prestige car market with the remarkably successful Lexus.[29]

The new information age economy requires eliminating all barriers to learning, even those that may have been well-intentioned efforts to help. National programs designed to give an advantage to some businesses or technologies over others, whether they come in the form of direct investment or indirect tax subsidies, remove the incentive to learn. Tax programs that fail to provide each individual with information about the amount of money he or she is really paying or that prevent him or her from having any choice about amounts paid in taxes also create impediments to learning. The flat tax of Dick Armey—even a well-constructed consumption tax along the lines suggested by Nunn and Domenici—fails to meet this information age criterion.

■ ■ ■

The only tax proposal that does meet this criterion is one that abolishes the income tax altogether. Proposed by Senator Richard Lugar of Indiana as part of his campaign for the presidency, and the favorite project of Bill Archer, chairman of the House Ways and Means Committee, a national sales tax strikes most pundits as a strange, if not shocking, idea. A sales tax, however, is not only more popular with the average voter, it is more efficient than an income tax, because it moves responsibility for compliance from a government bureaucracy to the retail activities of daily life. This proposal, under which the IRS would shrink to a shadow of its former self, is also, by far, the most effective system of taxation in an information age economy. Each individual would receive the full amount of his or her earnings, whatever the source from which it is derived, and would be fully accountable for how he or she spent it. Consumers would likely be more cost conscious than before as a result. A sales tax would increase and intensify the desire to get more for less—that is, higher quality at a lower price. Manufacturers and distributors would need to learn new ways to meet this demand, while buyers would develop expertise in finding the best bargains. This system would encourage all Americans to learn not only how to get them, but how to provide them. It would accelerate the downward pressure on prices into every aspect of the economy and that, in turn, would lead to expanded markets and increased economic growth.[30]

With a sales tax as the principle source of revenue for the federal government, American exports would become more competitive. Under the rules of international trade, a consumption tax, unlike an income tax, does not need to be included in the cost of goods sold abroad. Today's products currently include the cost of compliance with income tax regulations, even when sold in foreign countries. With a sales tax, therefore, American products would be sold for about 15 to 20 percent less in foreign countries than they would cost at home.[31] At the same time, imported goods would be subject to the same tax as domestic products when sold in the United States. The resulting gains in international trade would further boost economic growth in the United States.

A sales tax can be structured to encourage the kind of life-long learning necessary for success in the new age. College tuition or job-training services, even on-line database services, could be exempted to make them relatively cheaper than consumer goods. Investments for the information age, however, are not the only things that would need to be exempted. Necessities such as food and medicine must be excluded to avoid hardship for those who have barely enough on which to survive.

Not everyone seems to understand, however, the difference between creating a tax system for the twenty-first century and constructing a new instrument of oppression. Bill Archer, advocate of a universal national sales tax, was challenged on the fairness of taxing food for people who are hungry, to which he angrily replied, "No one is starving in America, and if they are, it's their own fault."[32] As the country struggled with the new lessons of the information age and searched for consensus on how to meet its challenges, Archer, and not just a few of his colleagues in the House, were still acting as if moral strictures similar to government policy in the Victorian age would solve the country's problems.

Richard Lugar had a more sound idea: no detailed regulations would be issued defining, for example, what constitutes junk food and is thereby not exempt, or whether diapers are drugs or food and entitled to an exemption. Instead, Lugar would let individuals decide for themselves what is and is not a basic necessity by simply exempting a threshold level of goods and services. "For example," he explained, "if the exemption level were $5,000, a family of four would have its first $20,000 of spending exempt from the sales tax. This figure is approximately 33 percent above the 1994 poverty threshold."[33] If the sales tax were set at 15 percent the family would receive a direct cash payment of $3,000, adding an element of progressivity and providing a substitute for the present earned income tax credit.

Before the invention of the microprocessor, this new system would have necessitated the creation of a new bureaucracy. Now, however, after the transformation into electronic information, this transaction, like nearly every other kind of financial transaction, could be made instantaneously. A "smart card," carried like a credit card, would keep track of how much money each person has to spend. It would combine money in a bank account and money that has been supplied by the government. The amount of money, or "E-cash," available would change whenever new instructions were downloaded over a phone line to the microprocessor on the card. No paper or administrative burden would be involved.

E-cash would not only make it possible to program exemptions into a sales tax, it will make the sales tax inevitable by rendering the income tax impossible. Electronic transfers would take place not only between financial institutions but between private individuals as well. Indeed, money would flow between countries at nearly the speed of light.[34] Through the use of encryption codes, which no government would be able to access, electronic bank notes will be certified without the issuer having any idea to whom they were issued.[35] Individuals who decide not to pay income taxes on interest, dividends, or capital gains would be able to do so with impunity. Anyone with a computer would be able to have a virtual Swiss bank account. The income tax, like the industrial age that produced it, is all but dead.

A tax system that facilitates economic growth in the information age will make the current debate over which government activities to cut to balance the budget a curiosity of history and a political irrelevancy. Claims by both the Clinton White House and the Gingrich Republicans to know what the permissible and necessary spending limit will be on health care seven or ten years in the future are just as much the product or machine age thinking as any of the five-year plans that ever came out of the Kremlin. The way to balance the budget is to free up the creative energy of the new economy, and the way to do that is to adopt a new system of taxation that corresponds to the requirements of the new age. The explosion of economic growth, in combination with the proper reengineering of the American government, will quickly close the gap between revenues and expenditures. Like solutions to the other public policy challenges we face, the answer will be found, not in new rules or constitutional amendments but in the courage to give up old ways of thinking and explore new possibilities for the future.

6

RETHINKING ENTITLEMENTS

The candidate was reluctant. The draft of his announcement speech said nothing about health care, and although his close friend and political ally insisted it was important, he objected that the subject was just too complicated and costly to talk about during a presidential campaign. "But you have to say something," the friend insisted. Harris Wofford, who had made health care reform his major issue, was running surprisingly well in the Pennsylvania senatorial race, and certainly someone running for president was going to make it an issue in the Democratic primaries.[1] "Besides," he added, "you don't have to be specific. Just promise that during the first year that you are president you will send to the Congress a proposal for a major overhaul of the nation's health care system."

Though Jim Blanchard had lost his bid to be elected to a third term as governor of Michigan, he was one of the most politically astute people advising the campaign. Based on his advice and that of others reviewing his announcement speech, Bill Clinton added a single paragraph on health care reform in the middle of the litany of policies that a Clinton administration would offer to the country. Standing on the steps of the Little Rock state house on October 3, 1991, and announcing his candidacy for president of the United States, Clinton pledged that "in the first year of a Clinton Administration, we will present a plan to Congress and the American people to provide affordable, quality health care for all Americans." It went mostly unnoticed and unreported.[2]

During the crucial New Hampshire primary, after listening to a long debate among several other Democratic candidates on the subject, all Clinton said was "the one thing New Hampshire voters should understand is that the only way you are going to get health care reform, is to elect any of the Democrats here President of the United States."[3] In the year before he became president, Clinton had not even considered health care an issue worth talking about; one year later, his promise to reform health care led him to propose the most expensive middle-class entitlement in a generation. Instead of increasing his popularity with "those who work hard and play by the rules," his attempt at health care reform would help elect a Republican Congress and endanger his own chances for reelection.

■　■　■

Clinton was never able to separate two very distinct messages from the public: what they wanted government to do and the way they wanted government to do it. Health care, as Jim Blanchard had predicted, became an important political issue when Harris Wofford used it to defeat Dick Thornburgh, former governor and U.S. attorney general, in a 1991 special election to fill a vacant Senate seat in Pennsylvania.[4] In his most effective campaign commercial, Wofford's statement, "If criminals have a right to a lawyer, I think working Americans should have a right to a doctor," played to the growing fear of the middle class that health care might not be there when they or a member of their family needed it.[5] Middle managers and blue-collar workers, thrown out of employment by nationwide corporate downsizing, suddenly found themselves without health insurance. Part-time workers, employees of small companies without insurance plans, and the self-employed were all faced with rapidly escalating health care costs and private insurance premiums they could not afford. Those who had the best jobs, and those who could afford it, were covered by the health insurance they needed and, because of Medicaid, so were the poorest of the poor. But those in between were in trouble, and they knew it. They wanted government to do whatever was necessary to make certain each individual had affordable coverage.

That did not mean, however, that they wanted government to take over the management of health care in America. During the height of the congressional debate over the Clinton health care plan, 53 percent of the public were more worried about government gaining too *much* control over health care than they were about universal coverage. Only 40 percent held the opposing view.[6] One year later, the voters of California defeated by a 73 percent to 27 percent margin a ballot initiative supported by teachers, nurses, and hospitals to create a single-payer, state-run system.[7] When congressional Democrats declared that passage of comprehensive health care reform would complete the "last unfinished business of the New Deal," it never occurred to them that they were giving Republicans all the ammunition they would need to capture Congress and begin the destruction of everything the New Deal had accomplished.[8]

Health care was an afterthought during the presidential campaign. When pressed to explain what he had in mind, Clinton first advocated what was called the "pay or play" solution, favored by many leading health care professionals. Under this plan employers would be forced to provide health insurance under requirements mandated by the federal government; if they did not, they would have to pay a payroll tax to support an expanded Medicaid program for the uninsured.[9] Clinton's endorsement, however, had wavered during the campaign, as the DLC urged him to consider an alternative approach, *managed competition.* Now that he was president he had to come up with a detailed proposal, and quickly. Clinton had promised he would send to Congress a comprehensive health care reform bill before the end of the first year of his administration. It was the only promise he made that should have been broken.

From the very beginning, it was clear that the Clinton health care proposal would fail to meet the essential requirements of the information age. Instead of sharing information with those who might have been able to contribute something to the solution, the administration approached the problem like an industrial age monopoly trying to conserve the trade secrets that had given it power. Hillary Rodham Clinton, appointed to lead the task force on health care reform, insisted that all meetings take place behind closed doors. Ira Magaziner is a social engineer who believed it was still possible to construct bureaucracies capable of managing complex social interactions. When Mrs. Clinton selected him to build a better health care machine, he coordinated the work of over five hundred health care experts in drafting a plan without public scrutiny. Both wanted to prevent those with the most to lose from any serious reorganization of the health care system from organizing opposition before the task force had finished its work. The result was just the reverse: those not included in deliberations attacked the proposal not only on its merits, but on the very fact that they had never been allowed to participate. This would have been a major political mistake in the industrial age; in the information age, it was nothing short of malfeasance.[10]

In a nationally televised address the president announced to Congress and the nation: "This health care system is badly broken and we need to fix it."[11] The speech was enormously popular; the public agreed that something had to be done. When Hillary Clinton, Magaziner, and the 500-member task force produced a health care reform bill 1,342 pages in length, no one in the administration was surprised that Republicans charged it would regulate out of existence the greatest health care system in the world. However, the president was not only surprised but furious when his old friend, Al From, president of the Democratic Leadership Council, informed him that the DLC would not be able to support his health care initiative.

From pointed out that the most recent ABC/*Washington Post* poll, taken in August 1993, showed a dangerously large number of Americans thought Clinton was too liberal. At the time of his nomination acceptance speech a year earlier, only 19 percent of the voters thought so; now the number was 41 percent. From warned that a health care program consisting of price controls and employer mandates could dangerously undermine Clinton's presidency by confirming Americans' impression of him as an old-fashioned Democrat. Rather than concern himself with the regulatory approach favored by labor, From suggested Clinton focus on principles and draft a plan that would appeal to moderates in both parties. The DLC, From made clear, would not support the task force's approach, but, he added, the president had no right to be angry or surprised. Not only had the DLC never been in favor of the kind of regulatory scheme the administration was proposing, it had gone on record in favor of managed competition during Clinton's own chairmanship.

Managed competition developed out of discussions among policy analysts and health care industry leaders at the home of Dr. Paul Ellwood in Jackson Hole, Wyoming, where the focus was on reforming the health care market by applying the new business principles of total quality management. These were the principles that formed the basis on which American corporations had begun to reengineer themselves, and they dealt with both efficiency (how to do things better) and effectiveness (which things should be done).[12] The Jackson Hole group wanted to lower health care costs, and they nearly hit on the right solution.

Their proposal was designed to create a more informed marketplace, but a marketplace made up not of individual patients but of experts organized into health insurance purchasing cooperatives, or HIPCs. These consortiums of experts would assess the relative costs and risks of each particular treatment for each patient and then make sure that the right medical treatment was provided at the lowest possible cost. In Orlando, the most successful of these alliances had reduced health care premiums below 1990 levels. Others reported similar—if less spectacular—results,[13] and there were other proposals to use information to improve the market. An "outcomes management standards board" would establish and promulgate patient outcomes and other quality measures through a national data system.

It was still a market restricted to health care professionals; those who used health care services would continue to have their decisions made for them. Furthermore, with its emphasis on HIPCs large enough to achieve "economies of scale in administrative costs," it was a market that still operated on industrial age assumptions.[14] Yet for all that, it was, at least in the eyes of Al From and the DLC, a vast improvement over the proposal made by the president, whom they had helped nominate and elect. Instead of an information clearinghouse of the sort envisioned by the Jackson Hole proposal, the Clinton bill established a "quality management council." Any physician who failed to provide it with data on "clinical encounters" would be subject to a $10,000 fine. Instead of voluntary HIPCs, the Clinton bill demanded compulsory physician membership and a fee schedule set by bureaucrats. Even universal coverage included a provision that imposed a fine on those who failed to pay the premium.[15]

Clinton believed it should be just as easy to change Al From's mind as it had been to change his own. He sent David Gergen, special advisor to the president and the leading moderate in the White House, to speak to the DLC's 1993 fall policy conference, asking him also to speak privately with From to persuade him to support the president on health care reform. Over lunch, From explained that the advice he had given Clinton, like the advice he always gave him, was based not on ideological zeal but on what he honestly felt was in the president's best interest; by that he meant his reelection. From restated his belief that managed competition was the best way to achieve health care reform, which was one of the reasons the DLC had decided to support the alternative introduced by Congressman Jim Cooper, Democrat of Tennessee, and Senator John Breaux, Democrat of Louisiana. Their plan made a lot more sense than what Clinton was proposing. From was not going to change his mind.

Nor was Bill Clinton, or so it seemed. Soon the insurance industry began to use television to campaign against health care reform. It was the most costly, and one of the most effective, efforts to influence legislation by changing public opinion ever undertaken. "Harry and Louise," the two characters featured in every ad, became as famous as Bill and Hillary. With wearied expressions, they derided health care reform as the latest in a long line of attempts to regulate everything Americans did at a cost no one could possibly afford. The debate began to shift from what could be done to provide health care for everyone to whether government had any business trying to change it at all. In the end, there was little for which Clinton was willing to fight. The principle of universal coverage, which he had insisted was a nonnegotiable immediate necessity, became, instead, an ultimate objective and an admission of weakness. Clinton, willing to settle for almost any reform, got nothing.

Clinton would have been better advised, and the country better served, if he had never proposed any regulation, much less the mind-numbing system of regulatory complexity contained in a bill not everyone could lift and hardly anyone could read. Had he followed his own better instincts and considered health care reform as an information age opportunity, instead of as an industrial age problem, he might have made the same immensely popular speech on health care, introduced the same set of six principles of reform, and then let the health care market evolve on its own into a more effective and efficient system.[16] Rather than attempt to reinvent or reengineer a system that contained some of the largest and most cumbersome private bureaucracies in the world, Clinton would have been well advised to reconsider the very nature and purpose of government.

■ ■ ■

Bill Clinton should have followed Dee Hock's lead. In 1968 the new credit card industry was a disaster. The authority to issue credit cards had been franchised to individual banks, without any oversight. Losses from operations, unwise credit policies, and outright fraud were already in the hundreds of millions of dollars and still growing. The very foundation of the American banking system was threatened. The Bank of America asked Dee Hock, then managing one of their credit card franchisees, VISA, to chair a seven-member problem-solving committee.

Hock, unlike Ira Magaziner and the Clinton health care task force, did not try to determine in advance what the conclusions ought to be. He suggested, instead, that the committee try to create the most orderly method for addressing the problems. It began by thinking through what money actually meant in an information age. With electronic exchange of information, Hock explained, money is "nothing more than guaranteed, alphanumeric data" that can be recorded as easily in electrons and photons as on metal or paper. A credit card is simply a device for exchanging these electronic particles, and if VISA could guarantee that exchange everywhere on the planet, it would have a market "that beggared the imagination." This realization changed our entire system of banking and finance. The question was how to organize a system that complex. The answer turned out to be quite simple.

Instead of writing a report recommending regulations the franchised card issuers would have to follow, Hock's committee spent a year reaching agreement about the principles on which the new organization would be built. Three of these principles deal with ownership and governance:

"1. *It must be equitably owned by all participants.* No member should have intrinsic preferential position. All advantage must result from individual ability and initiative.

"2. *Power and function must be distributive to the maximum degree.* No function should be performed by any part of the whole which could reasonably be done by any more peripheral part, and no power vested in any part which might reasonably be exercised by any lesser part.

"3. *Governance must be distributive.* No individual, institution, and no combination of either or both, should be able to dominate deliberations or control decisions."[17]

VISA thus became a self-regulating system with a membership that owned nothing but the perpetual nontransferable right to continue as participants. Less than five years after adopting these simple principles, VISA had cut its cost in half and gained the dominant market share in the business. Today, over a quarter of a century later, its products are created by 23,000 financial institutions and are accepted in more than 200 countries and territories. Every year 355 million people use VISA to make 7.2 billion transactions with a value in excess of $650 billion. Eleven hundred transactions are processed every second at a cost of less than a penny each, and the entire system is managed by a staff of fewer than three thousand.

Dee Hock created what he later called "the VISA Chaord." The word *chaord* was his own attempt to combine the seemingly opposite principles of chaos and order, a concept that can be applied to any complex adaptive system that is "on the edge of chaos."[18] Systems, even those as complex as health care, can be made orderly when they repeat themselves in recognizable and measurable patterns that oscillate between equilibrium and disequilibrium. Systems that remain rigid, like the regulatory structures put in place during the forty years Democrats controlled Congress, will fail to adapt to changes taking place around them and will eventually disintegrate. Systems become chaotic where no coherent pattern emerges and the system is always "boiling." When that happens, as it did with the escalating costs of health care over the last fifteen years, the system will spin out of control. A chaordic system is one that exists between the two types.[19] It concentrates on the rules governing the relationships among its parts; it is constantly changing and evolving; and it creates, in the process, coherent patterns that often resemble the fractal shapes of the new science of chaos. It is a complex system that is "rigid enough to permit efficiency and fluid enough to permit effectiveness."[20] It is this system that will reshape health care in America.

■   ■   ■

Next to social security itself, Medicare is the most expensive entitlement program administered by the federal government. At its origins, Part A of Medicare was Lyndon Johnson's proposal to make everyone who received social security eligible for government-subsidized health care. Part B was a Republican alternative in which participation in a plan to pay medical bills was strictly voluntary. Medicaid was a third proposal, initiated by the American Medical Association, under which the poor would be given the financial assistance necessary to buy private health insurance. Instead of negotiating a compromise among the competing ideas, Johnson, who was never accused of halfway measures, agreed with Wilbur Mills, the powerful chairman of the House Ways and Means Committee, that there was only one way to get anything passed.[21] Johnson combined all three proposals into a single bill, which thus offered something for every interest. The bill increased coverage for the elderly, and it gave some protection to the poor. More important than anything it actually accomplished in 1965, however, was that these original rules established a system that then took on a life of its own. Medicare created not only an entitlement, but a constituency more powerful than any other single constituency in the country. The elderly, whose numbers and propensity to vote become larger every year, have come to view both social security and Medicare as binding contracts between them and their government. Social security was expected to at least increase with the cost of living, and Medicare was expected to cover any medical expense they might incur. Thirty years after Medicare was introduced, the country could no longer support it, while senior citizens were certain they could quite literally not live without it. Everyone agreed that services provided by Medicare had to be reduced if expenditures were to be brought under control. Everyone was wrong.

All medical services, including those offered through Medicare and Medicaid, can be offered at a dramatically reduced cost by transforming the present industrial age command and control health care delivery system to an information age chaordic system. The new system, like any chaordic system, will be based on a handful of principles, some of which Clinton had outlined in his address to Congress.

The first principle is universal coverage. The problem of health care is a problem of insurance. The most cost-effective insurance system is one that covers everyone, rather than only those at greater risk. This requirement, however, can best be met not through employer or employee mandates, but by a citizen mandate: everyone who is old enough to vote must have medical insurance. Just as today proof of insurance is required in most states at the time a person obtains his or her driver's license, the social security system will confirm receipt of proof of health insurance. Those unable to pay for such insurance would become the only recipients of government-paid health care benefits, and only during those years in which their income fell below the poverty line.

The second principle is a rule prohibiting those who provide insurance coverage from denying it to anyone because of a preexisting condition. The third principle is a rule that makes all health insurance portable—that is, a change of employment, for instance, has no effect on coverage.

The first three principles require government to change the rules of the marketplace; the fourth requires a fundamental change in the tax law. Section 106 of the Internal Revenue Code provides that employer-paid health insurance is not considered part of an employee's taxable income. The section was added to the Code during World War II, when companies, desperate for scarce labor but prohibited by wage and price controls from raising salaries, began to offer "free" health insurance. When the war ended, however, the policy of offering paid health insurance continued.[22] As the cost of health care exploded, money that would otherwise have been available for wage increases had to be used to pay for health insurance premiums. Wages remained stagnant, but employees had no direct incentive to help control health insurance costs. Like the recipients of social security or Medicare, they viewed their benefits as something to which they were entitled. For years the United Auto Workers resisted a proposal by the auto companies that employees pay even *one dollar* for a visit to a doctor, for fear that they might eventually be asked to pay more.

In a normal market, the consumer decides what he or she wants and pays for what he or she gets. In the health care market, on the other hand, because of the consequences of Section 106, there is no direct market connection between buyer and seller. Purchase, payment, and receipt of service are separate from one another, and no information moves among the parts of the system to regulate the way it functions. This is precisely the opposite condition from that needed to begin and maintain a chaordic system. To do so, Section 106 would have to be repealed, enabling the marketplace to affect price and cost. This would also add more equity and progressivity to the tax code. The cost of exempting employer-paid health insurance premiums from taxation cost approximately $74 billion in 1994 alone. Nearly one third of that amount went to the wealthiest 13 percent of American taxpayers, those earning more than $75,000 a year.[23]

Until a national sales tax replaces the income tax, repeal of Section 106 would permit the use of subsidies or other forms of targeted tax relief to assist those who otherwise cannot afford health insurance, about 80 percent of whom are classified as "the working poor."[24] Those eligible for the earned income tax credit could exclude the cost of health insurance in calculating their income, and those with large family deductions could be given either additional deductions or tax credits. Labor unions could negotiate new agreements in which the employer would pay the money now spent on health insurance premiums directly to workers in the form of increased wages, which employees could then use to acquire the most affordable insurance they could find. Individuals would be free to choose the coverage they wanted, no matter where or by whom they were employed—the fourth principle required to establish a chaordic health care system in America.

The fifth, and final, principle creates an entirely new method of payment. The marketplace depends on information; the more people know about what is available and at what cost, the more efficient the marketplace will be. To be efficient, a health care market must provide incentives for consumers to learn everything about what health care should and does cost. Experts may argue that health care is simply too complicated, that people will not be able to exercise the same kind of judgment they use when shopping for a new appliance or car. In fact, people who paid for their own health care were found to spend 33 percent less than those who received free care, without any discernable difference in the quality of care each received.[25]

The present system is self-destructive because it prevents this kind of learning. Those who have health insurance are given an incentive not to decrease, but to increase the cost of health care. On a strict cost-benefit analysis, the more medical care they receive, the greater the value for every dollar spent on insurance premiums. Insurance companies, of course, have the opposite incentive—the less health care they have to pay for, the more money they make. The patient has no incentive to keep costs down, so costs go up. The health insurance company in turn is compelled to raise premiums, limit coverage, and exclude those who need health care the most. The solution is to create a new market in which those who use the services of health care providers and those who pay for them have a common incentive to bargain for the highest quality at the lowest price.[26]

In a new, chaordic health care system, the insurance company will become the payer of last resort, eliminating the existing incentive to exclude claims and deny coverage. The insurance company will be liable only for that portion of the bill not paid for by the patient. While this could be achieved through co-payments and deductibles, methods that are already being used, there is a much more direct and far more efficient way to accomplish it: health insurance policies must become insurance policies for life.

Like life insurance, these policies would be for a set amount. Unlike life insurance, the amount of these policies could be drawn upon whenever the policy holder incurred medical expenses. Whatever is not spent on health care will be converted to and paid for as life insurance. Patient and payer will both have the needed incentive to lower costs: the policy holder, by avoiding unnecessary medical expense, increases the size of his or her estate. The insurance company, by paying less for health care, has more money from premium payments to invest and a longer time over which to invest it. Patient and payer will want exactly the same thing—the best possible health care at the lowest possible price for the longest possible period of time.

This new form of insurance will require that everyone know more than just the cost of premiums and the limitations on benefits and coverage. Both patients and payers will need to know the cost of specific treatments and both the immediate and long-term outcomes. The patient will want to know in order to decide how much of the lifetime coverage to spend, and the insurance company or payer will want to know in order to decide which health care providers to recommend. Such information is available today—several companies have created databases from pharmacy and hospital medical information to measure outcomes and performances of specific health networks, clinical procedures, and treatment therapies.[27] Home pages exist on the World Wide Web to advise consumers where to find the best value in hospitals and managed care.[28]

The cost of the new health insurance policy will be formulated on the same kind of calculations that determine the price of premiums for a life insurance policy. Actuarial tables predict with reasonable certainty how many years of life are left to those who have reached a particular age. The new technologies, including phenomenal advances in genetic science, are producing vast improvements in our ability to predict the onset and duration of illness. Health statisticians, for example, have determined that 70 percent of the average's person's lifetime health care costs are incurred during the last ninety days of life. And while it is true that life insurance is paid only once and health insurance will ordinarily be used numerous times throughout one's life, this is a difference of degree, not a difference of kind.[29] Policies would be portable and competition among carriers would ensure competitive rates.

The new health care system would carry with it an incentive for technological innovation. Under the present arrangement, the use of advanced medical technology increases costs. Under a health insurance for life plan, everyone—patient, provider, and insurance payer—would have an incentive to use the technology that delivers the best outcome at the lowest price. The 1983 replacement of cost-plus pricing for Medicare hospital treatment with diagnosis-related group pricing provided the first demonstration of the effect that can be produced by incentives to reduce cost per treatment. Laparoscopic surgery, more easily administrable antibiotics, even gene therapy, suddenly became more acceptable. The rate of increase for health care expenditures was reduced by nearly $15 billion per year.[30]

A system based on chaordic principles will completely

change the way health care is administered. Complex forms and endless claim requests that are now so costly and time-consuming will be abolished. When patients go to a hospital or visit a physician they will simply present their health insurance debit card, which will be encoded with the amount of insurance still available. The health care provider will run the card through a magnetic reader and the amount billed will be deducted instantly from both the card and the insurance company's record and deposited directly in the provider's account.

Moreover, the debit card will be electronically encrypted with the complete health history and medical records of the patient. With the patient's permission, the health care provider will review the history and then add the new information concerning his or her own diagnosis and treatment. Thus, each time a patient sees a doctor or enters a hospital there will be a complete electronic record. While preserving the privacy of each patient, every treatment, procedure, and diagnosis will become part of a comprehensive database from which measurements can be made with unprecedented accuracy about the cost and efficacy of treatment. Those who use medical services will have at their disposal all the information they need to make informed decisions about where to find the highest quality for the lowest price. Those who provide medical services, forced to compete in the marketplace, will be compelled to constantly improve quality and lower prices.

■ ■ ■

The technology already exists. The administrative costs of the health care system, including both Medicare and Medicaid, can be reduced almost to the point of elimination. But this, as we have seen, requires that the new technology be put in the service of a new information age system. Newt Gingrich at least understood that the old system would no longer work. On the second day of the new Congress, in testimony before the House Ways and Means Committee, he described Medicare as a "large, clunky, inefficient government system. I believe we can design a Medicare program which gives every senior citizen greater choice of better health care at lower cost, and as a consequence, save a heck of a lot of money."[31]

Gingrich was still thinking about how to do that when he and the president surprised everyone and agreed to meet at a gathering of senior citizens in Claremont, New Hampshire, on a sunny Sunday in June 1995. Partisanship, at least for the moment, was thrown aside, as both men struggled with one of the most contentious issues facing the country. Clinton suggested that cuts in Medicare and Medicaid would be less severe if a balanced budget were achieved in ten rather than seven years and if tax cuts proposed by Republicans were either reduced or withdrawn completely. For his part, Gingrich promised new solutions to the problem of medicare by the time Congress passed legislation implementing the balanced budget resolution. Surprisingly, those solutions turned out to require more intrusion by government in regulating prices for health care than anything ever proposed by the Democrats. A more information age–like idea was floated by the Progressive Policy Institute, which advocated privatizing the Medicare insurance system to provide real market competition and choice, while taking the first steps toward eliminating the distortions in the tax code from the current system. Four leading Democratic senators signaled their intention to refocus the debate around these principles. But at least Clinton and Gingrich, by agreeing that balancing the budget meant something had to be done about Medicare, had set the stage for the ultimate demise of an outdated entitlement program.

The Republican victory in the 1994 congressional elections changed American politics forever. The debate over a balanced budget was over. There *would* be a balanced budget, and it would be achieved not by increasing taxes but by reducing expenditures, and by reducing them far enough to pay for a tax cut. The Republicans were succeeding in what had always been their plan—to require a balanced budget and then cut taxes to make it impossible for the federal government to play any significant part in the domestic affairs of the country.

They had done more than that, however. As Clinton pointed out in closing the New Hampshire meeting with Gingrich, they had begun a debate about what government was really supposed to do. "What is the role of the federal government as we move into the twenty-first century? . . . These fundamental, basic questions are now being debated all over again in Washington, maybe for the first time in fifty years."[32] But this time the debate would need to examine the kinds of policies required by the information age. Increased choice, restructured markets, and vast new quantities of information made possible by the new and developing technologies were all part of a new picture that was slowly coming into focus. The only thing lacking was the political will to turn the vision into reality.

7

REFORMING MORE THAN WELFARE

S omething had to be done: part of the reason Clinton had been elected was his promise to "end welfare as we know it."[1] Part of the reason for his dramatic fall in popularity was his failure to do anything about it. While the president delayed introducing his welfare reform proposal in response to the pleas of the Democratic congressional leadership, the public grew increasingly impatient. Eighty-four percent wanted those who were on welfare to work for their benefits. This was not the expression of harsh indifference to the plight of the poor it might have seemed; nearly the same percentage also favored providing both job training and subsidized child care to help welfare recipients find employment that would enable them to become self-sufficient. It was exactly what those on welfare wanted themselves.[2]

It was not, however, what the new Republicans wanted. Despite their avowed dedication to the principles of individual liberty and personal responsibility, they could not resist using the power of government to engage in some social engineering of their own. The Contract with America promised enactment of a "Personal Responsibility Act" with "a tough two-year-and-out provision with work requirements to promote individual responsibility." It would do more than that. It would also "discourage illegitimacy and teen pregnancy by prohibiting welfare to minor mothers and denying increased AFDC [payments] for additional children while on welfare." These provisions, the authors of the Contract promised, underscoring the obvious, would "cut spending for welfare programs."[3]

Traditional Republicans might view a cut in welfare spending as an end in itself, but Robert Rector, chief welfare strategist for the Christian Coalition, saw it as a means by which to attack rampant immorality. Working from his offices at the Heritage Foundation, Rector used his network of contacts among the religious right to change the emphasis of the Republican welfare reform proposal from work to ending illegitimacy. In the belief that without this, American "society will collapse," Rector tried to persuade House Republicans to add provisions banning food stamps, public housing subsidies, and cash payments to any unwed mother under the age of twenty-six. Assistance of this sort, he argued, "bribes individuals into courses of behavior which in the long run are self-defeating to the individual, harmful to children, and increasingly, a threat to society."[4]

Republican Representatives Jim Talent of Missouri and Tim Hutchinson of Arkansas incorporated Rector's suggestions and then, going one step further, called for the establishment of government orphanages to raise children born out of wedlock. Middle-class America was appalled. In a survey taken by the conservative think tank Citizens for a Sound Economy, 75 percent of those people earning between $20,000 and $60,000 a year agreed with the statement: "The current system is a failure because it encourages long term dependency on the government and does little to promote self-sufficiency."[5] Nevertheless, 59 percent of them thought that expenditures on welfare, instead of being reduced, should simply be allocated in a different, and presumably more effective, manner. They did not mean a reallocation that left out unwed mothers or paid for orphanages. Sixty percent opposed cutting off benefits for single mothers under the age of eighteen; 77 percent opposed putting children from welfare families into government-run institutions of any description. The middle class was all for hard work and independence, but it was also perfectly willing to do whatever was necessary to keep children with their mothers, even if that meant paying for a welfare system they had come to despise.

The Republicans did not give up. Clay Shaw, chairman of the House Ways and Means Subcommittee on Human Resources, tried a different tack. He proposed that the amount of money given in block grants to the states be made to depend not on increases in the number of welfare recipients who found employment, but on reductions in the rate of illegitimacy. Opposition was immediate, emphatic, and intense, particularly among one of the most reliable Republican constituencies. Pro-life groups attacked the proposal as nothing less than an "abortion bonus" for state governments. Conservatives now found themselves split between economic libertarians, who believed government should leave everyone alone, and cultural absolutists, who demanded that government in essence control the sexual practices of the poor.[6]

The governor of Michigan insisted that none of this was necessary. John Engler had created an image of himself as a radical reformer. After serving as the conservative spokesman in the state legislature he challenged the incumbent Democratic governor, Jim Blanchard, in 1990, in a race no one gave him a chance of winning. With bulldog intensity, Engler set out to convince Michigan voters he could lower the property tax level by chopping government down to size. In one of the biggest upsets that year, Engler defeated Blanchard by the slim margin of 17,000 votes. Four years later, after reducing property taxes through a referendum that raised the sales tax by 50 percent, he won a landslide reelection. During the campaign, Engler bragged about his tough stance requiring welfare recipients to work, claiming it proved that, when it comes to welfare, "Governors know best."[7] The only sensible way to achieve welfare reform, Engler announced, was to give the money to the states in block grants with no strings attached. Republican

Senator Nancy Kassebaum of Kansas suggested that Engler really wanted the federal government to "just leave the money on a stump in the forest so you can pick it up." Engler did not disagree.

Every time Republicans in the House started to split apart over welfare reform, Gingrich would bring in Engler to talk about the magical efficiencies that would result from moving welfare money from federal bureaucracies to state governments, conditioned only by the states' ability to write the rules for eligibility whichever way they wanted. However, House Republicans were not willing to go to such an extreme. They dropped all mention of orphanages but, though they lowered the assistance eligibility age from twenty-six to eighteen, they refused to abandon the prohibition on assistance to unwed mothers. And they insisted on a *family cap* provision to deny increased benefits to anyone who bore a child while receiving Aid to Families with Dependent Children (AFDC) payments.

Engler might have been willing to live with this; Henry Hyde was not. The new chairman of the Judiciary Committee and the most articulate pro-life Republican in the House, Hyde, of Illinois, regarded a prohibition on assistance to unwed mothers of any age an invitation to abortion. He broke with his own leadership and voted against the resolution establishing the rule for floor debate on the bill. House Democrats, in a rare moment of unanimity, introduced a substitute proposal emphasizing work requirements rather than morality. Only their original promise to pass the Contract's provisions in the first one hundred days saved the Republican version. After agreeing to include all of Clinton's requested provisions strengthening child support requirements for fathers, the House passed a welfare reform bill with the hope that the Senate would find a way to fix it.

Engler was similarly involved in the negotiations that went on among Senate Republicans. Nancy Kassebaum proposed a bill to end federal participation in the welfare system under which each state would establish its own welfare policy and raise the revenue to pay for it. What the states lost on welfare would be made up, at least in part, by what they would save on Medicaid; the federal government would take over the burden of that entire program.[8] At the urging of Haley Barbour, Engler convinced Kassebaum to drop her idea and support instead a bill by Senate Finance Committee Chairman Bob Packwood of Oregon to end AFDC as an entitlement. Unlike the House bill, however, this version would attach no strings to the use of the block grants each state would use for all welfare programs except food stamps.

Engler had been so successful in convincing House Republicans of the merits of block granting, he was even invited to speak in defense of this proposal to the Republican caucus. The funding formula adopted by the House rewarded states on the basis of reductions in the welfare rolls rather than by any increase in the number of welfare recipients who became gainfully employed. This favored two states more than any of the others—Wisconsin and Michigan. It was all Senator Phil Gramm, Republican of Texas, needed to bushwhack Engler, and, more importantly, efforts by Bob Dole, Senate Majority Leader from Kansas, to *end welfare as we know it*. Using Robert Rector's argument that "states will never make headway against welfare costs, unless Congress curtails eligibility,"[9] Gramm demanded of both Engler and the Republican Senate leadership why their proposal had none of the restrictions on unwed teenage mothers, legal immigrants, or related provisions from the Contract. Without those changes, Gramm announced, he would oppose the bill.

Alphonse D'Amato of New York thought he understood what Gramm and his junior colleague from Texas, Kay Bailey Hutchison, were really up to. Hutchison had collected the signatures of thirty senators on a petition to change the funding formula, all of whom wanted a greater share for faster growing states. D'Amato loudly denounced Gramm's supposedly principled objections as nothing more than a smoke screen, accusing Gramm of wanting to take money from New York and the other northern states for the benefit of Texas and the rest of the sunbelt. This combination of regional and presidential politics destroyed any chance for Republicans to agree on the best way to reform welfare in America.

Not long after this vicious debate among Republicans, an anonymous "Dear Colleague" letter was circulated in the Senate. "Mason Dixon" asked his fellow senators to support the "Restoring Values and Better Enforcing Efficiency in Rehabilitation" Act, better known as "RVs and BEER." With scathing satire, the letter described an alternative welfare reform proposal, which, among its other punitive provisions, would brand recipients with the letter *W* on their foreheads and cut off all benefits to any woman who divorced her child's father. The funding formula allocated block grant monies in "inverse proportion to state per capita public welfare expenditures." Southern states spending the least on welfare would receive the most money from the federal government.[10] No one asked Phil Gramm or Robert Rector if they thought it was a good idea.

■ ■ ■

No one had to ask Bruce Reed what he thought. The deepening divisions within the Republican party meant that the president had another chance to take the lead on welfare reform. Reed, domestic policy director for the Clinton campaign, after the election served as a member of the domestic policy group within the White House. He remembered that each time Clinton's polling numbers dropped during the campaign, television spots carrying the promise "to end welfare as we know it" drove them back up. The Republican attempt to use "family values" to win the support of the middle class had failed at least in part because Clinton—not Bush—was pushing for a radical revision of the welfare system. It seemed to confirm Clinton's claim that he was a New Democrat. Reed was convinced that what worked so well during the campaign would now work again.

Bruce Reed was interested in more than just restoring the

president's standing in the polls. As one of the original staff members of the Democratic Leadership Council, he believed without reservation that, in the words of the DLC, "the values most Americans share—liberty of conscience, individual responsibility, tolerance, work, faith, family and community—should be embodied in the policies of our government."[11] During the campaign, Reed stayed in regular contact with Al From; together they did everything they could to connect the candidate's promise to campaign on behalf of those who work hard and play by the rules to the formulation of a welfare policy that applied those same values to all citizens.

Clinton's plan had been simple, straightforward, and a radical departure from what had become the traditional, and largely meaningless, debate between conservatives and liberals. Conservatives, though they seldom said it out loud, seemed to believe that everyone on welfare was a cheat. They were almost certain that if welfare recipients were forced to work like everyone else, their numbers would fall precipitously. Liberals had illusions of their own. They believed the "welfare queen" made famous by Ronald Reagan, a woman who lives off welfare and collects multiple benefits to which she is not entitled, was the rare exception. There was a culture of poverty in America, and it required more than a dead-end job to abolish it. Democrats' solution was to create enormous state bureaucracies of social service professionals who could help people learn the rudimentary skills of daily life while supplying massive amounts of money for food, housing, training, and education to the millions of people who had never held a job and had no idea how to obtain one.

Clinton was convinced that both conservatives and liberals were simultaneously right and wrong. Conservatives were correct to insist that people on welfare work, while liberals were correct in claiming that many of those on welfare have neither the training nor the opportunity to find employment. But conservatives were wrong to punish the children for the mistakes of their parents and liberals were wrong to make welfare a perpetual offer of government assistance. Clinton refused to choose between the two viewpoints, instead proposing a two-year limit on the collection of benefits by able-bodied persons. This would supply recipients with a powerful incentive to prepare themselves to become self-supporting. Conservatives supported this idea of time-limited assistance, but they didn't like Clinton's ideas on how to help people move off the rolls. During the two years of an individual's eligibility for welfare, Clinton suggested the person receive not only cash payments, but employment counseling, job training, and day care for children. His goals for reforming welfare were to "reward work, establish time limits, and encourage responsible parenting."[12]

The Clinton proposal would have been logical in the industrial age; it had become essential in the information age. The social stigma connected with welfare was based on the widespread belief that those who were on it were "getting away" with something. The conservative solution, as often expressed by Phil Gramm, was to force everyone to carry his or her own weight. It was a solution with a certain plausibility. When work consisted of performing repetitive tasks on an assembly line or lifting a shovel to dig a ditch, anyone who was able-bodied could work if he or she was willing. But in the information age, the very nature of work has changed. Low-skilled jobs at middle-class wage rates are rapidly disappearing. The number of blue-collar workers continues to decline, not only as a percentage of the workforce, but in absolute numbers.[13] While every administration eagerly touts the number of new jobs created, nearly all of those jobs are either in the service or technology sector.[14] Good jobs that paid good wages in the industrial age could be performed by anyone; to make work pay more than welfare in the information age, people need to learn how to think and how to use the new technology.

Clinton's proposal could have been the first step in creating a policy that conformed to these new realities. He should have taken it. But the House Democratic leadership was consumed by the health care debate and pleaded with Clinton not to burden them with the additional task of reforming welfare. Despite the warnings of Daniel Patrick Moynihan of New York that there was a welfare, not a health care, crisis in America, Clinton decided to wait until the second year of his administration before sending a proposal to Congress.[15] Health care reform dominated the domestic agenda, and after it collapsed, the Republicans dominated Congress. Everything, including welfare reform, was now viewed in terms of what the Republicans were trying to do and whether the country was willing to let them do it.

▪ ▪ ▪

There were those inside the administration and at the DLC who thought the president ought to do more than simply join the Republicans in finding ways to reduce government. He needed to distinguish his own vision of how government should work from what the new Republican majority was talking about. While Gingrich and the new conservatives continued to insist on the paramount importance of personal responsibility, Clinton, his advisors argued, should return to the theme of reciprocal responsibility that had worked so well during the campaign. Gingrich and his followers believed that individuals were responsible for themselves, and that efforts by the federal government to help did nothing except spend billions of taxpayer dollars. Clinton believed government needed to help people help themselves, a difference he could exploit to his advantage.

A month after the 1994 election, Assistant Secretary of Labor Doug Ross suggested to Vice President Gore that the administration emphasize that difference and turn what the Republicans thought was one of their greatest strengths into one of their greatest weaknesses. After the midterm elections, Republicans not only controlled the House and the Senate, they also controlled thirty of the fifty state governorships. This, Ross believed, would lead Republicans to propose block grants as the way in which to make government smaller. The administration should point out there was no reason to think that giving money to fifty different bureaucracies would create any more efficiency, or any more choice for individuals, than having the federal bureaucracy spend the money, relative sizes of the bureaucracies notwithstanding. The point that needed to be made was that having *any* bureaucracy in charge is a mistake in the information age. "We should argue instead," Ross told Gore, "for turning all these programs into vouchers for individuals to spend as they see fit. It gives us a message with greater choice and more personal freedom, trumping the Republicans' own message."[16]

Several weeks later, Bruce Reed convened a closed-door strategy session at the White House. All those invited had connections to the Democratic Leadership Council. Ross was there, as was Will Marshall, head of the Progressive Policy Institute (PPI), the DLC's think tank. Paul Dimond, from the president's National Economic Council, was a longtime ally of the DLC. Ed Kilgore and Lyn Hogan, who would direct PPI's work on the program, also attended. Reed explained that he wanted them to form what would, in effect, be a surrogate White House staff to prepare a welfare reform proposal that the president could eventually support, but that would originate outside the administration.

By the end of the meeting, they had agreed on the principles that would form the basis of their proposal. No one disputed the need to *put work first.* In 1988, Senator Moynihan had authored legislation to create a program called JOBS. Clinton, who was then chairman of the Democratic Governors' Association, had supported its plan to train welfare recipients to become employable. It was a complete failure. The training seldom matched the requirements of prospective employers and, worse yet, the states were given additional federal funds for every person who attended training sessions, whether or not any of them ever became employed. Private firms who offered useless training sessions made money; the welfare recipients who were forced to sit through them were cheated out of a chance to learn.[17]

The lesson was obvious. Effective welfare reform had to concentrate not on activities, but on results. This, of course, was one of the established basic principles of quality management in the corporate world and had been a major emphasis of the vice president's task force on reinventing government.

Nor was it a new lesson in welfare. In New York, in Chicago, in Cleveland, in Milwaukee, private nonprofit groups were matching welfare applicants with job opportunities.[18] Even existing government bureaucracies were beginning to use this approach. California's experimental "work first" program is called Greater Avenues for Independence or GAIN. Larry Townsend, the GAIN administrator in Riverside County, the heart of Perot country, runs the most successful government attempt to exchange welfare for work in the country. His success flows from a belief in the effect of work on self-esteem, grounded not in some conservative ideology but in the childhood he spent in poverty. The program is based on the information-age assumption that there is no such thing as a mind that cannot become an economic asset. Once the counselors understand the competency levels of their clients, they tailor a training program to the specific needs of the individual. Nothing is taught in the abstract. Reading and math are taught around a curriculum based on news events and job opportunities. The Riverside chamber of commerce entered into a virtual partnership with Townsend to provide as many job opportunities as possible, and anyone who does not find a job after he or she has finished training helps teach new applicants. The object, Townsend explains, is to "provide an environment encouraging self-sufficiency and strengthening independent decision-making."[19]

Over a period of three years, the Riverside GAIN program increased the average total earnings of recipients by 49 percent and cut AFDC payments by 15 percent. While the most dramatic income improvement was among those who already had a basic education, even those who began without any functional knowledge of math or English increased their annual earnings by more than $2,500. Two thirds of those who moved off the welfare rolls were still working eighteen months later, and the number of placements increased even as the local unemployment rate went up.[20]

This was exactly what Bruce Reed and his small circle of welfare strategists wanted to achieve. While John Engler of Michigan and Tommy Thompson of Wisconsin, two of the most zealous advocates of devolution among the Republican governors, were pushing for block grants without any restrictions on the way they would be used, the Reed group devised what it called "performance-based grants." Each state would be given a bonus equal to six months of normal federal funding for every welfare recipient it placed in an unsubsidized, full-time, private-sector job over a six-month period.[21] But that was only part of what Reed and his colleagues had in mind. Welfare recipients would no longer be required to see case workers to receive their benefits. Instead, they would be given vouchers with which to pay for employment counseling and job training. The government bureaucracies that had monopolized these services would be replaced with a market in which any provider, public or private, could compete and the ability to find people work would make the difference between success and failure. In return for this new freedom, those who were on welfare would be responsible for using it wisely. Welfare payments would end after two years, or as soon as recipients turned down a job, whichever came first.

Their proposal was released in March 1995 by the DLC's Progressive Policy Institute under the title "Work First: A Proposal to Replace Welfare with an Employment System."[22] John Breaux, the senator from Louisiana who had succeeded Bill Clinton as chairman of the DLC, had already convinced South Dakotan Tom Daschle, Senate minority leader, and Barbara Mikulski, of Maryland, to co-sponsor legislation incorporating the Reed proposal. This was critical: Daschle's support signaled to everyone in the Senate that it was a mainstream Democratic proposal. Mikulski's support was equally important. She had led reform efforts within the Democratic party and had backed Edward Kennedy when he challenged Jimmy Carter in the 1980 presidential primaries. No one could question her credentials as a liberal, and certainly no one could attack a bill she sponsored as conservative. With Clinton's endorsement, the Senate Democrats entered the debate united in their ideological approach to welfare reform.

The bill they introduced not only abandoned the JOBS approach used by Moynihan in his 1988 legislation, it abolished the entire AFDC program. It went beyond what Clinton had proposed, and far beyond anything conservative Republicans had dared dream, by rejecting the notion of a two-year limitation on welfare in favor of an immediate obligation to work. Each applicant for welfare benefits would be required to look for a job. If he or she could not find one, he or she would sign a contract under which, in exchange for promising to take the first job offered, the recipient would be given a job placement voucher with which to get the kind of job counseling and training services he or she wanted. It was the most radical attempt to transform the welfare system the Senate had ever seen, and it had not come from any of the new Republicans but from a coalition that linked the most liberal and most conservative elements of the Democratic party around a strictly information age idea.

▪ ▪ ▪

It was too radical. Just as Doug Ross had predicted, the original Republican proposal was more interested in saving money than in ending welfare and suggested the way to do that was to give greater freedom to state bureaucracies. But this very freedom provided Phil Gramm an opening to attack Bob Dole for being soft on illegitimacy. Gramm conditioned his support and that of his followers on the adoption of amendments that would require states to adopt a family cap and to deny bene-

fits to any girl under age eighteen who gave birth to an illegitimate child. Dole agreed, but the Senate did not. Senator Pete
Domenici said anyone who believed a family cap that might
cost a mother an additional $64 a month in benefits would
cause her to change her behavior "must also believe in the
tooth fairy."[23] Twenty other skeptical Republicans joined all
forty-six Democrats in rejecting the proposal. The vote rejecting the second element of the Contract's attack on illegitimacy was even more lopsided. Seventy-six senators refused to
deny benefits to a child for the mistakes of a mother who was
barely more than a child herself.

The future of Dole's presidential bid, with its emphasis on
his ability to get things done, now depended less on the Republican majority than on Bill Clinton and two Democratic
senators with close ties to the DLC. Dole had included in the
original bill the job placement voucher favored by the DLC.
Joe Leiberman, senator from Connecticut and the new chairman of the DLC, now convinced Dole to add the job placement bonus plan for each recipient a state placed in an
unsubsidized job. John Breaux added a provision that required the states to maintain at least 80 percent of current
welfare spending levels for the next five years. To ensure that
work paid more than welfare, additional funds were added for
child care. Teenage mothers were given a chance to live in
"second chance homes," another concept developed by the
DLC's PPI. With all these changes, the most comprehensive attempt to reform welfare in line with information age requirements passed the Senate with bipartisan support, 87 to 12.[24]
But the conference committee cut children's eligibility for aid,
reducing support for the welfare bill below that needed to
override Clinton's veto.

▪ ▪ ▪

If there was one thing on which everyone should have been
able to agree, it was the need to prevent people from having
to be on welfare in the first place. As the country struggles

through the transition from the industrial to the information age, larger numbers of working families find themselves earning less and less. In 1977 the percentage of working families whose earnings actually fell below the poverty line was 7.7 percent; by 1993, that percentage had increased to 11.4 percent. The incentive to keep working for less than what welfare offered was in danger of diminishing; the remedy was the earned income tax credit. Ronald Reagan, who first suggested it when he was still governor of California, called it "the best anti-poverty, the best pro-family, the best job-creation measure to come out of Congress" when it was enacted in 1986 during his second term as president.[25] It provided the working poor with a refundable tax credit for every dollar earned up to a specified limit. It did not require a bureaucracy to administer it, and it did not pose the same threat to jobs that conservative economists claimed to find in every proposal to raise the minimum wage. George Bush expanded the coverage of the EITC in 1990; Bill Clinton did the same in 1993.

Republicans were far more interested in balancing the budget than in the problems of the working poor. Senate Republicans proposed restrictions on eligibility for, and reductions in the amount of, the earned income tax credit that would save $40 billion over the first seven years. The chairman of the House Ways and Means Committee, Bill Archer, had the audacity to include a $23 billion reduction in the EITC program in a bill ostensibly designed to respond to demands to end corporate welfare. This represented more than half of the increased revenues his committee found to help balance the budget. The House Republican proposal increased the tax burden on the 14.4 million working families who were "working hard and playing by the rules" and still barely surviving.[26] Welfare was wrong; poverty was not.

▪ ▪ ▪

The new Republicans not only wanted to take from the poor, they wanted to dictate that class's personal behavior. The best way to prevent increases in the welfare rolls, they were convinced, was to prevent conception among unmarried teenagers. They were correct in this belief—out-of-wedlock births account for most of the additional AFDC cases.[27] In 1980, one of every five children born in the United States was to a single mother; in 1992, the figure had risen to one of every three. Among teenage mothers, the illegitimacy rate was 69 percent.[28] Seventy-seven percent of them will apply for AFDC payments before their first child is five years old. The cost to supply AFDC, food stamps, and Medicaid to families with a single mother under the age of twenty was $34 billion in 1992,[29] and it continues to rise.

Welfare reform legislation in 1988 increased spending not only on education and training but on child care subsidies and health care. From 1987 to 1992 the birth rate among young girls and women between fifteen and nineteen years old increased by 20 percent.[30] Those conservatives who believe that financial incentives explain every form of human behavior thought they had all the proof they needed—welfare payments breed illegitimacy.[31] The conclusion rested on the premise, baldly stated, that teenage girls had sex not out of passion but because they first made a rational calculation of the economic advantage in having a child. Anyone who believed this was perfectly capable of dismissing as a minor irrelevancy the fact that what happened in the United States was happening everywhere in the Western world. Illegitimacy was rising, and it did not matter whether expenditures on welfare were going up, going down, or staying level.[32]

If conservatives believed teenage pregnancy was the result of the economic incentives supplied by welfare, liberals rightly insisted that teenage pregnancy was the result of the absence of economic opportunity. Teenage pregnancy was more closely connected with poverty than with anything else. They were right about something else: because poverty is far more pervasive in minority communities, the phenomenon of teenage pregnancy lent itself to the worst sort of racial stereotyping.[33]

Liberals were not right, however, when they suggested that poverty is not only a cause of behavior, but a condition in which the poor are simply victims. It was easy to taunt Newt Gingrich by suggesting he wanted to bring back orphanages and Victorian images of cruelty described by Charles Dickens; it was rather more difficult to admit that the central tenet of his attack on the welfare policies of liberalism was correct. Those policies not only encouraged dependency, they justified it on the ground that the poor were the victims of social oppression they were powerless to prevent. It was, like the conservative alternative, a theory that made economics the only thing that mattered.

Both theories had been tested, and both had failed. The state of New Jersey received a federal waiver in 1992 allowing it to deny increased benefits to any woman who bore a child while she was receiving AFDC. At the end of the first year, the birth rate of women on welfare declined, but the rate of abortions went up.[34] New Zealand adopted the identical requirement in 1991 and also achieved the opposite of what had been intended. Illegitimate births and abortions continued to rise and, after an initial decline, so did the welfare rolls.[35]

Both liberals and conservatives thought that only massive changes in the structure of society would do anything to improve the condition of the poor. The modest notion that government should do whatever was necessary to help the poor learn to help themselves seemed too little in the eyes of liberals and altogether too much in the eyes of conservatives. It was, however, both the single most important principle of public policy in the information age and the only intelligent alternative in the judgment of the new constituency.[36]

Just as industrial age corporations had developed huge bureaucracies to control the behavior of each member of the enterprise, American government employed thousands of people who designed regulations by which to define the eligibility of, and impose specific standards of behavior on, those who were to receive public assistance. The welfare bureaucracies were management, and welfare recipients, like blue-collar workers on an assembly line, were treated as the interchangeable parts of a system that would itself never be altered. In the well-run factory, the worker was an appendage of the machine; in a well-run welfare system, the recipient was an appendage of the bureaucracy. Both worker and recipient were taught the few simple repetitive tasks they needed to know to perform their functions. The worker was at the very bottom of the industrial hierarchy; the welfare recipient was at the very bottom of the social pyramid.

The information age has already destroyed the hierarchical organizations of the private sector; it is only a matter of time before it destroys the public bureaucracies. Place and position mean nothing; knowledge, and the means of acquiring it, mean everything. Blue-collar workers now learn to recognize problems and have the authority to make change to improve quality. Welfare recipients have to be given a similar opportunity and a similar responsibility. Blue-collar workers with the authority to stop the line when something is wrong no longer have management to blame if something does go wrong. Welfare recipients who are given authority to decide the best way to become self-sufficient will no longer think of themselves as victims and will have a powerful incentive to learn whatever they need to know.

Illegitimacy, especially among teenagers, will not be brought to an end either by drafting babies into orphanages or by lamenting the failure to eradicate poverty in America. Any serious attempt to do more than talk about the problem must begin with a change in both the nature and the quantity of information made available to the at-risk population. Moral standards that teach the virtues of self-restraint and the vices of promiscuity are essential, but they cannot be taught by government—even a democratic one—nearly so well as by the community and the family. Government can, however, help citizens learn about the consequences of their conduct, not by promulgating a whole series of bureaucratic regulations but by establishing a few simple rules.[37]

The first rule is that the costs and consequences of fathering a child are no less than the costs and consequences of bearing a child. Advanced technology in the form of DNA and gene research techniques makes it possible to identify the father of every child; technology in the form of computerized record-keeping makes it possible to reengineer the child support system so the income of the father can be applied directly to the needs of the child. Most of the fathers of children born out of wedlock to teenage mothers are men in their twenties and thirties. If the father is not working and has no income, the new rules will still hold him responsible for what the public has to pay and will electronically deduct payment from any income he subsequently receives. Vouchers for job counseling and training will become the property of the two-parent family with either parent providing the child care required for the other to take the steps necessary to get a job.

The first rule, then, is that fathers are financially responsible for their children. The second rule is that teenage mothers will not be eligible for any assistance unless they live under adult supervision. Payments will be made directly to the parents of the teenage mother if she lives at home and continues her education. If, because of abuse or neglect, she chooses not to stay at home, then the alternative will be for her to live in a home with other teenage mothers and their children. These modern-day settlement houses will provide an environment in which learning is not only possible, but necessary. Like knowledge workers who come together to solve a particular problem, young women and their children will help each other to improve.

The disparity between rich and poor has grown during the last twenty years[38] and is likely to grow greater still before the transition from the industrial to the information age is complete. As the middle class struggles to adjust to corporate downsizing and economic dislocation, the temptation to exploit resentment will only increase. Democrats will continue to criticize Republicans for giving tax breaks to the rich, while Republicans will continue to attack Democrats for giving too much to the poor. Their audience has heard it all before and no longer wants to listen.

As the proportion of knowledge workers continues to increase, and as this new constituency becomes the clear majority in American politics, a new set of politicians, perhaps even a new party, will propose a welfare policy that uses government to create market incentives and rewards responsible behavior. Unlike the rigid dichotomies of the industrial age, which have dominated the debate not only on welfare reform but on crime, affirmative action, and other social issues that so concern Americans, public policy in the information age will be based on the belief that the requirements of liberty and the requirements of community are ultimately the same.

8

☆☆☆

REPLACING CRIME WITH COMMUNITY

onservatives seemed to have the souls of accountants—all they could think about was money. They
were determined to balance the budget, and they
didn't seem to care if they were accused of doing it on the
backs of the poor. Welfare had been a terrible mistake that
had cost billions. It was time to end it and the only way to do
that was to dismantle the whole structure of financial incentives that made it attractive. Women on welfare would no
longer receive additional assistance the more children they
had. Mothers eighteen and under who had children would get
nothing at all; they alone would have to deal with the consequences of their irresponsibility. Illegitimacy would no longer
be anyone's problem but their own. There was one small difficulty with this solution: the children of unmarried teenagers
were more likely than anyone else in the United States to grow
up to be killers.

The numbers were staggering. Sixty percent of all violent
crimes in the United States in 1988 were committed by individuals between the ages of fifteen and thirty, 90 percent of
whom were male.[1] A history of childhood neglect or abuse increases the likelihood of later criminal behavior by 40 percent;
teenage mothers are three times more likely than others to
engage in some form of neglect.[2] More than 70 percent of all

juveniles arrested grew up in single-parent families. One study reported a correlation between single-parent families and violent crime so high that it rendered irrelevant differences based on race or income.[3] The correlation is inescapable: the greater the number of single-parent families—especially those headed by teenage mothers—and illegitimate male births, the greater the amount of violent crime.

Recent increases in the figures for both single-parent families and illegitimacy have been nothing short of phenomenal. In 1960, 243,000 children were living with a mother who had never married. Twenty-three years later, in 1983, the number had soared to 3.7 million. By 1993, 6.3 million children were living with unmarried mothers, a 70 percent increase over just ten years.[4] Teenage pregnancy rates, which had actually declined between 1970 and 1987, have risen ever since.[5] The birth rate for teenagers between fifteen and nineteen years of age rose by 20 percent between 1987 and 1991, from 51 to 62 per 1,000.[6] At the midway mark of the twentieth century, just 14 percent of teenagers who gave birth were unmarried. Twenty years later, in 1970, that percentage had more than doubled, to 30 percent. By 1991 the percentage had increased nearly two and one-half times again, to 69 percent. In large cities, the percentages were even higher—so high, in fact, that births among married teenagers had become almost unheard of. In Atlanta, 95 percent of teenage mothers were unmarried; in Cleveland, 90 percent; in Milwaukee, 92 percent; and in Richmond, 93 percent.[7]

The explosion of illegitimacy and single-parent families is mirrored by the increase in violent crime. For example, in 1960, a few years before Bill Clinton began law school at Yale, there were six murders, four rapes, and sixteen robberies in New Haven, Connecticut. Thirty years later New Haven, with 14 percent fewer residents than when Clinton had lived there, counted 31 murders and 168 rapes. The number of robberies had risen to 1,784, an increase of 10,000 percent.[8] What happened in New Haven was not the exception, but the rule. Violence had become a way of life. Crime was everywhere, and it was growing worse. Murder, once the quintessential crime of passion, was now perpetrated on strangers. The FBI estimated that in 1993 more than half of all homicides were committed by someone who did not know the victim.[9] No one felt safe anymore.

The number of children born to single mothers continued to increase. In the last eight years alone, the tendency of these kids to commit murder has risen an incredible 65 percent. By the year 2005, when the proportion of the population between the ages of fourteen and seventeen will have grown by 23 percent, the annual homicide rate may very well reach 35,000—or even 45,000.[10] It will be civil war by another name.

The United States government was failing to carry out the most fundamental function of any government—the protection of the physical safety of its citizens. Even though fewer than 100 Americans lost their lives to foreign enemies in 1994, the new Republican majority added $7 billion to the president's $261.4 billion defense budget request in 1995. Yet when more than 10,000 Americans were killed by other Americans that same year, the Republicans' only reaction was to reopen the left versus right debate on crime that inevitably reached a stalemate. Members of Congress debated whether depriving teenage mothers of public assistance might increase the number of abortions, and whether the right to bear arms includes the right to possess more firepower than a Marine battalion; despite their invocation of "family values," they did nothing to stop the disintegration of families and the consequent destruction of whole communities.

■ ■ ■

The terms of the debate have become chiseled in stone: liberals blame crime on poverty, while conservatives blame it on the moral decline of the country. Liberals insist that the only way to attack crime is to attack the conditions that give rise to it. Conservatives insist that the only way to attack crime is to incarcerate criminals. Liberals believe that everyone is a product of his or her society and that someone who commits a crime is, in essence, as much a victim as the person against whom the crime is committed. Conservatives believe that each person is responsible for his or her own actions and that any suggestion to the contrary is an open invitation to murder and mayhem. A conservative who opposes more spending on prisons has become as much an anomaly as a liberal who favors the death penalty. From Richard Nixon's law and order campaign in 1968 to George Bush's infamous Willie Horton ad in 1988, Republicans have attempted to define their differences with Democrats by a no-nonsense position on crime and criminals. It helped Republicans win the presidency, and it also gave them the tool by which to control the Democratic majorities in Congress. No Democrat, except those with overwhelmingly Democratic districts, could afford to cast any votes in Congress that might allow their opponents to label them as soft on crime. Liberals continued to believe that the causes of crime were economic, but it became progressively more difficult for them to do anything about it.

While liberal and conservative ideologues battled over crime in the well-lit, air-conditioned seminar rooms of Washington think tanks, the people who live every day with the consequences of their government's failure to protect them are beginning to reject the alternatives of both sides. The public appears to be as divided as the politicians over the question of whether the causes of society's problems, including crime, are economic or moral. By a margin of almost two to one (58 percent to 31 percent) women over forty believe they are economic. Only 39 percent of men over forty agree; another 50 percent are convinced the country's problems are the result of a loss of moral values. Among those who supported Bill Clinton because of their own partisan leanings, 55 percent believe the causes are economic, and only 33 percent believe they are moral. Among those who opposed him, the results are almost perfectly reversed: 55 percent believe they are moral, while 34 percent see economic causes. But among those without strong partisan affiliations who voted for Clinton, the group most likely to contain a high percentage of knowledge workers, the division was much less pronounced. Faced with a question requiring the selection of only one of the two alternatives, they split almost evenly, 45 percent choosing economics and 40 percent choosing morality as the cause of the country's problems.[11]

For the new constituency it was a false choice. Knowledge workers were far more interested in policies that combined increased economic opportunity with measures to ensure safer communities; such attempts had been made before. In 1989, Adam Walinsky, former chief legislative assistant to Senator Robert F. Kennedy, proposed a national police corps. It was a "ROTC for Cops," in which young men and women would be offered up to $10,000 a year for college in exchange for four-year postgraduate commitments to serve as local police officers.[12] This would accomplish two extraordinarily important objectives. Young men and women who might not even finish high school because they saw no future prospects would have the means to attend college. Police departments, where officers now have to deal with eleven and a half times as many violent crimes as they did thirty years ago, in turn would receive an infusion of well-educated and highly motivated recruits.[13] Some of the same young men and women who, without any hope for the future, might have become criminals would instead become police.

John Lewis, a leader in the civil rights movement before he was elected Democratic congressman from Georgia, was far less interested in the debate over the causes of crime than in doing something to combat it. Without the right numbers and kinds of police, violence would continue and there would be no community left to save. "All across the nation," Lewis passionately explained, "black communities are under an assault of crime and violence that is without precedence in our history. . . . The causes of the deterioration, the roots of our present crisis are many. But surely the most immediate and the most powerful is the fact of violence itself. . . . This widening gyre of destruction first stripped communities of businesses and jobs. . . . It is not only poverty that has caused crime. In a very real sense it is crime that has caused poverty."[14]

Like nearly every other crime bill introduced during the Bush administration, the Police Corps proposal went nowhere.[15] Liberals talked about economic opportunity, conservatives demanded personal responsibility, and crime continued to ravage the poorest communities in America. When Bill Clinton became a candidate for president he was one of the few politicians in the country who understood that the debate over whether prevention or punishment was the way to do something about crime had become not only irrelevant, but irresponsible. The way to fight crime was to combine tough sanctions with well-funded programs of prevention, not to choose one over the other.

■ ■ ■

During his presidency Clinton has frequently seemed incapable of making choices others saw as obvious. He has been criticized for his indecisiveness, and even some of his supposed political allies reworked Mark Twain's comment, claiming that if one wanted a change of policy from the White House, all one had to do was wait. But on the issue of crime, Clinton had come to certain conclusions from which, as president, he never varied. Those conclusions were based, at least in part, on what he had found as he had traveled the country in 1990 and 1991 trying to expand the membership of the Democratic Leadership Council.

Although Senators Sam Nunn, Virginian Chuck Robb, and the rest of the Southern Democrats who dominated the leadership of the DLC had wondered whether Governor Clinton might not be too liberal for the job, they eventually agreed that Clinton was the only one who had the time to lead a state-by-state organizational effort.[16] As its new chairman, Clinton became the spokesman for what the DLC thought were the two principles needed to inform any attempt to reconstruct the Democratic party—economic opportunity and reciprocal responsibility. He quickly discovered, however, that it was not a message that generated much excitement. There was something missing, and Clinton thought he found it when he began to speak about the need to rebuild America's communities. Politicians spent too much time dwelling on the divisions in the country and blaming one another for bringing them about. It was time to start concentrating on the things that brought people together.[17] Democrats looking for a new message to win the White House started to listen. Clinton had found the three notes of the chord—economic opportunity, citizen *and* government responsibility, and community. It was a chord he played right into the White House.

The crime bill the president proposed in his first year followed the same theme. The "three strikes and you're out" provision would impose life sentences on those whose propensity for violence demonstrated their apparent unwillingness to live by the rules of a civilized community. Federal funding for local programs designed to get young people off the streets was one method of prevention. Federal funding for an additional 100,000 police officers to patrol those streets was another. The bill was a vital first step toward what the community needed, and was just about the last thing Congress wanted to hear. Liberals, especially those who represented black majority districts, regarded "three strikes and you're out" as a new form of lynch law. Conservatives, especially those from white suburban districts in the South, dismissed prevention as another name for government waste.

The Democratic congressional leadership had come a long way since the respective days of the New Deal and the Great Society, when united Democratic majorities were produced by the force of the ideas of the party's presidential candidates. Those battles of principle had been replaced by small struggles over particular programs and specific appropriations. It was less a question of what someone believed; nearly everyone within the Democratic majority held the same views. It was, rather, a question of who could strike the best bargain for his vote when that vote became important, a game that all knew how to play. Those who played it called it the art of compromise; those who watched it called it politics as usual.

Members of the black caucus objected strenuously to any attempt to increase the severity of the sanctions of the criminal law, a reaction that had become almost instinctive. For too long police power had been used to harass and intimidate black citizens, and "law and order" had frequently been used as a racist appeal for white support. The congressional leadership did not even try to debate the question. Objections were overcome, not with argument but by raising the level of expenditures for programs in the districts of those who objected. It was a game in which no one but the taxpayer lost. Democrat Jack Brooks of Texas, chairman of the House Judiciary Committee, made certain the 1993 legislation appropriated $10 million for the creation of a criminal justice program at a university in his district. Everyone wanted something, and almost everyone got what they wanted, so long as it was only a question of money. When the crime bill passed the Senate, it had a price tag of $22 billion over five years, a figure that had risen by the time the bill passed the House. And when it came out of a contentious conference committee, the cost had gone up to $30 billion over six years.[18]

The conference committee report set the stage for the first serious confrontation between Clinton and Newt Gingrich. While the National Rifle Association lobbied against the bill because of its ban on assault weapons, Gingrich attacked it as another attempt by the federal government to tell local communities what they were supposed to do. In a stunning and surprising defeat for both the president and the Democratic leadership in the House, the rule governing debate on the conference committee report was shot down on a procedural vote. Clinton immediately consulted with both the Speaker and the House majority leader to decide on a strategy to save the legislation. Tom Foley and Richard Gephardt suggested that the only alternative was to win back the Southern Democrats who had voted with Gingrich by dropping the ban on assault weapons.

Michael Castle, a Republican from Delaware, had worked with Clinton when both men were governors and he now suggested an alternative. Delaware was almost a perfect microcosm of America and a bellwether of presidential politics. In the last eleven presidential elections, the state had voted for the winning candidate and had frequently done so by margins that came within a few percentage points of the national numbers.[19] While Clinton had gone on to become president, Castle had gone on to become Delaware's only congressional representative. Castle was a moderate, as was the majority of his constituency. He was all in favor of a ban on assault weapons, so he suggested that Clinton drop some of the more outrageous spending provisions from the bill. He also recommended responding to his suburban constituencies' newest fear of neighborhood crime—a fear shared nationwide—by adding more stringent reporting requirements for sex offenders who were released from prison. Once Clinton agreed to those changes, Castle delivered thirty-five more Republicans than had voted for it before. The bill passed in 1994 with the ban on assault weapons intact.

▪ ▪ ▪

The NRA was outraged, and the authors of the Contract with America were delighted. Republican candidates swore to replace much of the Omnibus Crime Control Act of 1994 with their own Taking Back Our Streets Act, designed to eliminate "specific funds for drug courts, recreational programs, community justice programs, and other social prevention spending."[20] Nothing was mentioned about repealing the ban on assault weapons. Nothing needed to be. Everyone, including Newt Gingrich, understood what was going to happen if Republicans took control of Congress. The NRA contributed twice as much to the campaigns of the seventy-three Republicans who were elected to their first term in the House as even the right-to-life movement did.[21] The bargain was sealed.

The allegiance of the new Republican majority to the NRA was evident right from the start. In one of the very first crime bills introduced they expanded the exceptions under which improperly obtained evidence could be used at trial, something conservatives had demanded ever since the "exclusionary rule" was adopted by the Supreme Court under Earl Warren. But they then immediately surrendered any claim of consistency by making their own new exclusion, which would not apply to evidence gathered by the Alcohol, Tobacco and Firearms (ATF) agency in the prosecution of anyone charged with illegally trafficking guns.[22] The exception was drawn as artfully as if it had been drafted in the offices of the ATF's greatest enemy, the NRA.

The notion that gun owners needed more protection from government agencies than did anyone else stemmed from one of the most deeply held principles of Newt Gingrich and his supporters. Using erroneous legal and historical arguments for interpreting the Second Amendment—an interpretation described in self-promoting terms as the "Standard Model" by its own creators—the Speaker declares in *To Renew America,* "The Second Amendment is a political right written into the Constitution for the purpose of protecting individual citizens from their own government."[23] Ignoring the most fundamental rules for building a community, Gingrich then passionately defends the right of individual citizens to take up arms against their government as the ultimate protection of freedom rather than the constitutional crime of treason most Americans consider such behavior to be. It was only after the national outcry that followed the bombing of the Oklahoma City federal building on April 19, 1995, and the subsequent exposure of the national private militia movement, that the NRA and its freshman Republican allies agreed to delay reconsidering the right of disgruntled citizens to take up even more powerful weapons against their government. Meanwhile, the president's appeal for a more civil tone in the nation's politics temporarily raised his standing in the polls by six percentage points.[24]

If consistency is the hobgoblin of small minds, the new Republicans demonstrated a mental breadth that staggered the imagination. The revolution Gingrich was trying to lead supposedly had as its principal aim the withering away of the federal government. The states, through the use of block grants and the elimination of unfunded mandates, would become the new centers of government power in a revitalized federal union. Henry Hyde called the idea of block grants "a defining issue between the Democratic Party and the Republican Party." But after forty years of opposition, the temptation to give orders of their own could not be resisted. As Bill Kristol, a key GOP strategist, admitted, "We are not for block grants if it means simply throwing the money out an airplane window."[25]

In the fervent belief that incarceration is the only real form of prevention, the Republican majority raised the amount of federal funding for new prison construction in the states from the $7.9 billion authorized in the 1994 bill to $10.5 billion. More money meant more regulation. Any state that wanted to receive the money the federal government was offering had first to pass legislation under which all those sent to a state prison must serve a minimum of 85 percent of his sentence before being eligible for parole.[26] It was legislation designed to appeal to the same emotions as "three strikes and you're out," but both attempts at severity ignored the most basic distinctions between the kinds of crime and the kinds of criminals. Though the difference between someone who puts a knife to a woman's throat and rapes her and an eighteen- or nineteen-year-old who is caught in possession of too much marijuana is obvious, the two would be treated in exactly the same way under these proposals.

■ ■ ■

The failure to distinguish between nonviolent and violent crimes has one ineluctable effect—it increases prison populations. There are only two ways to deal with this problem: either ever more prisons have to be built, or each time a new prisoner is added a resident prisoner must be released. Unless nonviolent offenders' punishment no longer involves prison time, their presence in the prison population will inevitably mean that ever-increasing numbers of violent offenders will be back on the streets. This was something that Nelson Rockefeller either never understood or never cared to worry about. Twenty years later, the next Republican governor of New York would have to deal with the consequences.

Nelson Rockefeller was considered a liberal Republican by friend and foe alike. But in 1973, with the crime rate spiraling out of control, it was Rockefeller who convinced the New York state legislature to pass two of the toughest sentencing requirements in the country. Under the first, either possession of four ounces or the sale of two ounces of cocaine or heroin suddenly became crimes that carried mandatory sentences of fifteen years to life imprisonment. Under the second, anyone convicted of a repeat felony, no matter what the two felonies were, had to serve a lengthy period of incarceration before there would be any possibility of parole. The only place you could still get three strikes in New York was at Yankee Stadium.

The effect was dramatic—not on the crime rate, but on the prison population. Ten years later, in 1983, Democratic Governor Mario Cuomo was forced to add an additional 33,000 prison cells to keep up. The cost of construction was in excess of $3 billion. And that was just the beginning. Each cell cost nearly $100,000 to build, and each inmate it held cost the state nearly $30,000 every year he was there.[27] It was more expensive to send a young criminal to Attica than to send a young student to Harvard. The New York state prison system became one of the most costly government-run programs in the country. Conservatives were caught in a conflict between two of their most cherished principles—less spending and more punishment.

Mario Cuomo had thought about and decided against running for president so often that he had become known as "Hamlet on the Hudson." Whatever his reasons for remaining in Albany, no one thought he would ever leave except of his own volition. He was the closest American politician there was to being an unbeatable incumbent. In 1994 the only candidate Republicans could find to oppose Cuomo for the office once held by FDR was an obscure state legislator from upstate New York. George Pataki's slogan never even mentioned his own name. It read simply, "Cuomo: too liberal, too long." And, in the year in which liberalism had become as attractive as leprosy, it worked. Pataki became governor of New York, Mario Cuomo became a radio talk show host, and Republican Mayor Rudolph Giuliani of New York City, who had endorsed Cuomo, was transformed from a political genius to a political idiot in the proverbial New York minute.

Pataki had promised to cut both taxes and spending. New York needed whatever federal money it could get, especially to build prisons, but coming on top of what the state spent to run prisons, the mandatory sentencing provisions of the House bill would bankrupt the state. In the twenty years since Rockefeller changed the law, the prison population had risen from 12,500 to 66,000. Pataki began to take a look at what the numbers really meant or, more accurately, what they concealed. Half of all inmates incarcerated in New York prisons were serving sentences for drug offenses. Only one third of them were there because they had committed violent crimes.[28]

The new governor proposed a change in the "two strikes and you're out" law that would restrict its application to violent felonies. Pataki was not interested in anything that resembled decriminalization of drug offenses, but he was willing to offer treatment as an alternative to imprisonment. It was a lot cheaper: outpatient drug treatment cost between $2,700 and $3,600 in New York. Even residential treatment, at between $17,000 and $20,000, was still less expensive than the cost of incarceration,[29] and it was clearly more effective. Approximately one in every eight individuals who receive treatment are free of drug or alcohol dependency one year later. Incarceration has not been shown to have even that minimal rate of success.[30]

Drug dealers, according to a Rand Corporation study, annually face a 1.4 percent risk of death and a 7 percent chance of serious injury.[31] As one criminologist put it, "Each day these people face dangers far greater than anything we can impose through the criminal justice system. If that doesn't deter them, I can't see how prison will."[32] Besides, as James Q. Wilson observed, every time a drug dealer is sent to jail it simply creates a job opening for another.[33] Instead of insisting that states put more people behind bars for longer periods of time, the federal government should restrict grants for prison construction to states that treat nonviolent drug offenders, either by placing them in alternative communities such as boot camps or halfway houses, where their treatment can be supervised, or by using new technologies such as electronic handcuffs to create *virtual* jail cells, where they can live without costing the state the money required to house, clothe, and feed them.

∎ ∎ ∎

The real battle in Congress was not over prison construction, however, but over the $5 billion appropriated in the 1994 Omnibus Crime Control Act for community-based prevention programs. This had been the subject of an intensive analysis by Republican pollster Frank Luntz, who found that the public perception of the crime bill would change if it were focused on a few specific and seemingly insignificant provisions. Luntz advised Republican members of the House "to redefine 'the Crime Bill' as . . . 'the Midnight Basketball Bill.' "[34] Designed to encourage what would normally be local community efforts to provide alternative activities for young people, to many this seemed like a perfectly good way to waste government money. Following his advice, House Republicans ridiculed the bill as another liberal misadventure that would spend billions and accomplish nothing. Once they were in the majority, Gingrich and the House leadership simply combined the appropriation for prevention programs with the appropriation for additional policemen into a single block grant program of $10.5 billion for local communities to spend as they saw fit.[35]

They might have learned from their own mistakes. During Richard Nixon's administration, the Law Enforcement Assistance Administration Act had also allocated billions of dollars to communities to use in the fight against crime. Those monies bought every imaginable type of equipment, from armored personnel carriers to helicopters, none of which had any discernible effect on the crime rate.[36] This latest Republican attempt to assist local communities was almost guaranteed to achieve the same result. To underscore their belief that only the police knew how to handle crime, Republicans insisted on the substantial involvement of local law enforcement authorities in any project that received money from a federal block grant. Crime prevention programs run by community, religious, or business groups did not have a chance.[37]

The new constituency of knowledge workers has a different and better idea. It has learned through its work the importance of participation and the beneficial effects of combining individuals into groups or teams that concentrate on the same objective.[38] It is willing—even eager—to join with others to help solve the problems in their own communities. A Times Mirror study in May 1994 discovered that within the same age group those who used personal computers were both more outgoing and more active than those who did not use them. Forty-eight percent of PC users participated in clubs or organizations, compared to only 38 percent in comparable demographic groups.[39] Even when the community is simply one that has formed among the users of an electronic bulletin board on the Internet, the members, like the members of any community who share a common interest and have learned to work together, want to protect both its security and its growth.

The most effective way to reduce the crime rate is to reduce the willingness of the community to tolerate its existence. If members of a neighborhood look the other way instead of reporting crime to the police, clearly crime pays. If neighbors join together in a voluntary association dedicated to ridding their neighborhood of crime, criminals disappear.[40] When drug dealers recently moved into the Five Oaks section of Dayton, Ohio, that once-quiet residential neighborhood became an urban nightmare of speeding cars and gunshots in the night. The residents decided they were not going to surrender, so they spent $693,000 to turn fifty-six roads into cul-de-sacs. The creation of these "defensible spaces" cut the overall crime rate by 25 percent and the violent crime rate by 50 percent in the first year alone. Housing prices rose 15 percent, and the neighborhood felt like a community again.[41]

There was an even more dramatic turnaround at Paradise Gardens in Washington, D.C., one of the most crime-ridden public housing projects in the nation. There, residents hired members of the Nation of Islam to protect them against the gun-wielding drug dealers who had turned their complex into a war zone. The Black Muslims did what law enforcement should have been doing, through a community-based policing scheme; they took on the drug dealers and worked with members of the community, both to lower their tolerance for self-destructive behavior and to increase their commitment to improving life in the project. The new sense of increased safety and self-esteem among residents persuaded a private developer to renovate that half of the project that had been abandoned and boarded up. Residents began to attend monthly meetings, where they made decisions about other ways to improve their community together. Paradise Gardens won the fight against crime: 70 percent of the residents now pay market-based rent, and all of them can take advantage of on-site day care, comprehensive health services, after school study programs, including one for college-bound students; recreation programs for children; and a high-technology jobs program for teenagers.[42]

The survival of any community depends entirely on the commitment of each of its members, and that commitment will exist to the degree that there is frequent interaction among members over an extended period of time.[43] Community policing is designed to provide just this kind of opportunity. In accordance with the principles of the best quality programs in the private sector, it attempts to prevent the problem from happening in the first place, instead of trying to fix it after it has already occurred. The police get out of their squad cars and into the neighborhoods. In Houston, Texas, where community-based policing first earned its reputation, the community was fully engaged. The 1,000 police officers added since 1991 are supported in over 100 neighborhoods by the city's Citizen Patrol Program, which has the authority to track down parole violators and crime suspects. Houston joined New York, which also has an aggressive community-policing program, in leading the nation's cities in reducing the rate of crime between 1993 and 1994.[44] In Oakland, California, each neighborhood was urged to "take control of the situation, talk to your neighbors and friends and get organized." Neighbor joined with neighbor to clean the streets, ridding them of both litter and graffiti. It was a signal that the community was ready to support police efforts to close down the drug houses; indeed, using the city's zoning and housing codes, the police proceeded to shut down seven hundred of them in five years.[45]

The very act of creating a partnership between the police and the neighborhood, to both explore the problem and decide upon a solution, increases the likelihood of success— participation produces commitment.[46] Self-directed work teams that have the authority to make decisions achieve results no system of command and control could ever accomplish.[47] It is the lesson of the information age, applicable not only to private business but to every area of public policy, but only so long as there is a community in which to apply it. Where there is no community, it becomes the responsibility of government to help create the environment for one.

It is especially important to create new communities for individuals who demonstrate an unwillingness or an inability to conform to the rules of the larger community. It is possible to predict with some certainty the likelihood that a particular individual who has committed a crime will be a repeat offender. A teenager from a single-parent family who was the victim of abuse, or whose parents engaged in criminal activity, is more likely to be a recidivist than is a teenager whose parents both work and are married to each other.[48] The solution is not to lock up the offender with other individuals, whose penchant for repetitive criminal conduct may be even higher and more violent than his own, but to make him a member of a different kind of community—a community in which the values and expectations carry clear and decisive consequences for improper behavior.

The "scared straight" programs that expose juveniles to the reality of prison and the "boot camps" that employ Marine Corps–style discipline to change the behavior of first-time offenders are first faltering steps toward the comprehensive solution now required by the burgeoning new generation of likely young criminals.

Though usually thought of as the ultimate hierarchical organization, the U.S. Army has become the most advanced information age institution in the federal government. The army knew it had to change once it understood that it had lost the Vietnam War "became of a failure to appreciate and apply basic military fundamentals."[47] Maintenance and management were no longer the basis on which commanders were appraised. Training became the principal activity of the peacetime army, and readiness for battle became the standard for evaluation and promotion. Officers and those under their command were graded on their collective ability to perform each task they were assigned.[50] Young soldiers were taught the value of teamwork and learned the use of advanced technologies in the most fully integrated organization in the world. Certainly the army can do the same thing with first-time offenders.

When the country decides it can no longer tolerate the criminal civil war it daily experiences it will begin to remove dangerous people from the community before they commit more crimes. Upon the first conviction for a nonviolent felony, those who are determined most likely to offend again will serve two years in the new community corps, where they will receive the same training given army recruits. They will be taught the discipline needed to follow the rules of both military and civilian life and the skills that will enable them to continue to learn. At the end of two years they will be allowed to choose among volunteering for a career in the regular army; using their military training and discipline to enroll in a training program such as "ROTC for Cops" and become police officers; or reentering their old communities, where they would become role models for the kind of change their two years of discipline and training have made possible. Some traditionalists will argue that the military's role should be limited to protecting. the country from foreign aggression, but they should recall that branches of the military frequently provide relief for the victims of natural disasters. Crime produces far more victims every year than do hurricanes and earthquakes, and it poses a threat to the future of the American community grater than any we face today from foreign aggressors. By asking the army to mold the characters of those young people most at risk, America will have its best chance to win the war against crime and restore communities to places where families can live and children can learn.

9

RETHINKING
RACE RELATIONS

esse Jackson went to Cleveland looking for revenge. On the opening day of the first national convention of the Democratic Leadership Council, while delegates inside were listening to a speech by Bill Clinton, Jackson joined a picket line. Labor had formed the line to show that it wanted nothing to do with an organization that would even think about supporting NAFTA and Jackson was there to protest the decision of the DLC to have nothing to do with him. All of the other prospective candidates for the 1992 Democratic presidential nomination had been invited to speak to the convention.

There was never any debate about whether to invite Jesse Jackson. Al From, president and executive director of the DLC, was in charge of organizing the convention. The whole purpose in having a convention in the first place was to "promote a new agenda and a new politics." The agenda was a new approach to public policy in the new information age. The "new politics" was a deliberate attempt to move the Democratic party away from the left so that it could once again appeal to the middle class.[1]

The chief spokesman for what Al From meant by the "old politics" was none other than Jesse Jackson. No one else symbolized, in quite the same way, the continued commitment of the Democratic party to the welfare state policies voters had rejected in one presidential election after another. The DLC had to establish its own identity, and that identity, to be useful to what those who believed in it were trying to do, had to separate itself once and for all from what Jackson, and those who followed him, demanded in almost every speech they made.

No one had ever really said *no* to Jesse Jackson before. Though he had never held an office and, before the 1988 presidential campaign, never run for one, Jackson was the self-proclaimed leader of every one of the more than 20 million Americans of African descent. Like Northern politicians who had once wrapped themselves in the "bloody shirt" of the Southern rebellion, or conservative politicians who had blamed everything on communists and communism in the 1950s, Jackson held himself out as the embodiment of the civil rights movement and the legitimate heir of Martin Luther King, Jr. Anyone who disagreed with him almost certainly faced the charge of racism. It was a weapon he had used to close off the very debate on policy Democrats needed to engage in if they were to have any chance of regaining the presidency. Crime, welfare reform, and the whole range of social policies that were tinged with the issue of race were held hostage to Jackson's point of view so long as his leadership of the black community went unchallenged.

Clinton, then chairman of the DLC, was tempted to avoid confrontation by inviting Jackson to serve on a panel without letting him address the convention. He decided instead to go along with From's decision. They both knew Jackson would protest his exclusion in every way he could, and that those protests would be given as much coverage as the convention itself. For Al From, at least, that would be all to the good. No one would doubt that the DLC and Jesse had nothing to do with each other.[2]

▪ ▪ ▪

The DLC was formed in 1985, after Walter Mondale managed to carry only a single state against Ronald Reagan and after Paul Kirk, longtime aide to Edward Kennedy, was elected chairman of the Democratic National Committee. The size and scope of Mondale's defeat seemed to suggest that unless something were done, Republicans would not only continue to control the White House, but by taking formerly safe seats in the South, they would win control of the Senate as well. The election of Paul Kirk was understood by many moderates as a signal that the Democratic party simply refused to face reality.

Every political analyst knew that the Democrats had been steadily losing the white vote and Democrats knew white moderates in the South and ethnic whites in both urban and newly suburban areas of the North were primarily responsible for that decline. Almost every one of them had a theory about why this was happening. Busing to achieve integration in the public schools had alarmed and then antagonized many of the white blue-collar workers who lived in the Northern suburbs, a point that anyone who remembered the Wallace phenomenon in 1968 understood all too well. Drugs and violence had been used to separate those who claimed to be tough on law and order from those who were supposedly soft on crime, a distinction almost always advantageous to Republicans. The war in Vietnam and the 1979 seizure of American hostages in Iran had left an impression of Democratic impotence when it came to involving the ultimate use of force. Everyone might have had a theory, but Paul Kirk wanted a definite answer. He did what every politician was in the habit of doing—he commissioned a poll.

The results left no room for doubt. White flight from the Democratic party was not only real but, without substantial and even radical changes in what the party stood for, irreversible. Southern moderates and Northern ethnics had become convinced that the Democratic party was now the special province of ". . . liberals on the one hand, and . . . blacks, gays, Hispanics, feminists and labor" on the other.[3] There was no room for the "common man" and, worse yet, the party had become a threat to everything the "common man" stood for. Gays and feminists were, in their judgment, "outside the orbit of acceptable social life," and constituted a "social underclass" that endangered their children. This "underclass" made up one faction of what the Democratic party had become. There was only one other part, also an "underclass," an economic underclass that "absorbs their taxes and even locks them out of the job, in the case of affirmative action."

The Democrats had become "the giveaway party. Giveaway means too much middle class money going to the blacks and the poor." The only way left to recover the lost allegiance of the white middle class, in the prosaic language of survey research, was a "demarketing of the party to the economic and social underclass." This could be done by "segmenting black and Hispanic voters into underclass and middle-class sectors, and targeting Democratic identification with middle-class blacks and Hispanics." It would do no good to simply talk about fairness. In the mouths of Democratic politicians "fairness" had come to mean, in the minds of white moderates, policies to help minorities.

Kirk read the report, reviewed it with some of the party's congressional leaders, and then suppressed it—a traditional industrial age response to bad news. Though he would later claim that he had not believed the findings were valid, he also expressed concern that release of the report might lead to a division in the party over what should be done about the problem. The problem only worsened.

By the 1988 presidential election, it was no longer a question of winning back those Democrats who had been defecting to Republican candidates. There were not enough Democrats left. While everyone pointed to the Republicans' negative campaign tactics, and though no one could find anything nice to say about what the Democrats had done, Michael Dukakis ac-

tually won the votes of a greater percentage of those who identified themselves as Democrats than Jimmy Carter had in 1976.
An analysis of the election results further suggested that he
had done better with members of his own party than Lyndon
Johnson had in the electoral landslide of 1964. Had the same
number of Democrats voted in 1988 as had in 1976, George
Bush would have been defeated, and Dukakis would have been
elected president of the United States.[4]

Reagan Democrats were still voting Republican, but now
they were doing it as both Republicans and Independents.
And they were doing it with a vengeance. Among all voters in
the 1988 election, Dukakis lost every income category above
$20,000. Even this statistic was misleading, however. When vot-
ers were categorized by race, white voters supported Bush in
every income category above $10,000.[5] The middle class,
much of which had been created by the policies and programs
of the New Deal, had come to view the Democratic party as an
irrelevancy at best and as a danger at worst. The hard-core
constituency of the Democratic party was now made up almost
exclusively of minorities and the poor, a coalition that, in both
the public mind and in his own, was led by Jesse Jackson.

The emergence of Jackson as a political force within the
Democratic party and the progressive disenchantment of the
white middle class shared a similar origin. Jackson and those
he led were zealous in their insistence that past discrimination
could only be remedied by an enforced system of quotas.
Wherever there was a discrepancy in the number of African
Americans, or women, or virtually any definable minority in
education or employment and their numbers in the population as a whole, government had a duty to set the balance
straight. Those who asserted this argued that it was nothing
more than what they were entitled to because of past oppression. Those who found their own jobs and educational opportunities at risk because of such policies rejected entitlements
as thinly disguised demands for preferential treatment. The
two camps agreed only that the Democratic party was respon-

sible. Those who wanted quotas as a means of achieving equality of result complained that the Democrats had not been willing to go far enough; those who found in quotas the ultimate denial of equality of opportunity were convinced that the Democrats had gone much too far.

The division of the Democratic party and the beginnings of the disaffection of the middle class began in the troubled and sometimes violent convention of 1968. The Vietnam War had driven Lyndon Johnson from the race for reelection, transformed Eugene McCarthy from a quixotic challenger for the nomination into an apparent front-runner, and convinced Bobby Kennedy that he could wait no longer. Hubert Humphrey won the nomination but, those who had supported either McCarthy or Kennedy insisted, only because the rules had been stacked against their candidate. In many states no presidential primaries were held, and delegates were selected in a process that virtually assured the exclusion of anyone who had not participated in local and state conventions two years earlier. In some of the states the procedures guaranteed delegations that were predominantly, if not exclusively, white and predominantly, if not exclusively, male. Every Democrat, except those, like Chicago Mayor Richard J. Daley, who still believed in the old politics, demanded something new. Hubert Humphrey and the leadership of the national party promised to give it to them. What they got was the McGovern Commission.

The new rules drafted by the McGovern Commission applied to the selection process for delegates chosen for the 1972 Democratic National Convention and eliminated the procedures by which the reformers had been denied the chance to become delegates to the 1968 convention. They did this, in part, by applying the new logic of entitlement to every aspect of the selection process. To determine whether the composition of a state delegation was the result of discrimination, the credentials committee was authorized to look at its composition in terms of race, sex, and age. While the report stated in a footnote that the representation of minority groups was "not to be accomplished by the mandatory imposition of quotas," if the proportion of blacks or women within the delegation did not correspond to that group's proportion of the population as a whole, the delegation was subject to challenge.[6] Quotas were not required, they were simply the standard by which to determine if discrimination had occurred.

If anyone had a doubt that the so-called reform rules, with their insistence on equal outcomes rather than equal opportunity, had contributed to the crushing defeat of George McGovern, Robert Strauss was not among them. As the new chairman of the national Democratic party, Strauss made certain that the rules were changed for the 1976 convention to eliminate every reference to quotas or to anything that could be construed as requiring a quota. But not everyone shared his enthusiasm for the change. When the convention opened, a minority of the Rules Committee issued a report calling for the abolition of the changes Strauss had made. On Sunday evening, just after the convention began, Strauss convened a private meeting with Jimmy Carter and state party leaders. Strauss explained that the forces opposed to Carter's nomination were going to use the minority report as a chance to demonstrate their strength before the roll call vote on the nomination.

Carter, who for all practical purposes had won the nomination weeks before the New York convention opened, thought the whole thing arcane and irrelevant. There was more at stake in his quest for the presidency than some minor point of procedure. Politely, Strauss disagreed. He glanced around the small conference table where Carter and some of the most influential state party leaders sat and tried to explain the effect party rules sometimes have on elections. After reminding them all about what had happened in 1972, he looked directly at Carter. "You see, Governor," he concluded, "the people don't understand any of this either. But if you get tagged with the quota label it can cost you votes. The American people don't like quotas."[7]

■ ■ ■

If the American people did not like quotas, American Jews found them an abomination and a hateful reminder of how quotas had once been used to keep them out of full participation in the institutions of America. It was, in its way, an American tragedy. African Americans, who had been brought to America as slaves, and Jews, who had fled enslavement in Europe, had trusted one another to understand what it was like to search for freedom. In the early days of the civil rights movement, when it was considered an act of courage for John F. Kennedy to express his concern as Martin Luther King, Jr., sat in the Birmingham jail, American Jews risked their lives fighting for the rights of African-American citizens in the South. But as the civil rights movement became more militant, some leaders began to view Jews as part of the white establishment they had come to despise. What had happened in Germany in the 1930s was history—ancient history—that no longer held relevance to what was happening in America and throughout the world.

African Americans felt that they were oppressed in America, and that Jews were not. Moreover, in Israel Jews had become the oppressors of Palestinians. The PLO, like the civil rights movement in America, was doing everything it could to reclaim its freedom. For a long time, the American Jewish community dismissed this hostility to Israel as the ignorant posturing of a small number of black extremists. It was not so easy to dismiss it, however, once it began to appear that this same policy was being observed by the Carter administration.

The signing of the Camp David accords between Menachem Begin and Anwar Sadat, the Israeli prime minister and Egyptian president, respectively, the first concrete step toward peace in the Middle East since Israel came into existence, should have eliminated any lingering suspicions about Carter's commitment to the survival of Israel. Instead, it only increased the anger and feeling of betrayal among American Jews when it was learned that, in direct violation of American policy, Andrew Young, American ambassador to the United Nations and one of Jimmy Carter's closest African-American friends and advisors, had met secretly with the PLO. Young was forced to submit his resignation, and the debate between African Americans and Jews became more openly hostile than it ever had been before.

Carter had asked for Young's resignation in response to the cries of outrage that had descended from almost every Jewish leader and organization. The African-American leadership retaliated in kind. Meetings were held to defend what Young had done and then, with rhetoric that on occasion foreshadowed the kind of virulent anti-Semitism that would become a hallmark of the speeches of Nation of Islam head Louis Farrakhan, to denounce Jews for tearing Young down. Alarmed at the African-American reaction, and afraid of further alienating Jews, Carter decided to act. On September 5, barely two weeks after Young had been asked to resign, the president invited Ted Mann, president of the Presidents of Jewish Organizations, to lunch. He also invited Robert Adams, an old friend from Georgia; Bob Washington, chairman of the Democratic party of the District of Columbia; a labor union president; a member of Congress; and the president of the Association of State Democratic Chairmen.[8]

Carter spent most of the meal talking about his recent trip down the Mississippi and the attack by the famed killer rabbit the media had treated like a story of alien abduction. It was not until after dessert that the conversation finally turned to the main topic. Robert Adams began by asking the president about recent developments in the Middle East, to which Carter responded by observing that the former enmity between Sadat and Begin had resolved into a genuine friendship. Right on cue, Abrams expressed the hope that something similar would now happen here between Blacks and Jews. With a quick smile, Carter readily agreed, and then, as if to prove the point, mentioned that his good friend Young had slept at the White House just the night before. He then remarked that while the Jewish leadership had been "getting a bum rap" for Young's resignation, it would all be resolved "with the proper dialogue."

Ted Mann seemed to agree. He mentioned that he would be meeting that very weekend with Vernon Jordan, Jesse Jackson, and Benjamin Hooks, head of the NAACP, to engage in just that kind of dialogue. Others were less confident. The relationship between blacks and Jews, they suggested, rather than ameliorating, had decayed, and there was no reason to think that it was going to change. Between the increasing conservatism of the Jewish vote and the argument over quotas, seen as a means of discrimination by Jews and a means for greater economic opportunity by blacks, there was "less and less common ground." This was the last thing Jimmy Carter wanted to hear. "Given each group's traditional support for the underdog, and their mutual opposition to bigotry," he insisted, "this current dispute will be short-lived."

Carter was wrong. The antagonism between the two only increased as Jesse Jackson became a more formidable force in American politics and the issue of quotas and affirmative action continued to divide the Democratic party. During the 1984 campaign, Bob Beckel, campaign manager for Walter Mondale, met with Jackson seventy-two times to resolve potential differences between what Jackson wanted and what Mondale was prepared to do. When it was over Beckel still was not quite sure "what Jesse wanted." Four years later Jackson became a candidate himself, and after winning the party-run Michigan primary found himself as the last challenger remaining to the nomination of Michael Dukakis.[9] He was in the perfect position to bargain and he knew his price.

In 1985, at the quadrennial meeting of the Democratic National Committee's rules commission, Jackson had testified:

"The rules under which the Democratic Party operated to se-lect delegates to the 1984 convention had a discriminatory in-tent and effect among delegates. . . . We are also obligated to raise the continuing inequities of access by women, Blacks and Hispanics—and all other elements in our [National Rainbow] Coalition—to equal participation under the rules of the Dem-ocratic Party."[10]

Despite Jackson's plea for strict proportional representa-tion, the commission had continued the practice of selecting "superdelegates" from among the elected leadership of the party and its public officials. Jackson now made it clear that he would endorse Michael Dukakis only if the Democratic party revised its rules so that any state delegation that failed to in-clude blacks, Hispanics, and women in strict proportion to their percentages in the general population would be deemed to have failed in its efforts at affirmative action. Desperate to avoid the trouble Jackson had caused Mondale, Dukakis agreed. The rules commission decided that to "overcome the effects of past discrimination," the Democratic party would give preference to women and minorities not only in the se-lection of delegates, but in "all party affairs."

No one could have done more to antagonize the vast ma-jority of Americans for whom quotas were anathema than Jackson himself. His 1988 description of New York as "Hymietown" only confirmed the Jewish community's belief that Jackson was an anti-Semite. His reluctance to reject the embrace of Louis Farrakhan only intensified that segment's distrust of a political party that would countenance the possi-bility of putting him on a national ticket. Jesse Jackson came to symbolize everything the white middle class disliked and ev-erything Jewish Americans feared.

Jesse Jackson may have thought that his insistence on racial quotas had nothing to do with the Democratic defeat in 1988, but George Bush knew better. Two years after he was elected president, Bush used his veto power to strike down civil rights legislation on the ground that it would establish quotas in the hiring and promotional practices of private business. While Jackson picketed the DLC for its refusal to let him speak, inside the convention the issue exploded. One of the resolutions proposed for adoption summarized the DLC's professed belief in "equal opportunity—not equal outcomes." The draft had been worded to set the stage for a compromise bill the DLC leadership intended to offer in the next Congress: "We believe the role of government is to guarantee equal opportunity, not mandate equal outcomes. We reaffirm the Democratic party's historic commitment to secure civil, equal, and human rights. We oppose any discrimination of any kind—including quotas. Where others seek to exploit racial differences for political advantage, we support a broad opportunity agenda to give all Americans the tools to get ahead."[11]

Clinton, chairing the convention, was immediately faced with an amendment from the floor deleting the phrase "including quotas." While he had no interest in doing anything to give credibility to Jackson's characterization of the DLC as the "southern white boys' caucus," he understood, as well as Bob Strauss ever had, the danger of being associated with anything that even resembled a quota. Without the slightest hesitation, he asked his friend, Senator John Breaux, to do whatever necessary to kill the amendment. Breaux came up with what he called a "perfecting amendment." It retained the reference to quotas as a form of discrimination but then added a sentence that read: "But as Democrats we believe it is fundamental that women and men who suffer the burden of injustice and discrimination be afforded the legal means and economic opportunity to right those wrongs." The Breaux amendment carried on a voice vote.

The Cleveland convention of the DLC was the beginning of the end for Jesse Jackson's role as a dominant force within the Democratic party. Clinton would accept an invitation to speak at a 1992 meeting of Jackson's Rainbow Coalition but, to Jackson's astonishment and anger, he would use it to attack what he called racist lyrics of the black rap singer Sister Souljah.

Jackson would again be invited to speak at the Democratic National Convention, but this time, with Bill Clinton the nominee, the speech would not take place on prime-time television. Once the convention was over, Clinton campaigned as if he had never heard of affirmative action and as if the only vote Jesse Jackson could deliver was his own. After the election everything changed again.

■ ■ ■

President Clinton, who had abandoned Jesse Jackson, suddenly embraced George McGovern. Affirmative action was out; quotas were in. Insisting that the new administration would "look like America," Clinton chose a cabinet as if race and sex were the major qualifications. When the new president announced his intent to lift the ban on gays in the military, much of the country became convinced that the "New Democrat" they had elected was no different than any of the old ones when it came to the question of preferential treatment for women and minorities.[12]

Republicans were quick to respond. Phil Gramm soon began his campaign for the presidency announcing that he would abolish affirmative action. Not to be outdone, Bob Dole, who as recently as 1985 had joined with other Republican senators to ask Ronald Reagan not to discard racial preferences, now called for their elimination. All the major candidates for the Republican nomination wanted to be on the right side of an issue that, quite suddenly, seemed to be the key to the one state without which Bill Clinton could never be reelected.

Glynn Custred and Tom Wood had tried for years to eliminate the use of quotas in the admissions and promotional practices of the state university system in California, where they taught. Just before the 1994 election they convinced two members of the state senate to sponsor a proposal to put before the voters the California Civil Rights Initiative (CCRI), a proposition designed to restore the original intent of the Civil

Rights Bill of 1964. During the debate on that bill in the U.S. Senate, Hubert Humphrey had promised that nothing in the Act "will give any power to the [Equal Employment Opportunity] Commission or to any court to require hiring, firing, or promotion of employees in order to meet a racial 'quota' or to achieve racial balance."[13]

Richard Nixon broke Humphrey's promise when his administration began to use racial quotas as a means by which to measure integration in the construction unions in Philadelphia. The labor movement was opposed to this, as was the leadership of the civil rights movement. On December 23, 1969, in what Nixon called "an historic and critical civil rights vote," Congress rejected a rider to an appropriations bill that would have banned the use of such quotas.[14] George Bush, then a member of the House of Representatives, voted in favor of quotas, like most Republicans.

Racial preferences and minority set-asides quickly became a part of American life. Now Custred and Woods wanted to return California, if not the country, to the principles of equal opportunity. Their ballot proposal was direct and to the point: "Neither the State of California, nor any of its political subdivisions or agents shall use race, sex, color, ethnicity or national origin as a criterion for either discriminating against, or granting preferential treatment to, any individual or group in the operation of the State's system of public employment, public education, or public contracting."[15]

After the 1994 election, Custred and Woods had more friends than they knew what to do with. Republicans were eager to sign on with an issue that would help defeat Democrats generally and Bill Clinton in particular in 1996. Democrats, who could see the disaster that awaited them, proposed a compromise. If the backers of CCRI would agree not to start a petition drive to put it on the general election ballot in November, Democrats would provide the necessary votes in the state legislature to have it placed on the March primary ballot instead. The offer was tempting. Organizers would not have to raise millions of dollars for the petition drive, and the promise of bipartisan support removed any serious possibility of defeat. All that remained to consummate the deal was the agreement of two powerful politicians, Bill Clinton and Willie Brown.

Clinton seemed to be ahead of the game. He had already formed a task force, headed by George Stephanopoulos, to examine all of the federal government's affirmative action policies. The Democratic Leadership Council was doing its own review of the same programs to provide the president with intellectual cover for any decision he might make. But neither the president nor the DLC was moving fast enough. In early February 1995, the California chapter of the DLC sent an urgent memo to Stephanopoulos telling him that if the legal deadline for placing a proposal on the March 1996 ballot were going to be met, a decision would have to be immediately forthcoming.

Before Clinton could decide anything, Willie Brown did it for him. The Speaker of the California Assembly asked to meet the leadership of the petition drive in his office. After keeping them waiting long enough to signal his disdain, Brown launched into a lecture in which he dismissed what they were trying to do as racism in its latest disguise. There would be no deal, let alone a vote, to put their proposal on the March ballot. Brown had previously given his word to the Senate majority leader, Bill Lockyer, that he would go along with the Democratic plan to keep the initiative off the November ballot.[16] But now Willie Brown was running for mayor of San Francisco, where affirmative action and quotas were still popular. The promise had become inconvenient.

The White House review went forward. When it began, it was generally understood that affirmative action was a policy that "should be given a gold watch and retired." The review identified some programs such as the military's that were very successful, while others, which applied strict quotas without any cultural change, failed to achieve the goal of increasing minority participation. When it was complete, Clinton reaffirmed his belief that government should grant preferences in employment, in public contracts, and in education on the basis of race and gender. Like nearly every Democrat for the last twenty years, the president was careful to draw the obligatory distinction between programs that increase opportunity and those that impose quotas. "Affirmative action," he explained, "is an effort to develop a systematic approach to open the doors of education, employment, and business development opportunities to qualified individuals who happen to be members of groups that have experienced long-standing and persistent discrimination. . . . It does not mean, and I don't favor, the unjustified preference of the unqualified over the qualified of any race or gender. It doesn't mean, and I don't favor, numerical quotas."[17] He sounded like he meant it, and the civil rights community breathed a sigh of relief. Clinton had stunned congressional Democrats by coming out in support of a balanced budget; nearly everyone had expected him to follow it up with a rejection of affirmative action.

Dick Morris, whose political advice had rescued Clinton's political career after he lost the governorship at the end of his first term, had become the president's new pollster and chief strategist. Morris believed that on most issues, the best position was somewhere halfway between Newt Gingrich and liberal Democrats.[18] Jesse Jackson and the Congressional Black Caucus sought to combat this process of *triangulation* by staging a series of high-profile events indicating a willingness to launch an independent campaign for the presidency.[19] The threat worked. Morris's polls showed that if Jackson ran as an independent he would take up to half of the African-American vote and 13 percent of the white vote, destroying any chance Clinton had to win reelection. And that, in turn, destroyed any chance that Clinton would run the risk of a Jackson candidacy by ending affirmative action.

This was almost more than Pete Wilson could have hoped. Wilson had used the Democratic addiction to group equality in his successful campaign for governor of California in 1990.

His opponent then was Dianne Feinstein; by the time he was through with her, a majority of the California electorate knew her as the "quota queen." It was a lesson neither of them forgot. In 1994 Wilson fought back from what seemed certain political extinction to defeat Kathleen Brown by strongly supporting a ballot issue designed to reduce illegal immigration. One year later, he entered the race for the Republican presidential nomination and focused again on affirmative action. He issued an executive order banning racial, ethnic, sexual, or any other preferences in state hiring and in state contracts. He then urged the University of California to prohibit the use of race in determining who to admit as a student or who to hire as a member of the faculty. The meeting of the university's regents was scheduled for the day after Clinton announced his continued commitment to affirmative action.

Jesse Jackson arrived in San Francisco threatening to disrupt the meeting of the Board of Regents on July 20, 1995, in the hope that he could reverse the likely outcome of this review, as he had Clinton's. One hundred fifty people signed up to speak at the meeting; Jesse Jackson was careful to be last. He was allotted the same three minutes as everyone else; he took thirty. He began by asking everyone to join him in prayer, and when it was over, he launched into the same speech he had been giving for thirty years. With the rhythmic cadences of a Baptist minister, Jackson described what affirmative action had done. Everyone was talking about having a color-blind society; he had grown up in one—"I was invisible." He had never seen a black policeman, he claimed, "until I was an adult," nor a black fireman. It was the best case for ending racial preferences anyone could have made.

Jesse Jackson never saw a black policeman or a black fireman when he was a child; today more than 9 percent of firemen are black, and black policemen patrol the beat in every major city.[20] Every child, black or white, has seen them. Jesse Jackson had been, like the title of Ralph Ellison's famous book, an "invisible man" growing up in a segregated society;

that day in California he was one of the most visible people in the country, even the world. Before the civil rights laws in the early 1960s, African Americans were effectively deprived of the vote in the South and routinely excluded from housing and employment in the North. Now, more than thirty years later, there were more African-American members of Congress, including many from the South, than had ever been elected in the nation's history. Because of the gains in registration of African Americans spurred by passage of the Voting Rights Act of 1965, tens of thousands of African-American officials served in leadership positions throughout the country. By 1995, Colin Powell had served as chairman of the Joint Chiefs of Staff, become a national hero, and garnered more support than anyone since Dwight D. Eisenhower to become president without ever having announced a candidacy.

America had changed, and perhaps nowhere so much as within the African-American community itself. During the long night of segregation in the South, the black Baptist church was the black community, and the black Baptist minister provided the leadership. From Martin Luther King, Jr., to Jesse Jackson himself, the pulpit was the school of politics. It was no accident, then, that the anthem of the civil rights movement was, in the words of Dr. King, the "old Negro spiritual, We Shall Overcome." And overcome they did. By the early 1990s, thirty years after the legal abolition of segregation, 60 percent of African Americans belonged to the middle class whereas only one in twenty had prior to World War II.[21] The percentage of African Americans living in poverty declined from 55 percent in 1959 to 33.1 percent in 1993.[22] As the African-American middle class emerged, it joined the rest of America in the movement to the suburbs. African-American suburban populations grew by 70 percent in the 1970s; 73 percent of the African-American population growth occurred in suburbs from 1986 to 1990. Young African-American college graduates have median family incomes indistinguishable from the median family incomes of young white college graduates,[23] and the number of African-American families earning more than $50,000 a year has climbed from 266,000 in 1967 to over a million in 1989.[24]

The civil rights movement made all this possible but it paid a price for its own success. The growing African-American middle class, well educated and ambitious, no longer needed anyone to tell them they could not make it on their own. Affirmative action—to say nothing of racial quotas—had become, for its supposed beneficiaries, what it had been intended to abolish—a badge of inferiority.

Ward Connerly thought so too. He had introduced the proposal to abolish affirmative action policies at the University of California. After twelve hours of acrimonious debate, the regents voted 14 to 10 to eliminate racial preferences in student admissions and faculty hiring. Connerly, who is African American, harbored no illusions. It was time, he said, for everyone to do more, not less, for the disadvantaged. The place to begin was in the elementary schools, where children could still be taught not only to learn but to want to learn. For Connerly, the issue remained equal opportunity, the challenge still to give each child as much opportunity as possible. For Jesse Jackson nothing had changed. He led a protest march on a cold evening after the vote, but the sixties were now ancient history. No one would be arrested. It ended with a laugh. "Go home," he told a new generation, who had never known what it was like to be beaten by Birmingham cops. "The only thing you're gonna catch tonight is the flu."

■ ■ ■

Affirmative action had been designed in the 1960s to help African Americans overcome the effects of past discrimination; it was being used in the 1990s to give preferential treatment to groups that had never experienced slavery and, in some cases, to people who had only recently arrived in this country. In California the logic of multiculturalism was used to expand the protection of affirmative action programs to any group that could point to any history of discrimination, no matter what its form or how long ago it had occurred. Japanese Americans had been sent to detention camps during World War II; Chinese laborers had been exploited to build railroads in the nineteenth century; Mexicans had been deprived of part of the land from which California was formed. At the time the UC regents voted to end the use of racial and other preferences, no less than 75 percent of that state's population could claim membership in a group entitled to special treatment.[25]

The demographic changes leading to a new "majority minority" were taking place all across the country. Unless new restrictions are put in place, by the year 2010 half of all population growth in the United States will come from legal immigration. New York City, which now has a white plurality, at the end of another generation will become 35 percent Hispanic, 27 percent African American, and 27 percent white, and African Americans will be replaced by Hispanics as the largest racial minority in the country by the year 2015. The Hispanic population is growing at four times the rate of the white population but only half the rate of the Asian population. At the end of two generations from today, the Asian proportion of the population will triple, from 3 percent to 9 percent.[26] Asian households already had higher earnings than white households in 1994, and only the very affirmative action programs established to keep minorities from being shut out by a white majority prevented them from becoming a majority of the student body at the University of California.

Defenders and opponents of affirmative action ignore the changes transforming the very definition of "opportunity." The question of whether anyone should be given preferential treatment might have made sense when the number of jobs and the number of places in an entering class were limited to what was available in large, hierarchical institutions. It makes no sense when those same institutions are in the process of becoming extinct. Status and position were matters of importance in the industrial age; learning is the only thing that matters in the information age. Earlier, status and position depended on exclusion; now, success depends on sharing knowledge as broadly as possible. In the new information age community, both economic and educational institutions will become chaordic systems that take advantage of new technologies to eliminate the physical restrictions of mass and distance. Everyone—regardless of race, sex, ethnicity, or cultural differences—will have the same opportunities to engage in the process of continuous learning that will be as much a part of the future as the performance of a single repetitive task was a part of the past.

No governor ever did so much for higher education as Pat Brown of California. During his two terms in office in the late fifties and early sixties, Brown created a system of public education that gave each citizen the right to attend school from kindergarten through high school—and even college and graduate school—without charge. Any student who graduated from high school with the required grade point average could attend the University of California. The commitment to universal higher education still exists in California but, as Ward Connerly saw it, it is simply not possible to give everyone a chance to attend the system's two most prestigious schools, UC Berkeley and UCLA. But that, of course, was precisely the reason why the advocates of affirmative action were so much against the elimination of minority preferences. The percentage of African Americans was higher at those two schools than on any of the other seven campuses of the University of California system in 1994.[27]

Connerly was wrong, and the advocates of affirmative action missed the point. It is possible to provide anyone who wants to attend Berkeley or UCLA the opportunity to do so. Some universities already teach all of their courses, and an increasing number are teaching many of their courses, through a combination of audio and video conferencing, E-mail, fax, and other systems for remote distribution of materials. To make electronic participation as effective as physical attendance, universities only need add the latest in interactive technology so the students can electronically raise their hands and engage not only the instructor, but the rest of the class in dialogue. This type of distance learning can increase the capacity of existing faculty and physical facilities by a factor of seven, simply by an investment in the right technology.[28] The University of California could admit everyone who was qualified and give all of them access to the best faculty to be found on any of their nine campuses, were their vision as generous as Pat Brown's.

The inclusion of everyone who can contribute is no longer an objective of social policy, but an unavoidable necessity. Admission to the new knowledge class must never be conditioned on race or gender. There will be no place for what is now understood as affirmative action in the educational system of the information age; each student will be given all the assistance he or she requires to obtain the education needed to keep learning throughout his or her life. There will be no place for simple timetables and goals as a means to guarantee the absence of discrimination in employment. The self-employed contractor or those working in a newly empowered organization will find work from informal networks established to bring together people with the requisite skills to accomplish a specific job.[29] But to create that world as quickly as possible requires radically changing the way we educate both our children and our workforce.

10

EMPOWERING AMERICA'S SCHOOLS

The Republican Contract with America never even mentioned it, but income and education were now inextricably linked. Between 1979 and 1993, real hourly wages increased for those who graduated from college, from $15.85 to $17.05, while for everyone else they went down. Real hourly wages for those who did not finish college fell from $12.24 to $11.37. This was nothing compared to the economic devastation suffered by those who never studied beyond high school. Real hourly wages of high school graduates declined from $11.23 to $9.92, and the wages of high school dropouts, who were once able to find jobs on the assembly line, fell from $10.06 to $7.87.[1]

Most of these income disparities that have characterized recent decades could be attributed to the failure of America's educational system to change quickly enough to provide the kind of learning now needed for success. This growing gulf threatens to destroy the middle class and divide the country between the few who have more than they could ever want and the many who have less than they need. Without the moderation of the middle class, a nation's political system can easily dissolve into chaos. Today the greatest threat to the middle class's continued existence and the harmony of our civil society is an educational system that has not changed its basic assumptions since the assembly line of Henry Ford first created the need for a new kind of worker.

At the turn of the century most American workers— roughly 80 percent—were either farmers or domestic servants; by the start of World War II, 40 percent were blue-collar workers.[2] The transition from the kitchen or the field to the factory was facilitated by the willing cooperation of the public schools, where pupils were trained to read, write, and add well enough to follow the instructions of a foreman. They were taught to be prompt and responsive. They were trained to perform the same tasks in endless repetition without any loss of efficiency.

The most serious challenge facing the new industrial age schools was how to create a sufficient capacity in the system to meet the increasing demand for these workers in the economy. In 1906 in Gary, Indiana, a city built by US Steel and named after that company's founder, Superintendent of Schools William A. Wirt devised a solution. The Gary Plan used a "platoon system" in which half the student body spent the morning in class and the afternoon in shop and gym classes or on field trips, while the other half did the opposite. This arrangement effectively doubled the capacity of Wirt's educational factory. The superintendent wanted "an educated populace, but educated to take orders cheerfully and positively; above all he desired order, voluntary or otherwise."[3] This was about as far from Thomas Jefferson's independent and self-sufficient yeoman farmer as it was possible to imagine. Wirt ran his schools with an efficiency that rivaled the most successful industrialist. He had students repair and maintain physical facilities, in a sense doubling his investment by simultaneously instructing the children in the work ethic and reducing maintenance costs.

John Dewey, who today is known somewhat erroneously as the father of progressive education, was the most prominent contemporary critic of the new industrial age schools. He advocated and defined a school curriculum designed to teach children how to think. Full participation and choice were at the heart of Dewey's notion of a democratic education. Just as today's school-to-work programs are a key to ending the "two-track" approach, which determines the economic capability of a child while he or she is still in high school, Dewey wanted nothing in the educational process that limited the potential of any individual to learn. Wirt's system failed, in Dewey's opinion, because in neither its academic nor its vocational education did it teach the scientific method of inquiry—a pattern of thinking that required testing all purported truths against the individual's own experience and experiments.[4] This, indeed, was the exact opposite of what the industrial giants wanted in their local educational establishments.

Dewey criticized Wirt in his book *Democracy and Education*, published in 1918, which was considered by one critic too difficult for the average educator to read. Far from lamenting this fact, the critic was positively grateful few of them would read Dewey: "While it is true that citizens of a democracy need to be taught to think, it is ever more important, especially in the present crisis, that they be trained to revere and obey."[5] This sentiment, expressed before the end of World War I, remained the predominant view of American education even after the collapse of the Soviet Union and the beginning of the end of the industrial age.

During the first half of the twentieth century, schools became assembly lines for turning out well-behaved citizens who knew that their civic duty was to vote and that their own well-being depended on following the rules and being punctual at work. The highest marks were given to those who demonstrated the necessary aptitude for becoming dutiful—and therefore productive—employees. The high school graduate who did not go on to college accepted his position as a newly minted blue-collar worker with little reluctance. He could look forward to a decent life and, after World War II, a steadily increasing standard of living, especially if he was a member of a powerful industrial union that routinely extracted from management some portion of the monopoly rents for labor. This system fed on itself. Educational expenditures were routinely supported by all classes and seldom became a partisan issue. Local school board elections were, for the most part, nonpartisan exercises in civic virtue. All citizens wanted the education of America's children to be run by the best people possible.

Public education thus became all that could be expected from a monopoly. Quality was irrelevant because demand was constant. Every year students enrolled in the only public school they were allowed to attend. School districts concentrated their efforts on inventing new rationales for larger budgets and larger administrative bureaucracies. The National Education Association became one of the largest and most powerful unions in the country, demanding more money for teachers and explaining the decline in educational achievement as the result of not giving teachers even more. Parents who could afford it gave their children a private education, and middle-class parents moved to wherever good public schools could still be found. But there were no private schools for the poor, who lacked the means to move or to improve their children's education. Their economic futures were being threatened by an educational factory badly in need of retooling and redesigning.

▪ ▪ ▪

The president of the American Federation of Teachers knew things had to change. Al Shanker had been advocating reform of America's schools on the new principles of quality longer than most corporate chieftains had been using these principles in their own businesses. There was one business, however, that had used them to change not only the way things were built, but the whole system of designing, manufacturing, and marketing. General Motors and the United Auto Workers had created a new kind of car and a new kind of company by rethinking every assumption about the automobile business.[6] In just a few short years, the product, Saturn, had achieved unprecedented success with its customers. Al Shanker wanted to do the same thing for the children of America. He went to Spring Hill, Tennessee, to observe the Saturn project, hoping to find some kernel of an idea that could be used to change the way public schools worked.

If anything, the crisis facing General Motors in the mid-1980s was even more critical than that facing public education—its entire future was at risk. Customers were leaving in droves. The dramatic drop in market share could not be denied, nor could it be attributed any longer to a temporary demand for more fuel-efficient cars.[7] In meeting after meeting, GM's new chairman, Roger B. Smith, made it clear that GM was losing to Japan because the Japanese were producing a superior product. GM had to go back to the beginning. Instead of making minor changes in what they were already doing, they had to build a car from scratch. To signal that this new product would be from a different world, GM named it "Saturn."

Smith assembled a team of ninety-nine people, fifty-five of them GM management and forty-four from the UAW. After visiting successful car-manufacturing sites around the world, the group decided that GM needed to develop an entirely new car company, completely divorced from what Alfred Sloan had created. Saturn would be an information age company built on the fundamental principles of quality. It would not be run by a command and control bureaucracy; instead, teams of workers on the factory floor and in the dealers' showrooms would decide the best way to satisfy customers. Management would help assure survival by studying the environment for changes that might affect it in the future and then communicating what they found throughout the organization. Every one of these teams, including the top-level "strategic action team," would include representation from the UAW. This flat, nonhierarchical system would concentrate on its objective, despite the absence of rules or regulations, by maintaining a continuing stream of information to all parts of its operations. The culture of the organization would drive it toward success because of the values and vision it had been given.[8] Saturn embodied every organizational requirement for success in an information age; the team created a chaord.

The laws of chaos demonstrate that chaordic systems produce vastly different outcomes based on very small differences in the conditions under which the system is first formed.[9] In Saturn's case, the initial conditions were teamwork, empowerment, and quality. Smith created Saturn to help take back market share from the Japanese. While never losing sight of this objective, the original team created a more inspiring vision founded instead on the values and beliefs of the people who would make and buy their cars.

Biological systems and markets do not have any inherent values. Governments can inform markets with public purpose, however, by deciding which societal goals the workings of the market should accomplish. So too can chaordic systems be given values to guide them, thus serving as the human analogy to the mathematical strange attractors, which create boundaries within which such systems operate. In complex corporate organizations, this process of creating boundary conditions comes from enunciating a clear statement of values and providing a long-term vision to inspire each member of the team. The clearer the boundary conditions, the greater the amount of empowerment and creativity the system will produce. Beyond any brilliant new manufacturing technique, product innovation, or financial scheme, corporations that achieve the greatest long-term success are those that have best inculcated their values into the daily habits of all of their employees.[10]

The Saturn system is built on five core values—commitment to customer enthusiasm, commitment to excel, teamwork, trust and respect for the individual, and continuous improvement. As Saturn's CEO points out, the initial training for all new employees begins with a thorough discussion of each of these core values.[11] These five values are translated into a set of four principles that describe the kind of partnership Saturn wants to have with each of its key constituencies. For its members, it pledges to "create a sense of belonging in an environment of mutual trust, respect, and dignity. We believe that all people want to be involved in decisions that affect them. We will develop the tools, training, and education that each member needs. Creative, motivated, responsible team members who understand that change is critical to success are Saturn's most important asset."[12] The four principles focus on Saturn's relationships, thereby finding the exact place to create performance improvements in a chaordic system.[13]

These principles were translated into a 3,400-word, eleven-page memorandum of agreement between GM and the UAW establishing the basic charter of Saturn. This memorandum was deliberately written so that it could change and evolve over time as conditions in the outside world necessitated. It stated the mission of the corporation and bound all the signers to its accomplishment. It declared Saturn to be independent from any GM–UAW national agreement unless the terms of the agreement were adopted by all members of Saturn. In place of a detailed contract specifying work rules, job categories, and regulations on every anticipated conflict, it established a network of teaming and training among all Saturn members, dedicated to making each successful.[14]

Every employee of Saturn is a member of at least one team. On the factory floor workers are grouped into teams of eight to fifteen people, depending on the task to be performed. Work traditionally done by a supervisor, such as budgeting, scheduling, or training, is done by the team instead. The team also elects a leader who can call on work-unit module advisors to help with any problems it can't solve. The original "charter team" members were selected from among laid-off UAW employees in other plants for an ability to team well with others rather than for any manufacturing skills they might possess. Each Saturn employee becomes a knowledge worker whose values and beliefs are shaped by the experience of working together with others to accomplish a goal.[15]

Not only were all decisions to be made by joint management and labor teams, but all such decisions were to be made by consensus. Consensus meant that 100 percent of the team had to agree to abide by any decision that had the support of at least 70 percent of its members. Saturn pledged that—short of economic catastrophe—at least 80 percent of its workforce would have a job for life. Employees could, however, *fire* themselves by deciding they couldn't live with a team decision. To make sure a team functions well as a unit, members hire their own new members. There is no human resources staff or personnel bureaucracy to screen candidates. Instead, the workforce has grown by a careful evaluation by the team of each new member based on the skills he or she possesses and his or her ability to fit in with the rest of the team.[16]

To help every team make the best possible decisions, Saturn instituted a rigorous and continuous training process. Each charter member received over 300 hours of training in 650 different courses, ranging from technical to interpersonal skills training to management concepts and theory. New employees spend the first three months learning the job from their future teammates as well as in classroom settings. At least half of that time is devoted to teaching skills such as conflict resolution or problem solving that will make them effective players. And everyone, from the CEO to the worker on the line, receives a minimum of 92 hours of classroom or on-the-job training each year. Since 5 percent of their time is spent in training, 5 percent of their quarterly salary is paid only if the entire team has completed that quarter's training requirements.[17]

Information is the key to the system's performance. One of the core principles of the company is that there will be "total open information sharing." Every worker has access to computer terminals that contain more financial data and company performance statistics than most companies would share with their middle management. Meetings to solve specific problems are scheduled throughout the workday; rather than treat them as "interruptions" to their work, teams are structured and staffed to accommodate this "normal" way of doing business. Like the lean production lines of the best Japanese automobile companies, any member of the team can halt production on the assembly line if he or she believes the immediately preceding team has failed to turn over a product free from all defect.[18]

The results of this chaordic system have been spectacular. During its first two years of production, Saturn sold more cars per dealer than any other manufacturer, even surpassing the traditional winner, Honda.[19] J. D. Power and Associates, which conducts the official customer satisfaction surveys for the automobile industry, found Saturn's dealer satisfaction index second only to Lexus, whose cars sell for three times the price.[20] And a *Popular Mechanics* survey of Saturn buyers, most of whom would have bought a foreign make had Saturn not been available, showed that 83.4 percent would buy another Saturn, just short of the 87 percent repeat buyer mark registered by Lexus.[21] By creating a system that utilized the knowledge of its entire workforce with maximum flexibility and authority, Saturn delivered what every consumer wants today—a superior product for less money.

After visiting Spring Hill, Tennessee, Al Shanker declared, "Everyone must go to Saturn. There may be another way to build a quality car, but why not follow Saturn's example and do it in a way that works for people?" His visits in 1993 and 1994 were "transformational experiences."[22] The factory of the industrial age could be restructured into a more productive and humane place to work. If America's factories could be reconceptualized, so could its schools.

■ ■ ■

Deborah Meier had proven just that at Central Park East Secondary School (CPESS), established in 1985 as an educational experiment. Not only was it established at roughly the same time as Saturn, its focus on relationships and empowerment is a mirror image of Saturn's chaordic principles. Like Saturn, the selection process for this innovative seventh- through twelfth-grade school requires its members (in this case both student and parent) to agree to become a part of its unique culture and abide by its democratic values. Like the originator of Saturn, Meier sees her task as the creation of "environments where all kids can experience the power of their ideas."[23] She has produced comparable results. More than 90 percent of the student body attends four-year colleges after graduating. In the heart of East Harlem, the school operates with total safety and security provided, not by a ubiquitous police presence, but by the community's culture, which tolerates nothing less.[24]

According to Meier, students "learn habits of mind—logic, perspective, making connections, being concrete, using evidence, building a case."[25] Each person who earns a diploma from CPESS must first complete a final demonstration of mastery, including a portfolio of his or her work in each subject and a rigorous oral exam.[26] The approach produces what the information age demands—people who can think for themselves and make decisions based on the facts of each situation. What took place at Saturn took place at CPESS, and that can happen in every school in the nation.

Bureaucracy is all that stands in the way. The public school bureaucracy has a monopoly on providing K–12 education. "This is a system that can take its customer for granted," Shanker said in addressing what he believed to be the root cause of the problem.[27] It is not motivated to restructure itself because, unlike the situation General Motors faced, there is no immediate threat to its future. If America's schools are going to teach future knowledge workers how to think, it will take more than a few lost millage elections and the continuing loss of their most affluent students. Nor will efforts to restructure what exists, for example, by moving authority to local teachers and administrators or site-based decision making be any more successful than decentralization efforts of corporations.[28] Without a change in the rules of governance, the cultural change required to produce what Saturn was able to do will simply not occur. Only when workers have been empowered to satisfy customers without interference from bureaucratic regulation and only when those decisions have a real consequence for the future of their institution will the necessary transformation of our nation's schools take place.

But just changing the organizational structure of American education is not enough, as the attempts to provide vouchers for parents to use to send their child to any school, public or private, demonstrate. In California in 1992, a ballot proposal to institute a system of vouchers was defeated handily, principally on the argument that the initiative provided no safeguards on the criteria by which children were admitted or the curriculum they would learn. Given a choice between the freedom to choose any school they wanted with no restrictions on what children would be taught or continuing the admittedly inferior system of public education, the state with the greatest number of knowledge workers in its population voted for the status quo. The public sees private school vouchers as a threat to the ability of the school system to instill a common understanding of American values to all members of the next generation. Because the American ideal is the cultural glue that holds the national community together, rather than bonds of race or language, this intergenerational learning experience becomes even more critical in the information age. Knowledge workers do not want private school vouchers to further divide their increasingly fragile communities.

■ ■ ■

Saturn and CPESS suggest the right way to bring about the development of an information age educational system. Each team or school needs a clear understanding of what it is expected to accomplish, the resources available to it, and both the authority and the freedom to decide how to accomplish the mission itself. These are the basic principles of the charter school movement, which is rapidly gaining support in states throughout the country.[29] Charter schools are created by public entities and maintain a commitment to ensuring the values of the community are reflected in the schools' curricula. Unlike the school voucher approach, they provide individual choice for parents in making decisions of how and where to educate their children without further dividing the community. Charter schools combine increased individual freedom with a stronger community and produce the effectiveness and efficiency required in an information age educational system.

Located in the poorest Latino neighborhood in the San Fernando Valley, Vaughn Elementary School was just another item on the casualty list of failed schools in the Los Angeles Unified School District. Test scores were among the lowest in the state and the attrition rate for both teachers and administrators was over 50 percent. As the school's new principal, Yvonne Chan took advantage of the 1992 law creating charter schools to "take the handcuffs off the principal, the teacher and the parents—the people who know the kids best. In return, we are held responsible for how kids do."[30] Parents now must sign a three-page contract pledging involvement in their child's education and promising up to thirty hours of voluntary work. This mutual commitment to a common goal, freely decided on by those who can make it happen, is the key to teamwork and empowerment in this elementary school, just as it was at Saturn and CPESS.

Chan focused on the two elements of quality—efficiency, as measured by how many services she could provide the children within the same budget, and effectiveness, as measured by higher student achievement. She privatized nonteaching functions—activities like payroll and cafeteria services for which the school had no core competency—and with the savings hired more teachers and introduced computers and after school programs. Per pupil teacher ratios dropped from 33 to

27 without any increase in funding. Teachers are working longer hours than before, but they feel better about their jobs as test scores improve rapidly. The entire school community has much to do with this feeling of satisfaction. Every faculty member serves on one of eight parent-teacher teams that meet weekly and, in a real sense, run the school.[31]

The Saturn focus on teaming can be found at another charter school, Fenton Avenue Elementary in Lake View Terrace, California, which also serves a poor and minority neighborhood. Joe Lucente changed his title from *principal* to *executive director* and turned over policy making to seven working councils of staff, parents, and community members, coordinated by an umbrella group of fifteen co-equal team members. Even the "plant manager," James Parker, can see the differences in output and behavior that this team commitment to achievement produced. "Before the charter I often felt like an outsider; now I have a vote on everything, and I feel like part of a team. I've seen us go from bickering to all getting along and getting things done for the school."[32]

This story is repeated wherever local communities have been freed from the heavy hand of bureaucracy to pursue a dream to which all participants are mutually committed. In San Francisco, the Chinese community organized the Charter Early Childhood Elementary School to teach learning through art. Both the children and the community had to assist in renovating a building just to get the school opened, but it was accomplished with the community's pride of having overcome the challenges that confronted it.[33] In Oakland, California, the local district school board and union were so hostile to Clementina Duron's idea for a charter middle school that they refused to admit it into their low-cost pool for insurance, payroll, or legal services. Despite these added costs and no suitable building, the other Latino parents sharing Duron's dream convinced the local Roman Catholic diocese to at least provide them the space in a park to start their school. Parents dug ditches to put in the sewer and electrical lines for the eight portable classrooms wheeled onto the site three weeks before school was supposed to open. That it did at all was a tribute to the community's and Duron's "commitment and passion."[34]

Colorado has more experience with charter schools than any other state in the union. These range from the Academy Charter School in Castle Rock, with a strict dress code and a back-to-basics curriculum, to the Community Involved Charter School in suburban Denver, with an experimental learning environment and a dress code that accommodates Mohawk haircuts and earrings. As parent Sherri Budge says, "Not every child learns the same way but if your child does not have the learning style of the teacher he's assigned to, you're stuck in most schools."[35] Not with the choices that come with charter schools. Colorado Governor Roy Romer, vice chairman of the DLC, was an early champion of charter schools. He was also one of the few Democratic governors to easily win reelection in the anti-Democrat, anti-incumbent election of 1994. The popularity of charter schools does not surprise him, though it does most members of his state's educational establishment.

Parents in the Cherry Creek school district have the opportunity to send their children to the best schools in Colorado. Each year its students score significantly higher on standardized tests than both the state and national averages. Nevertheless, parents in the district requested a charter school that would provide a more fundamental education and more discipline. Despite the defeat of the most recent millage request, the school district had been surprised to hear from the parents—only after it received an application for a competitive school did it bother to survey its customers, as it were, to determine their level of satisfaction. The survey revealed possible support for a magnet school along the lines being suggested by the charter school advocates.

The charter school system in Colorado was working just the way a chaordic system should. By creating new rules in the relationship between parents and educators the system, without any preestablished directives, was evolving to produce a better result. As one parent remarked, "I'm not criticizing Cherry Creek Schools. They're preparing my children to compete with anyone. I'm just proposing with this charter school that we raise the bar a little bit."[36]

Some members of Colorado's educational establishment saw in charter schools not a promise but a threat. Under state law, school boards have the authority to grant charters after a review of proposals submitted to them. The power to review is the power to delay, and it is one many school boards have used to great effect. Their underlying attitude was expressed by one board member, who told a group of parents trying to start a charter school that she had "a problem with you taking public dollars to experiment."[37] That, of course, is the whole purpose of charter school legislation. Faced with a conflict of interest between preserving their monopoly in the provision of education and their pledge to provide the best education possible to their constituencies, most school boards fall back on what has worked in the past and ignore their responsibilities for the future.

The problem is not unusual. It is faced by Saturn's leadership as it tries to preserve its unique culture in the face of skepticism and sometimes outright hostility from existing bureaucracies. The new leadership of General Motors, anxious to spread the success of Saturn, has suggested it market other models, not produced in Spring Hill, under Saturn's nameplate. It also wants Saturn to report to one of the existing business units rather than remain an independent entity that reports directly to the chairman. The leadership of GM is under the erroneous impression that the remarkable customer loyalty and quality output Saturn has achieved owes more to production and marketing techniques than to the chaordic synergy produced by its vision and values. If Saturn can sell cars in dealerships without haggling, then other GM dealerships should be able to do so as well. Customers walking into the other dealerships, however, don't do so with the same relationship to the company that Saturn's customers do. So *no-haggling* pricing or *value bundling* seems more a marketing ploy than a sincere expression of concern for the customer's needs. The experience of buying a car whose attributes do not include all of the cultural aspects of a Saturn won't be the same. As Saturn's UAW local president and a member of its Strategic Action Committee said, "It won't be a Saturn. The customer will see through it."[38]

Management was not the only bureaucracy envious of Saturn's success. Don Ephlin, then head of the UAW's GM division, negotiated the first Saturn contract and was responsible for its precedent-setting provisions. In return for the increased role of the UAW in the management of the company, he agreed to a significantly smaller number of work classifications or job descriptions. The contract also paid the assembly line workers a weekly wage rather than an hourly salary. Some of their pay was also put at risk, that is, made dependent upon the company achieving a variety of performance goals. Steve Yokich, who had negotiated a different kind of employee involvement contract with Ford, was skeptical. He was afraid the union would lose its ability to protect the worker from management's control of the speed—and therefore the productivity—of the line. Indeed, concerns about the degree to which the Saturn local was too cooperative with management in the decision-making role led to a challenge to the local's leadership. It survived, but only by the narrowest of margins. The election of Steve Yokich as president of the UAW in 1994, along with changes in top management, brought into question not only whether what had been done at Saturn would be done elsewhere, but even whether it would continue to be done at Saturn itself.

The same mistake General Motors made when it began to talk about abolishing the distinction between Saturn and its other divisions is made by educators who talk about charter schools. They frequently suggest that if all public schools were only given the same freedom to make decisions at the school site level they, too, could produce the kind of passion, commitment, and results that charter schools have created. The key to success at CPESS, however, was the freedom it was given to experiment without concerning itself with any oversight from the local or state school board. Charter schools can do this; standard public schools cannot. The real problem is that the Coalition of Essential Schools, of which CPESS is a member, numbers only 178 after ten years of effort.[39] The charter school movement had no more than two hundred schools operating in nineteen states by 1995.[40] Neither has been able to grow quickly enough to meet the demands of the new economy. If thousands—indeed, tens of thousands—of individual school cultures are to be free to create the kind of results Saturn has produced in one factory, they will need a new organizational design and governance structure to guide their evolution that is as innovative as Alfred Sloan's pyramid was in its day.

▪ ▪ ▪

The redesign of America's educational system must be based on the successful quality models used to transform manufacturing facilities like Saturn. The process begins with a clear vision of the new world, followed by the establishment of a continuous conversation among all the members of the team, each with his or her own specialized knowledge necessary to carry out the task, so that each can learn from the others.[41] The overall governing structure integrates research and design with the communication and dissemination of new techniques and training to maximize gains in effectiveness and efficiency. The need for this redesign has been noted by experts from other fields, such as Nobel Prize–winning physicist Kenneth G. Wilson, who have turned their attention to the problem of education. However, as with most situations requiring major paradigmatic shifts, this one is almost invisible to most of those within the educational establishment. For that reason, the redesign of American education will need to be an effort that involves the entire national community.

The vision for this new educational system is rooted in John Dewey's belief that public education should teach students both how to think and how to value democracy. People of all ages, from elementary age to adult, make judgments, attach meaning to things, or sort through conflicting information when learning new skills.[42] In other words, they engage in what cognitive scientists call "higher order thinking." Because these skills will determine the future success of each student, this context-connected learning approach must be the foundation for the information age educational system and will require changes in every aspect of a school's culture, from selection of the students to the testing of their mastery of the subject matter, just as it did at CPESS. The increased freedom to explore and learn about new worlds while working in teams with other students will create a context for learning democratic behavior in these new schools essential to this country's future.

The role of government will be to create the environment and tools necessary for a continuous conversation among all parts of the system. The Department of Education, as part of its own transformation, must initiate a dialogue between the two national organizations of teachers, the NEA and the AFT; the leadership of each state's educational establishment must find consensus on a new vision for education similar to Saturn's original charter. Those American schools currently producing the best students will have to be studied to help inform the work of this "team of 99." The resulting vision statement must be accepted and agreed on by Congress and the president so that the interests of all citizens will have been incorporated into the design. The bureaucratic oversight currently conducted by DOE can then be ended and its staff's time and attention directed to ensuring that a constant stream of information circulates between and among every school and educational element in the new system.

State departments of education in turn must establish research and development sites to examine and test the latest ideas for improving the classroom experience. Just as today's medical research centers are connected to the country's leading medical schools, these state-sponsored educational research facilities would provide a model for training and retraining teachers that will drive all teacher training to new standards of excellence. While the country's "learning enterprise" spends an estimated $400 billion to $600 billion a year (counting both in-school and at-work education), less than one tenth of 1 percent of those dollars appears to be spent on research to improve the actual process.[43] By comparison, most American businesses invest at least 2 percent of their revenues in research and development. To bring educational expenditures to this level—roughly $5 billion per year—will require states to invest every dollar saved from increased classroom productivity in these new research and development centers.

The dissemination and communication of the best techniques for improving learning will necessitate the development of a whole new category of expertise, what Wilson calls "educational architects and instructional designers."[44] Their role will be to produce better classroom materials and teaching techniques and to earn their livelihood by selling them to individual schools. The rapid success of companies like Future Kids, which teaches computer literacy to children in after school settings with a unique, content-connected curriculum, demonstrates the enormous potential market for this. By contrast, current attempts to privatize the operation of entire schools have failed to demonstrate significant improvements in real student learning. Resistance by both teachers and parents to such schemes underlines the importance of reflecting the community's values in any redesign of the educational system.

Local school districts will determine the educational needs of the community in the information age and then bring the best learning technologies to each of the schools operating within that community. The district will become the broker between those who have curriculum or technique ideas to sell and those with authority to buy. This will only work, however, if schools are deprived of their monopoly over public education.

But the prospect of choice and competition in education is viewed by the educational establishment as a direct threat to its existence, so it continues to wage an intense struggle to stop even the public school chartering movement from gaining ground. The desire of parents to decide what type of schooling their own children receive and to choose between schools of increasing quality is too strong, however, and political support for charter schools continues to grow.

The idea of choice only loses public support when it is extended to private schools in ways that threaten the acculturation function of primary education. The solution is to create a VISA-like chaord for American education. Those who have a stake in providing educational services to America's kids must agree to a few simple rules of governance that distribute the functionality and the authority to offer the service to the end points of the system—the schools. New schools should be added to the chaord whenever they express an interest so long as they agree to the fundamental values of the organization, such as a nondiscriminatory acceptance process, a commitment to produce students who have mastered the required skills and knowledge for the particular age group, and a learning environment that supports democratic values such as teamwork and tolerance. All members of the new educational chaord would agree to be paid at the same level for the same services, with payment coming to them from state-funded vouchers for public education. The individual states will provide a uniform level of funding for each pupil, thus ending one of the most insidious remnants of segregation in housing while at the same time providing an incentive for each school to maximize its productivity.

Just as business first used computers to automate existing tasks without restructuring the work itself, the introduction of technology into schools has mainly been used to automate rote drills and tests without changing the nature of the teaching experience itself. The redesigned educational system will develop and train teachers in entirely new ways to teach particular skills. With access to global databases and video demonstrations that can create contexts for the lessons to be learned, teachers will be able to focus on providing the unique counseling and individual attention their profession demands. Programs such as Reading Recovery, which have isolated the best coaching approach to teach every student how to read, suffer only from the time it takes to train each teacher and assure mastery of the technique.[45] Expert systems can capture the best practices of such programs and create both aids for the teachers and supplemental experiences for the students so the program can be taught to more students quickly and with fewer costs. In addition, information technology can provide simulated experiences, continuous and more timely learning, and connections to students and teachers throughout the world. Technology per se is not the solution to solving the country's educational crisis, but it does provide the possibility that the problem can be fixed at a cost the country can afford and before even more children are lost to ignorance and illiteracy.

Peter Drucker has observed that "education will become the center of the knowledge society, and the school is the key institution."[46] With the nation's economic value dependent on the knowledge of its citizens, demand for a redesigned system of education will produce changes even more radical than those envisioned by John Dewey at the turn of the century. Al Shanker's hope that every school learn the lessons of Saturn will then become a reality.

RETRAINING AMERICA'S WORKFORCE

he campaigning never seemed to end. When Clinton gave his second state of the union address in 1994, Stan Greenberg and the Democratic National Committee, on behalf of the White House, had assembled a focus group to measure reaction. The proposal for a "three strikes and you're out" sentencing provision brought the most positive response. The second most favorable reaction came when the president, in congratulating Congress for passing NAFTA, said it was now time to complete the preparation of America's workforce for the new world economy by creating "a reemployment system, not an unemployment system."[1] Doug Ross was ecstatic. For more than a year he had been trying without success to find someone in Congress who thought this was a good idea.

Ross, who was one of the leading theoreticians of the Democratic Leadership Council before Clinton's election, believed that the key to higher-paying jobs was an understanding of the source of economic value in the new world economy, where what one knew mattered a whole lot more than what one could do. Ross believed completely in Peter Drucker's argument that "true investment in the knowledge society is not in machines and tools but in the knowledge of the knowledge worker."[2] Nothing was more important than providing the means by which to transform an industrial age workforce into one that could compete in the information age; Ross began with a focus group of his own.

Recently unemployed workers in the Baltimore area were asked to participate in a discussion about the current government-run employment service. Laid-off workers are supposed to go to the service, both to learn about new job opportunities and to collect unemployment benefits, but the system failed to serve either the workers looking for new jobs or the employers looking for new employees. There were 1,800 employment service offices in the country at the time, but only 30 percent of employers nationwide listed job openings at any of them, and fewer than 7 percent used the offices more than twice a year. Only 20 percent of all such listings related to skilled positions. It is thus not surprising that the process accounted for only 4 percent of the civilian nonfarm job placements annually.[3] But that was not the only reason—or even the most important—why those who used it came to hate it.

Ross's focus group's discussions were often raucous and always pointed. The most emotional moments inevitably came when members were asked to talk about their experiences in trying to use a system designed to help them find jobs and pay their bills until they were able. Their comments might have been written by a quality consultant; one unemployed worker made it clear he was tired of being treated like a "client. That makes them talk down to you like they know better. I want to be treated as a customer instead." When asked why the idea of a customer-focused approach might change this attitude, one of the participants explained, "If private industry was running this then they would have an incentive to make it work. As a customer I'm always right and they have to serve me and try and sell me something I want." These laid-off workers, with the economic and ethnic backgrounds that had once made them the most reliable constituency of the Democratic party's New Deal coalition, had learned what every knowledge worker already knew, the fundamental lesson of quality—competition for the customer creates the most effective and efficient system, even when it comes to government services.

When the moderator described an alternate system in which computers provide information about real jobs, counselors gave instructions on how to acquire the skills necessary to get those jobs, and the recommended training could be purchased from anyone who offered it, the group seemed interested. But then one participant commented, "You're not going to have the government run this, are you? If so, it will never work." Someone else added, "It would be just like the VA hospital, where they are only interested in pushing people through to fill their quotas in order to get more government money."

As soon as the idea of government providing these services was raised the men and women around the table became agitated. "The problem with government is they don't try and make a profit. All they do is spend money." And all agreed with the summary provided by one of the more senior members of the group: "The employment system hasn't worked for the last twenty-five years and there is no way they could make this work either." The unemployed already understood the information age requirement that organizations must learn from their customers before they can respond to them.[4]

■ ■ ■

The industrial age was over, and so was the promise of job security from its most powerful and successful corporations. In the 1980s more than 3.5 million workers were laid off by Fortune 500 companies. Every year, two million full-time workers are displaced by plant closings, production cutbacks, or layoffs, as the economy rewards those engaged in technological activities and punishes those organizations that have not adapted to the new realities. For the most part, those who were laid off were not going to be recalled when the economy recovered. In 1992 and again in 1993, 75 percent of all laid-off workers were permanently laid off, the highest percentages recorded over the twenty-seven years in which the statistic has been tracked.[5] In 1994, almost 24 percent of the unemployed were out of work for more than six months, twice the 1989 level. From 1992 to 1994 America experienced levels of long-term unemployment not seen since the end of World War II. The number of middle managers among the ranks of these unemployed had risen to 11.3 percent from only 9.4 percent five years earlier.[6] A year after losing their jobs, 80 percent of them were still either unemployed or earning less than they had before.

Doug Ross was determined to create a new system based on the twin principles of competition and choice. Writing in the DLC's book *Mandate for Change*, published as a suggested agenda for the incoming Clinton administration, he outlined a proposal to consolidate dozens of government training programs into a single chaord. Each of these programs had developed its own bureaucracy and is own institutional support. The idea of creating a one-stop center for any worker needing job counseling, as logical as it may seem, was still seen as an immediate threat by both the government agencies who ran the programs and the public employees who staffed them. When Ross further proposed that government compete with private companies who wanted to provide this service, he set off a firestorm of criticism and resentment from every bureaucracy the system touched, all of whom were adamantly opposed to competition.

Under the various job-training programs, state and local bureaucracies spent enormous amounts of administrative money determining the reason for each dislocated worker's layoff. The worker who lost his job because of a free trade proposal and the worker who lost her job because a defense plant had been closed would be sent to different places for help. The states, who also ran the employment offices for people who were laid off for no other reason than changes in the economic needs of their employers, admitted that this was unnecessary and costly. Their proposed solution, however, was simply to consolidate all the existing training and employment counseling programs into one large block grant states would administer, eliminating duplication and thereby saving money.

In the end, the problem was bureaucracy itself, and block grants would do nothing to change that. "No one suggests that there be only one supermarket in a city in order to produce the greatest efficiency," Ross argued.[7] Competition from multiple types of grocery stores, each emphasizing a different approach to its customers—from the low-cost, no-frills club warehouses to the local gourmet food shop—produced the best deal for the customer. Specialization and diversification parallel the process of biological evolution that provides a template for the kind of growth chaordic systems offer.[8] A system that is not only efficient but effective provides choices for customers, thereby compelling producers and providers to compete for every sale.

State and local bureaucracies were afraid that private providers of job counseling services would threaten their monopoly; members of public employee unions who staffed those offices saw the proposal as a direct threat to their jobs. The American Federation of State, County and Municipal Employees (AFSCME), the Service Employees International Union (SEIU), and the United Automobile Workers (UAW), through its state employees division, were determined to protect the 20,000 jobs of their members that might be lost when the employment system faced competition for the first time.[9] At its 1994 annual meeting the AFL-CIO passed a resolution denouncing the competitive model and calling for the establishment of a permanent government monopoly. "The Employment Service should be the center for job opportunities, with the requirement that all employers list their job openings with the Service."[10] Command and control was still the preferred solution.

Serving his last term in Congress, Bill Ford, Democrat and chairman of the House Labor and Education Committee, was not about to desert the union allies who had supported him throughout his career in Michigan. Ford's passion for the working man was unquestioned. His own father had died in a workplace accident, searing into his soul the need to protect workers from exploitation. During his thirty-year career in Congress, no one had done more to advance the legitimate interests of organized labor. Ford, Pat Williams, a labor Democrat from Montana who chaired the House Subcommittee on Labor-Management Relations, their staffers, and especially the union lobbyists who worked closely with them, were convinced that the rank and file would fall prey to unscrupulous private providers of job counseling and brokering services. Even though the draft legislation required states to set up a screening process providers would have to pass before being "chartered" as authorized vendors, the legislation never made it out of committee.[11]

Democrats were equally opposed to the use of vouchers by which workers could acquire these services directly. The idea that government might bypass bureaucracies altogether and provide each citizen the wherewithal to acquire a particular service on his or her own was first raised in the context of education. Vouchers that could be used to pay for a child's education at any school, private or public, was the premise of the school choice movement, an idea that was also applicable to other kinds of social services. In 1992, PPI pointed out that "while most Americans enjoy the freedom to obtain needed services on the market, this option is ordinarily not available to the poor who must obtain social services through a quasi-monopoly maintained by departments of social services."[12] Policy experts, as diverse in their political orientation as Stuart Butler, of the Heritage Foundation, and David Osborne, of Clinton's unofficial campaign policy organization, advocated vouchers because they "place the control of services into the hands of the consumer," which "increases the accountability of providers, depoliticizing their selection; stimulates innovation, giving consumers more choice; . . . and reduces waste, creating greater equity for the poor."[13]

Under the plan originally devised by Doug Ross, each unemployed individual would be given a voucher, called an "opportunity card," with which to buy needed reemployment services. The cost of the program would be paid for by savings from the elimination of the job-training bureaucracy, forcing large numbers of public employee union members to lose their jobs. Bill Ford was a staunch defender of public education who believed vouchers for education were wrong; he did not believe vouchers for job training were any better. The idea that he was opposing the president of his own party did not bother him much: in 1992 he had supported Mario Cuomo right up until the night the governor of New York nominated Bill Clinton in a speech Ford thought only proved the Democrats had selected the wrong candidate.[14]

Faced with determined congressional opposition, Labor Secretary Robert Reich and Ross negotiated a more acceptable alternative that might still redeem Clinton's state of the union pledge. Under the Reemployment Security Act of 1994, the idea of vouchers was dropped and states were permitted—but not required—to charter private companies to provide employment services. If a state did decide to charter private firms, state employment offices would be given time to bring their services up to par with their new competitors. This provision, designed to placate the interests of the public employee unions, sacrificed critical elements of choice and competition. This bill also died in committee. Democrats were too wedded to the working assumptions of the New Deal to tolerate any threat to the monopolies enjoyed by public bureaucracies.

The idea of creating a new reemployment system was enormously popular everywhere but inside the beltway. A 1994 pre-election Times Mirror poll identifying the new taxonomy of the American electorate asked respondents what they most wanted to see from the federal government in the immediate future. While their first priority was adoption of the "three strikes and you're out" criminal sentencing law, their second priority, with more than 80 percent respondent support, was the idea of increased federal expenditures to provide job skills to workers who need them for new or better-paying jobs.[15] Again the public understood, better than any elected official in Washington, the changing nature of work in the information age.

The national economy was now sharply divided between those working in the new global economy with the latest information technology and those still trapped in jobs untouched by this change. Companies, both large and small, collectively spent more money in 1991 on computing and telecommunications equipment alone than they did on equipment for industrial, mining, farming, and construction work combined. Only 25 percent of American workers used computers in their jobs in 1983; 47 percent used them in 1993. According to the latest Department of Labor statistics, the hourly pay rate at plants with advanced technology was $11.84, compared to only $8.62 in plants lacking such equipment. Jobs that required the use of computers paid 10 to 15 percent more. Two thirds of college graduates took advantage of their training to obtain these jobs, but only one third of high school graduates were so employed, and of those who dropped out of school, only 10 percent qualified for such high-skill, high-wage opportunities.[16] This phenomenon even extended to the self-employed, among whom those using PCs for their work earned 40 percent more in 1994 than those who did not.[17] As wage rates declined for industrial age work, the median income of American families fell from $38,129 in 1991 to $37,668 in 1992 to $36,959 in 1993, even as the incomes of knowledge workers went up.[18]

While the shortage of skilled workers created higher wages for those with technological know-how, this increase in the incomes of the top 20 percent of Americans only aggravated the inequalities of income distribution already threatening the nation's social cohesion. The answer to the problem of income inequality is not to be found in the redistribution of wealth through new taxation schemes, however, nor is it to be found by letting entire generations suffer during the transition from the industrial to the information age. Rather, the answer is to retrain workers for high-skill jobs and invest in their education, no matter how difficult the task or how high the immediate cost.[19]

Without any organized constituency to support this solution, Congress refused to act. Reich suggested Ross, under the aegis of the Labor Department, establish demonstration projects to test the effects of chartering employment services. Only one governor, Republican William Weld of Massachusetts, was interested. Weld had been reelected in 1994 by the enormous margin of 71 percent to 28 percent. In the same year and state that Senator Ted Kennedy had to fight for his political life against an unknown challenger, Weld carried every category of voter by education, age, or income (with the exception of those earning less than $15,000 per year) by over 70 percent. Those who had voted for Bill Clinton in 1992 gave 58 percent of their votes to the Republican; Perot supporters provided him 79 percent of their votes.[20] From tough work requirements for welfare recipients to charter schools, Weld had pursued policies designed to move his state into the new economy.

Weld was clearly ahead of other state governors. The employment system he proposed permitted providers of training and counseling services to bid for the right to become temporary franchisees for a particular office. The City of Boston's employment services produced twenty organizations, including the state's own employment service, willing to run the operation. But even as Weld moved forward with the idea, supported by matching money from the Department of Labor, Democrats in the state senate, allied with AFSCME, sought to block any expansion of the concept of privatization. The legislation they passed, while not affecting this program, required proponents to prove in advance the savings the government would receive before "outsourcing" public employment jobs.[21]

Bill Ford retired from Congress in 1994, the year in which many of the most ardent New Deal Democrats were defeated. The Contract with America said nothing about retraining or enhancing the skill base of America's workers, but the threat to the appropriations of virtually every government program caused a sudden new interest within the administration in anything to reduce the cost of government. The secretary of labor wanted to hear any idea that might protect America's ability to prepare for global competition from the "block and cut" tactics of Gingrich's House. Ross had a second chance, and he was determined to take advantage of it.

■   ■   ■

With the same people from the DLC and the Clinton administration who helped Bruce Reed write the Senate Democratic welfare reform voucher proposal, Ross created a "GI Bill for American Workers." The first idea in a list of ten that was the DLC's response to Gingrich's Contract with America promised every laid-off American the right to purchase with a government voucher the job training and counseling he or she needed from public and private providers of such services. These vouchers could be used to buy up to $500 worth of job search aid and up to $2,000 worth of training and education. The voucher would be given to any unemployed person as soon as he or she applied for it. Application would be made at one-stop information centers that would contain the kind of job counseling services the focus groups had considered with such enthusiasm. The proposal would eliminate bureaucracy, save money, and increase services.[22]

The Democratic defeat in 1994 was the best thing that ever happened to Ross's idea. It went from being the nerdy idea nobody liked to the most popular in its class. The Democratic minority in the Senate made it one of its top five legislative priorities. Just before Christmas, when Clinton pulled together his Middle Class Bill of Rights proposal, he not only borrowed the title to describe his overall plan, he made the idea of vouchers for job training for unemployed workers one of the four principal points. Ross knew none of that made a difference unless Gingrich and his cohorts could be convinced to support an idea that came not from the Contract with America, but from the Clinton administration.

During the first one hundred days of the new Congress, the House, operating under instructions from the new Speaker, did nothing but scurry to enact the provisions of the Contract with America. Ross used this time to begin a dialogue that focused on Gingrich's and Clinton's frequently proclaimed interest in nonbureaucratic solutions to the challenges of the new economy. With some members of the original "New Paradigm Society" as his allies,[23] Ross secured an invitation for Reich to discuss the president's reemployment proposal on the talk show Gingrich hosted on his "empowerment network." When the White House heard of the plan, George Stephanopoulos moved quickly to stop it. David Bonior and the Democratic leadership had launched an attack on Gingrich, his lucrative book deal, his political committee, GOPAC, and the monies that helped finance the TV network. The president's political advisors were not about to have a cabinet member grace such a potentially illegal operation with his presence. A heated debate on the importance of policy over politics failed to change Stephanopoulos's mind.

Undeterred, Ross arranged a meeting between former Republican Congressman and HUD Secretary Jack Kemp and Al From to discuss their mutual interest in advancing what both liked to call an "empowerment agenda for America." The result was a jointly authored opinion piece that first appeared in the *Los Angeles Times* on June 20, 1995, supporting the concept of vouchers for job training. Kemp and From summarized the philosophical dogmas each party would have to give up for this new political concept to advance. "For the right, it requires stepping back from the notion of every individual for himself or herself—and from the ideal that devolving from one bureaucracy to 50, somehow empowers working families. For the left, it requires weaning from a powerful addiction to government entitlements for every needy group—and getting Democratic constituencies that now control job-training programs to yield that control."[24]

All of this helped smooth the way for the first bipartisan legislative initiative in a year to come out of the House that was not initiated by the Republican majority. The chair of the Committee on Economic and Educational Opportunities was Howard "Buck" McKeon, a Republican from Tujunga, California. The owner of a chain of cowboy boot stores, McKeon had once served as mayor, an experience that convinced him that turning federal programs over to the states was no solution at all. His California colleague, Republican Frank Riggs, joined him as the prime sponsor of the new program. More surprisingly, Pat Williams, now the ranking minority member on the committee, had concluded on his own that the current program wasn't working and was in desperate need of reform. He agreed to provide bipartisan support for vouchers in the full committee on one condition—he wanted the name changed from *skill vouchers* to *skill grants*. With that change, the problem of accepting a good idea with a politically incorrect name disappeared. The GI Bill for Workers went to the floor of the house with an overwhelming 29 to 5 bipartisan majority in its favor.[25] One Republican staffer called the bipartisan support for the bill "really pretty amazing in this new world order."[26] Its passage marked the beginning of the transformation of American politics into the information age.

Unfortunately the Senate and its roster of Republican presidential candidates failed to get the message, proposing yet another block grant solution to the problem as part of their welfare reform proposal. But this linkage meant that if these aspiring political leaders had their way, no state would be obligated to spend *any* money retraining America's workforce.

The money could instead be used to cover each state's shortfall in welfare expenditures. As part of the bipartisan agreement on welfare reform, the job training provision was split off from the legislation and left to stand on its own merits.

The Senate voted for not much more than the original compromise offer from the states. Most of the job-training programs were consolidated into a single program to be offered in one-stop shopping centers to the unemployed. States were encouraged, but not mandated, to establish a voucher system for the provision of such services. The bill passed with overwhelming bipartisan support, but laid-off workers would be dependent on the ability of each state's political leaders to overcome the resistance of their own bureaucracies before experiencing real choice and competition in the employment services they might receive. For once President Clinton's program depended on the House version prevailing in conference.

▪ ▪ ▪

If retraining the American workforce is an important part of the transition from the industrial to the information age, then providing a college education for everyone who wants it and can benefit from it is essential. In 1988, Michigan Governor Jim Blanchard was convinced the key to future Democratic victories required a new social contract in which government played a major role helping citizens realize the American dream. He defined it in terms of four goals—"home ownership, a college education, health care, and a secure pension when they retired."[27] Later, as head of the 1988 Democratic National Convention's Platform Committee, Blanchard commissioned a book describing the efforts of Democratic governors to this end. But even his party's nominee that year, fellow Governor Michael Dukakis, failed to push the idea—preferring instead to focus on the issue of competency. He would have done well to listen to Blanchard.

In his state of the state address in 1986, Blanchard promised to create a state-sponsored savings plan to help Michigan parents and grandparents afford college tuition for their offspring. The state treasurer, Robert Bowman, now president and chief operating officer of ITT Corp., devised a plan under which the state would accept lump sum or monthly contributions to a trust fund called Michigan Education Trust, or MET. These funds would be invested by the state so as to provide enough of a return that college tuition payments would be fully paid by the time the designated child was ready to attend. The plan guaranteed tuition payments at any of the state's four-year institutions, even though the cost varied widely from its three major universities to the twelve smaller specialized colleges and the twenty-nine community colleges.[28] If the student chose to attend college in another state, the plan still contributed the average tuition cost of Michigan's colleges by giving the student a "refund" of the contributions made by his or her parents.[29] By August 1988 the plan had been approved by the legislature and was ready to accept applications.

Based on experiences of previous government programs and public interest, it was expected that about 5,000 applications would be received in the August 1 to August 5 enrollment period. Instead, the state treasurer's office was swamped with 82,495 applications.[30] In the end, 54,547 parents signed up.[31] The only requirements the investors had to meet was to maintain a regular schedule of contributions. The level of contributions was set at roughly the current price of college, with the state betting that it would be able to make investments over the years to cover the difference. The fact that it also controlled the level of appropriations the universities and colleges would receive gave the state some leverage on mitigating the impact of inflation, but each university and college had the legal authority to decide its own tuition. Bowman knew something that most investors did not—investments in the stock market over any given fifteen-year period, no matter what the underlying economic conditions turn out to be, have historically provided the best possible return to the investor.[32] By moving the state's investment portfolio for this trust fund out of the restrictions that normally applied, he was able to hedge his inflationary bet with little risk. The benefit to Michigan's citizens was enormous, and the program continued to grow in popularity. At least ten other states eventually adopted the idea of the Michigan Education Trust fund in one form or another, most recently Texas under the direction of its new governor, George W. Bush, Jr.[33]

When Blanchard was defeated, the new Republican governor, John Engler, moved quickly to suspend the entire MET program. He asked his state treasurer, Doug Roberts, to commission an audit of the fund's solvency. The audit found that its investment portfolio, with a return of almost 10 percent, actually had a surplus of over $30 million, compared to its expected obligations. This was good news to Engler's new treasurer, who had purchased MET contracts for his own two children during the first enrollment period, but it was not what the governor wanted to hear. Engler was opposed to any government involvement in something that banks and insurance companies did for profit, so he commissioned a second audit. It came back with the same answer. He did not bother with a third; he simply closed MET to any further enrollments, promising to honor only those contracts already purchased.[34]

Engler based his decision on a disputed ruling by the Internal Revenue Service, which threatened to tax the state's investment income, thereby reducing its potential surplus though hardly jeopardizing its solvency. Shortly after Engler's reelection in 1994, the IRS ruled that the state owed no additional taxes on the monies invested in the fund. Popular pressure was hard to resist. In October 1995, Roberts unveiled the new MET plan. It was hard to decide whether he was more a banker without a heart or an entrepreneur without a brain. Roberts announced the new fund would limit its investments in what he termed "the safety of bonds" and would therefore be unable to guarantee complete coverage of future tuition.[35]

Further, each enrollment would require payment of a lump sum in advance without the opportunity for installment payments. And the size of the investment requested was much higher than the existing costs of a four-year college education. Roberts's apparently more prudent investment strategy created a MET program that significantly diminished the competitive threat to banks and insurance companies while serving the political interests of the governor. When it came to encouraging more competition, his supporters in the banking community were no different than his state's employment system's bureaucrats. In both cases political paradigms of the past prevented people from being given more choices and brighter futures.

■ ■ ■

Returning to his DLC roots, on the one hundred and first day of his new administration Clinton traveled to New Orleans to announce a plan that not only eliminated banks as middlemen in the provision of student loans, but also included a provision under which the loan's repayment would be made on a schedule contingent upon the income of the borrower. The initiative was first tested for public approval. Stan Greenberg's polling showed it would be enormously popular.[36] However, Greenberg had not polled the nation's bankers. Clinton's proposal touched off a fierce lobbying battle in Congress from the same people who convinced Engler to suspend the MET program in Michigan.

On March 2, 1993, before Clinton had made any public statements, the Consumer Bankers Association scheduled a "Lobby Day" to educate Congress on the evils of direct student loans. The bankers were determined to keep the existing "Sallie Mae" system under which student loans are not administered by colleges and universities but by a bureaucracy of secondary investors, loan officers, and others. The lobbying effort backfired. Media accounts portrayed the arrival of mid-level bank executives as a gathering of vultures bent on preserving their bloated salaries. Three days later, Clinton formally agreed to include direct lending, with income-contingent loans, as part of his legislative initiative to increase access to educational opportunities.[37]

Opposition came not only from Republicans but from Democrats as well, and among them few were more adamant than Bill Gray, former congressman from Pennsylvania and now president of the United Negro College Fund. His organization opposed direct loans not only because of the administrative burden they would create for small colleges, but also because reliance on personal loans and the limited grants envisioned in the national service bill threatened Pell grants, which had traditionally financed college education for the poor. Clinton's proposal, it was feared, would shift student aid from an entitlement to something each individual had to earn, either by performing public service in the community before attending, or by paying back the loan after college.

This strange coalition of white bankers and black college administrators convinced large numbers of congressmen and senators from both parties to oppose any immediate alteration of the existing program.[38] After much legislative horse-trading that at one time threatened the entire national service proposal, direct lending was authorized for up to 40 percent of all student loans in the second year of its implementation and 50 percent or more after that if enough colleges were interested. Republicans, however, prohibited permanent authorization, demanding reconsideration in 1998. But they couldn't wait, moving in 1995 to restrict the proportion of direct student loans in 1996 to 20 percent and simultaneously to place additional administrative costs on them to further discourage their use. Once again, powerful interest groups threatened to delay the benefits of the information age for everyone in order to prolong their own survival.

▪ ▪ ▪

While the merits of direct lending were being debated, a far more radical proposal became law almost unnoticed. As adopted in July 1994, the bill contained a "pay-as-you-can" provision that based the amount owed on a student loan on current income. If, after twenty-five years of payments, total loan repayments did not equal all that was due, the government would wipe out any remaining liability.[39] The bill captured one of the new economic realities: because education is directly related to income, it is possible to create a "career line of credit" for each person based on that individual's decision about how much of the line of credit he or she is willing to draw down. In the industrial age businessmen were able to obtain bank financing for new equipment based on the revenue stream that would be created by the new productivity from the machines. In the information age every young American can similarly capitalize his or her own future revenue stream by financing a college education at any institution involved in the direct loan program. The education itself virtually guarantees the future income stream needed to pay back the loan, as seen through wage comparisons. This revolutionary approach to student aid ensures that anyone—no matter what sex, no matter how poor, no matter what racial or ethnic background—can have the money to pay for college. It was too good an information age idea for DLC members of the administration to ignore and too big a governmental intrusion into the world of private enterprise for Newt Gingrich's troops to tolerate.

The president did little to advance the idea of Individual Education Accounts until after the 1994 elections. On December 15, 1994, Clinton addressed the nation on his Middle Class Bill of Rights and, at the urging of Reich, Ross, and Paul Dimond, he announced a program to combine the education accounts with the skill grants to be provided under his GI Bill for Workers. Ross and Dee Hock, who had created VISA on chaordic principles, wanted to combine all the various loans and scholarship funds into a single account that could be used by individuals with their own separate debit cards. It was the original opportunity card idea relaunched as one of the president's key proposals. But Gingrich—for all his talk about information age policies—wanted nothing to do with it.

By preventing individuals from financing their lifelong learning, Republicans showed themselves to be every bit as short-sighted as the Democrats who blocked the creation of a new labor market system. Both were responding to constituencies uncertain of their ability to compete in the new era. Fear of the future, however, is no policy. Lifelong learning, no longer an activity for dilettantes, has become an imperative for economic, even national survival. Competition and choice are as necessary in other levels of education as they are in elementary and high school. Despite the resistance from the old-world institutions that continue to provide the principal support for the two major political parties, the movement toward a new system of education has already begun.

In order for these embryonic efforts—such as charter schools and direct government loans—to grow rapidly enough to help each individual attain the education needed to succeed in the new economy, entirely new structures will have to be created. These structures will be neither in government nor outside of it, neither in the private sector nor divorced from it. They will involve the civic sector of our society, yet fulfill what we might today consider to be governmental purposes. Their creation will occur as government at all levels, profit and nonprofit organizations in the private sector, educational institutions from school boards to unions, and political leadership with enough vision and courage come together to form new chaords. As Dee Hock discovered, it will be necessary to rethink the fundamental notion of learning and make it the central purpose of the nation's work. Then an institutional governing arrangement will follow, which, based on a few fundamental rules of decision making and participation that fully embrace competition and choice, will prepare every American for the challenge ahead.

CREATING A
LEARNING ECONOMY

A mong the many remarkable things that have
occurred on the Sinai Peninsula few have been
more surprising than the sudden success of the
Egyptian army in 1973 as it broke through Israeli defense lines
in a complex maneuver across the Suez Canal. The Israelis
had constructed what was thought to be an impregnable line
of defense against a tank attack, but the Egyptians, who had
never won a battle against Israel, breached the Bar Lev line
and found nothing between them and the Negev. As the offensive gathered steam and the superpowers began to make
their first diplomatic moves, the Egyptian troops reached the
critical mountain pass that was the last obstacle in their push
across the peninsula—and then they stopped. The Israeli
army gained precious time to regroup and create a stalemate
that eventually led to a negotiated settlement.

Israeli and Egyptian generals met and quickly worked out a
plan for the withdrawal and transfer of authority required by
the Camp David peace accords. While the politicians exam-
ined each tiny detail of land and location, the military were
left to wait for further instructions. After eight months of lan-
guid discussions, a certain level of trust had developed between the two sides. Andrew Marshall, head of a top-secret
analysis agency in the Pentagon, had been curious why the

Egyptians had halted so soon after their initial victory. At his urging, the Israelis asked their Egyptian counterparts just what caused them to stop when they did.

The Egyptian officials explained that because they had never won a battle with the Israelis, they spent months rehearsing every detail of their battle plan. Their Russian advisors had taught them how much force needed to be amassed at the front lines and what was needed to cross the Suez. Each objective and its accompanying tactics were drilled into the Egyptian officers. In accordance with Soviet military doctrine, they were told that under no circumstances could there be even the *slightest* deviation from that script. They were sufficiently confident in their chances to formulate a plan to follow in the case of an initial victory—they were to regroup and establish the proper supply and logistical support operations for the next phase of the battle—and after they crossed the Suez, that is precisely what they did. But no one had given any thought to what to do next. There were no plans, and without instructions to follow, the army ground to a halt.[1]

By contrast, in November 1980 General William E. DePuy predicted the type of warfare that the American army was being prepared to wage. "Future wars will probably be fought under nonlinear circumstances. . . . The Middle East represents the clearest possible example of that probability." An entirely different approach to training, emphasizing the simulation of real battlefield conditions using the latest in technology to ensure the reality of the experience, would prepare the next generation of battlefield commanders for exactly this type of warfare. "Accustomed to open flanks, to operating on the basis of ambiguous intelligence, seeking the enemy and not the terrain, concentrating rapidly, and adapting constantly to the flow of events—these leaders have maneuver in their bones."[2] That leadership led to almost instant victory in the Gulf War.

Marshall's office conducted an assessment of the performance of the military in the Gulf War and came to some disturbing conclusions. America had won by doing the right thing—using high-tech weapons to enable the leadership on the ground to gain the advantage through surprise tactics and superior maneuverability—but they had gone about it the wrong way. The military's command and control processes had not changed since World War II, so this war, like others, was fought with separate army, navy, and air forces, limiting the effectiveness of the new "smart" weaponry. On future battlefields, tanks would become anachronistic death traps, just as they were for the Iraqis.

Tank vulnerability to long-range smart weapons would not be the only military change produced by new communication techniques. With the proliferation of cruise missiles and the work that pilotless drones could now accomplish, aircraft carriers would lose their central role. The new American military would need less logistical support but better targeting intelligence. Information about the enemy and where to strike could no longer trickle down through the military bureaucracy; it would have to go directly from "sensor to shooter." Marshall envisioned such information being transmitted from a satellite to a tiny screen on each pilot's headset.[3] Organizational boundaries between functional groups like the army and the air force did not make sense in a world where the main offensive strategy was an integrated AirLand battle doctrine. The United States is now, according to Marshall, "in a period with the technologies available that will lead to a difference of how we will fight. The initial tasks will be intellectual—to understand where the new technologies will take us."[4]

Each combat activity consists of a cycle that moves from

1. Observation—the participant tries to determine what the situation is; to
2. Orientation—the soldier needs to understand his or her relationship to that situation; to
3. Decision—he or she determines what to do about it; to
4. Action.[5]

This cycle represents one learning experience each time it is completed. Learning can be accomplished by the individual in hand-to-hand combat or aerial dogfights, or by a team as small as a platoon or as large as a naval task force. The cycle is the constant. Moving through it as rapidly as possible determines the learning rate for the organization or, in its entirety, the system. Cycle time thus becomes the key to victory.

In a linear world where one action causes the next, planning and concentration of force are very effective. But almost any activity in an information age operates in nonlinear space, where each action can cause a variety of different reactions, setting off a chain of events as unpredictable as the weather. To be effective in this chaotic environment, a system must be able to adapt quickly to take advantage of changes on the battlefield without losing sight of the ultimate objective. Such a system requires a robust flow of information and the ability of each of the parts to learn from the data presented. Speed and agility become the decisive determinants of success.

Creating self-directed systems in place of command and control hierarchies is the central organizational imperative of the information age. Whether it be moving information from sensor to shooter, from customer to product developer, or from welfare recipient to job counselor, the problem is the same. With speed of cycle time the key to rapid learning, operational concepts and organizational structures both need to be redesigned to move information as quickly as possible to those who need it. To maintain American leadership in the new world economy, new chaords are needed to govern our *system of systems*.[6] Just as the human body organizes all its complex systems into a single functioning whole in which information is moved to each part to act on it, America's economic and political systems need to be reshaped to become adaptive learning organisms, constantly in touch with the changing environment around them.

American car companies discovered this in the 1980s.

Ford's response was to adopt the techniques of total quality management. They learned from the Japanese how to focus on people and integrate technology into the new manufacturing process, now termed "lean production." General Motors applied the best practices of management, marketing, and production to create a brilliant new organizational design with Saturn. They were less successful in changing their already-existing culture and company. Neither Ford nor General Motors, however, learned as quickly as Chrysler how to take advantage of speed.

After Lee Iacocca left Chrysler in 1992 the new leadership team was determined to take advantage of one of his more lasting legacies. Iacocca had authorized the construction of a brand new building in Auburn Hills, a suburb of Detroit, to house Chrysler's design, development, and marketing organizations. The new leaders used the intimate design of this new Technical Center to adopt Honda's lean product-development approach to creating a new car, a process that incorporated all four key elements of lean design—leadership, teamwork, communication, and simultaneous development. Under the old system each group (designers, marketers, manufacturing engineers, or finance types) would do its work on a new car project and then, in standard linear fashion, throw it over the wall to the next. Under the new system, everyone needed to complete the project is brought together as a team from the beginning, working on a single floor of the building.

This new nonlinear system reduced the development cycle from six years to four. The Neon went from design to first build in just thirty-three months; the new target is twenty-four months. Creating the LH series of cars (Intrepid, Concorde, and Eagle) required only 741 engineers, whereas the old process involved 1,400 people. The new system significantly reduces the overall cost and price of new cars while creating a much faster turnaround time for new product development, producing more choices more frequently for the customer.[7] Increasing the speed of development also increases quality, since each person is in constant communication with everyone else working on the project. Chrysler's customers gave its new cars 15 percent higher marks on quality than customers of the older models.[8] The crucial issue is no longer which company is bigger than another, but which is faster.

It is not a lesson most American industry has learned yet. As information technologies expose the lack of creativity in serving customers and increasing economic value that exists among companies in the less competitive sectors of the economy, the first instinct of the leaders of those businesses is to merge with others to further reduce competition while gaining the traditional economies of scale. Without any more purpose than wanting "to see what being big is like," as one CEO described it, the mergers only put off the day of reckoning for management's failure to learn how to adapt to an age in which innovation rather than size determines success. The merged Chase Manhattan and Chemical banks might rank in the top twenty-five of all such enterprises in the world, but their new size did not help those laid off by the combination, or the customers who were no longer served in their own neighborhoods. Gas and electric utilities threatened by the prospect of deregulation and intensified competition thought they would find protection by becoming bigger, but other companies had already gone that route and found they were better off smaller. Just as the new economic principles determine the proper organizational system for private enterprise, so do they determine the requirements for the country's economic system as a whole.

▪ ▪ ▪

The United States will have the fastest learning economy only if it is constantly open to competition from the rest of the world. The desire to protect American companies from the threat of foreign competition may be understandable, but it is misguided. It is an industrial age policy that has lost all relevance today. It is, however, a policy that still has enough support to energize presidential campaigns and jeopardize every step the country attempts to take to reduce international trade barriers.

As the number of industrial jobs declined, the opposition of organized labor to free trade increased. Large manufacturers in particular shed workers dramatically, as the full force of new technology and quality improvement techniques hit their industries. From 1987 through 1992, the 500 largest industrial concerns in America reduced their collective workforce by 1.3 million jobs. This decline was partially offset by the 483,000 jobs that smaller manufacturers created in the same period. Nevertheless, labor unions were in no mood to support the creation of a free trade zone in the Americas while their membership rolls were being depleted at record rates.[9] The idea that the United States would put further pressure on this employment problem by eliminating tariffs on goods produced by Mexican or Canadian workers struck union leadership as ludicrous, irresponsible, and a vindictive move by President Bush. In 1991, at the urging of organized labor, the Democratic National Committee's executive committee went on record in opposition to Congress's granting Bush the fast track authority he wanted to negotiate such a treaty. Almost immediately thereafter, the Democratic Leadership Council, with Clinton as chair, emphasized its New Democratic commitment to free trade by adopting a resolution supporting fast track authority for NAFTA on a roll call vote.

Once he had become a presidential candidate, Clinton was pressured to come out against NAFTA as it had been negotiated by Bush. Clinton was told that the crucial swing states heavily dependent on manufacturing—Michigan, Ohio, and Illinois—hung in the balance. The issue was debated hotly within both the campaign and broader Democratic circles. Jimmy Carter called Clinton to urge him not to cave to protectionist sentiments.[10] Al From argued vigorously that if Clinton backed off his support for NAFTA, his credentials as a New Democrat would be ruined and the charge by presidential candidate Paul Tsongas that he was a "pander bear" confirmed. Clinton did not abandon the position he had taken with the DLC, but he conditioned his support for NAFTA on the adoption of side agreements on worker safety and environmental protection that his administration would negotiate. Contrary to the warnings of union leaders, Clinton's pro-NAFTA stance did not persuade the automobile workers of Michigan or any other midwest state to vote against him.

This willingness to take on the Democratic establishment and fight for the principle of free trade also turned out to be the high point of Clinton's first two years in office. The fight over ratification of NAFTA, however, revealed more about the coalition of forces focused on the past than about the effect decisive presidential leadership has on public opinion. Four supposedly different political points of view agreed that passage of NAFTA would be disastrous for the country; they were all wrong.

Congressman David Bonior used the offices of the Democratic whip to directly challenge the president. Stan Greenberg first went in 1985 to Macomb County, which Bonior represented, to investigate the phenomenon of Reagan Democrats and what motivated them to desert the party that had brought them middle-class prosperity.[11] For Bonior, expanded trade with Mexico and Canada was a threat not only to the incomes but also to the jobs of the automobile workers in his district. If the auto companies could hire Mexican workers for less than two dollars an hour to produce cars that could then be sold in the United States without any tariffs to increase the cost of importing them, it would only be a matter of time before there were more auto workers in Mexico than in the United States.

Ralph Nader saw NAFTA as an attack on the protection that his advocacy efforts had long helped create for American consumers and workers. If companies could move their production facilities to Mexico and not have to abide by any of the environmental or worker safety regulations he had played a part in creating, the threat to American jobs would undermine the political support for such regulations in the United States. Nader dismissed as a sham the side agreements that Clinton had negotiated on these issues.

For Pat Buchanan it was a simple matter of national interest—America must look out for itself. The loss of even one American job to a foreigner as a result of the passage of NAFTA was unacceptable. Ross Perot, meanwhile, saw it as a simple matter of economics. He told anyone he could get to listen that passage of NAFTA would suck jobs out of the United States, as CEOs like him opened plants wherever the lowest-priced production happened to be. Under this reasoning Haiti and Bangladesh were economic powerhouses just waiting for their economic ships to come in.

The country's leading political iconoclast found himself in a strange alliance with three politicians whose views he would normally scorn. When Perot returned to the place where his presidential campaign started for a debate with Vice President Gore on the issue, the scare tactics and disinformation he was using were exposed under the hot lights of the television studio. The opposition in Congress soon melted away. But the alliance of Bonior, Nader, Buchanan, and Perot revealed a strong desire among unrelated factions to impose order and control on an economic system that seemed to be increasingly unpredictable and chaotic.

All of these players failed to understand that information systems will not support the imposition of order from an authority outside the system. As noted international economist Paul Krugman points out, "the world economy is a system—a complex web of feedback relationships—not a simple chain of one-way effects."[12] The case for freer trade rests less on an understanding of international economics that it does on an understanding of how such chaordic systems thrive and grow. The first principle of such systems is that interactions inside them are information driven.[13] Those that grow and expand are open to information about their environment and use that to find patterns to explain how the outside world works. Information that signals a change in that environment is the basis for learning and growth.

The learning cycle here is much like it is on the battlefront. The system scans its outside environment, compares it with memory, and decides whether any action is required. A properly functioning system observes the consequences of its action, a process usually called feedback, to determine its next move. This kind of iteration and rapid cycling made possible by the ability to parallel process multiple inputs distinguishes high-performing systems from those struggling to survive. When change appears to threaten the existing order, systems may attempt, as protectionists do, to restrict the flow of such information. Yet the very act of attempting to avoid disruption will bring about the death of the system. To grow and evolve, the system needs to continually recreate its own order after each learning experience. The disequilibrium brought about by new information causes it to reconstruct itself in a new and better form.[14] Free trade, which permits and therefore encourages the continuous introduction of new competitors, produces new information. This is the best way to guarantee that the American economic system continually expands and thrives at this point on the *edge of chaos*.

That potentially chaotic future struck fear in the hearts of the four preachers of protectionism whose dependency on paradigms of the past blinded them to the possibility of creating both more freedom and more order. After the 1994 election, when Clinton took the case for ratification of the more-comprehensive Global Agreement on Tariffs and Trade (GATT) to a lame-duck session of Congress, the members used the power of talk radio to attempt to defeat the bill. The battle over NAFTA had centered in the House; the battle over GATT, which would create a new world trade organization, centered in the Senate. Because of the strident criticism by right-wing radio, both Phil Gramm and Bob Dole hesitated to give their support. Pat Choate, who had organized Perot's anti-NAFTA effort, was also behind the anti-GATT movement. Behind him was the money of Roger Milliken, whose textile empire depended on the protection his industry had enjoyed almost since the country's founding. The involvement of these special interests did not seem to bother the grass-roots activists Perot recruited to the cause. Confident that the agreement would create a new world bureaucracy that would endanger the nation's sovereignty, they flooded Washington with their phone calls and faxes.[15]

In the end, they were no more persuasive with the new Republican majority than labor had been with the old Democratic majority. Two thirds of the GOP senators supported the pact, along with two thirds of their Democratic colleagues. As with NAFTA, the opposition was not really so much partisan as it was parochial. Senators from the textile regions of the country, and mountain states' senators where the Perot support was most intense voted no. Because there had been little if any political repercussion in the 1994 election against those who had voted for NAFTA, even senators from the Midwest knew it was safe to vote yes.[16]

■ ■ ■

Just as the campaign against NAFTA united all those interested in creating order from outside the system against all those interested in seeing the system grow and learn, the debate over immigration unites all those who believe in freedom from government as the most important political priority against those who see yet another role for government in protecting the system from too much disruption by outside forces. Immigration policy has become an important issue whenever there has been a dramatic change in the economic circumstances of the country. In the late nineteenth and early twentieth centuries, immigrants flooded to America's cities to escape ethnic and religious persecution and to take part in the economic boom created by the new opportunities of the industrial age. Public schools taught them the skills needed in the factory, settlement houses taught them the skills needed to raise a family, and they were assimilated into the booming American economy. When the economy began to falter, immigrants became the first target of those seeking to restrict disruptions to the system. In 1924, six years before passage of the infamous Hawley-Smoot tariffs, which temporarily shut down imports to the United States, Congress enacted legislation sharply reducing permissible levels of immigration. It remained law until 1965 when Congress, with broad bipartisan support, increased the limits of permissible legal immigration. Twenty-five years later, Congress raised the limits again. From 1971 to 1990, this open-door policy encouraged twelve million people to legally immigrate to the United States, more than had done so in the previous fifty years.[17] But in 1994, as hundreds of thousands of Californians were thrown out of work by the economic dislocations that accompanied the transition from the industrial to the information age, immigration once again became a partisan issue.[18]

Governor Pete Wilson, who as a senator had sponsored an amendment to the 1990 legislation making it easier for California farmers to obtain immigrant labor, declared illegal immigration the real cause of the state's problems and announced his support for Proposition 187. Designated the "Save Our State" proposition by its supporters, 187's provisions would deny access to education and all but emergency health care to anyone illegally in the state. Unlike Democrats, who believed Mexicans came to America looking for work, Republicans made it clear that they believed Mexicans were here looking to cash in on the generous public welfare benefits the state provided. Both sides agreed that the presence of too many illegal immigrants took jobs away from American citizens. Democrats suggested the solution was more strict enforcement of the existing laws prohibiting employers from hiring illegal workers, while Wilson argued that the problem be attacked more directly by eliminating the incentives that supposedly caused them to come here in the first place. The constitutional questions raised by Proposition 187 allowed its opponents to use the courts to block implementation after passage, but the groundswell of anti-immigration sentiment its presence on the ballot created rescued Wilson's 1994 reelection campaign.

▪ ▪ ▪

After the 1994 election, Republicans of all types suddenly decided the issue was too important to be left to Californians alone. In Congress new Majority Leader Dick Armey expressed the libertarian point of view on immigration. "I'm hard-pressed to think of a single problem that would be solved by shutting off the supply of willing and eager new Americans. If anything . . . we should be thinking about increasing legal immigration."[19] Government, according to Armey, has no business interfering with the free flow of people across national boundaries as they search for a better economic future. This point of view is shared by members of the "freedom left," who see any attempt by government to restrict residency in the United States as an infringement on personal liberty. The American Civil Liberties Union, for example, opposed Proposition 187 on the grounds that people who had entered the country illegally nevertheless had a "constitutional right" not to be prosecuted. When former Congresswoman Barbara Jordan's Presidential Commission on Immigration Reform suggested the creation of a national database from which employers could discover which of their prospective employees were in the country legally, both freedom right and freedom left opposed it, even on a trial basis.

Pat Buchanan had no patience for any of this and demanded a temporary moratorium on legal immigration for five years, exempting only the spouses and children of those already here. In his words, "the country has got to regain a measure of social cohesion and assimilation of the 25 million who have come in here in the past 20 years. To do that, people have to be acculturated and assimilated, just as they were when we had a 40-year hiatus from 1924 to 1965."[20] Buchanan supported a constitutional amendment to deny citizenship to children born on U.S. soil to illegal immigrants. Phil Gramm refused to go quite so far, but he did want to deny even legal immigrants access to welfare benefits, Medicaid, or Supplemental Security Income (SSI) payments. The proposal was part of the House-passed welfare reform proposal, though Gingrich, in one of his more libertarian moments, suggested perhaps it was not such a good idea.[21] None of the new Republicans could find a better way to produce some of the promised welfare reform savings. What others attacked as heartless, Gramm defended on the eminently conservative principle that only citizens should receive the benefits of citizenship. Principle was one thing, political reality quite another. Cuban Americans in Florida were furious. Candidate Bob Dole decided to let Phil Gramm take responsibility for including the provision in the Senate's welfare reform proposal.

All of this political posturing demonstrated a lack of understanding about how to create an information-driven economic system that succeeds. A 1993 poll showed that 60 percent of Americans believed increased immigration was "bad for the country."[22] But if refugees and elderly immigrants are eliminated from the data on all immigrants, only 5.1 percent of immigrants are receiving welfare benefits compared to 4.9 percent of native-born citizens, hardly an indication that they have somehow inflicted serious damage to the American economy.[23] To the contrary, immigrants are far more likely than average citizens to take business risks. In Los Angeles County, which with the possible exception of Miami has the highest ratio of immigrants to citizens in the nation, the number of Latino- and Asian-owned businesses tripled in a decade, with the number of Latino businesses growing three times faster than the total number of Latinos in the population.[24] The same phenomenon is occurring in cities like Miami, San Francisco, Houston, and San Diego, all of which have experienced substantial growth in both immigrant population and economic activity.

The rate of increase in household income among immigrant groups also reflects a dedication to hard work. In the 1980s, both Latino and Asian household incomes in California increased at rates ten times that of the overall population.[25] This success has not come at the expense of other parts of the population but has, instead, created more growth for everyone. In cities with large immigrant populations, African-American household incomes are demonstrably higher than in cities that have not benefited from an influx of new immigrants.[26] The value such populations bring to an economic system goes beyond their entrepreneurial attitudes and economic prowess.

These populations come to America neither for strictly economic reasons, as suggested by liberals, nor just to live on welfare, as suggested by conservatives. According to a survey of *legal* immigrants in 1992, they come to this country to be a part of what they see as the American Dream. Seventy-seven percent of those surveyed who were not already citizens intended to become citizens. This had less to do with economics than with the American ideal. Eighty-four percent wanted to be citizens so they could vote, 75 percent said citizenship would enable them "to be a full part of American society," and 71 percent said they wanted to achieve the American Dream. Their definition of becoming a part of American society was to get a college degree, become involved with their child's school, or own their own home.[27] These survey data are verified: during the 1980s, Latino and Asian groups in Los Angeles County bought homes at rates equal to or greater than the population as a whole.[28]

Opposition to immigration stems from two entirely different causes—one based on a question of values, the other based on perceptions of relative economic standing. Knowledge workers learn the value of reciprocal responsibility as they work in teams and as each experiences the benefits that come when everyone contributes to the outcome. The idea that illegal immigrants, who violated the law in the manner in which they entered the country, should somehow be given the same benefits as citizens strikes them, along with most members of the middle class, as fundamentally wrong. Pete Wilson's focus during his reelection campaign on the need to reward those who "play by the rules" captured this notion precisely. Illegal immigrants should be given no more benefit from the law than their own behavior warrants. Legal immigrants, on the other hand, obeyed the law; those who seek to become citizens should be given every opportunity to contribute and participate in the community. Opposition to their participation can only be ascribed to jealousy of their higher economic success and the disruption, however beneficial it might be to the overall system, that it causes to an individual's sense of security.

Traditional notions of left and right don't explain political divisions on the issue of immigration, nor do they provide any guidance to the right information age policy. A system of systems that can meet the challenge of a constantly changing environment must remain perpetually open to information about the outside world. Immigrants who come to this country with a desire to apply that knowledge in their daily lives are an essential and valuable resource. The use of information technology to identify illegal immigrants and deny them access to jobs, as suggested by Barbara Jordan's presidential commission, is a first step in reducing illegal immigration. The use of other types of technology to close the borders and require a process for legal application to enter the country is another. But the debate about how many or how few legal immigrants to "accept" misses the point. America should welcome every person whose skills and knowledge would contribute to the economic value of the country. The number of immigrants admitted each year should be determined by how quickly they can make that contribution as citizens. Welcoming them helps guarantee the openness, and therefore the success, of an economy in the information age.

·   ·   ·

Vigorous competition from abroad under today's relatively free trade approach and the unintended benefits of an open-door immigration policy have produced an American economy more competitive and productive than it has been in a decade. The Lausanne Institute of Management Development annually compiles a report for the Geneva World Economic Forum rating each industrialized country's economic competitiveness. In 1994, after eight years as an also-ran, the United States regained its ranking as the most competitive economy in the world.[29] By 1995, Japan had fallen to fourth place behind Singapore and Hong Kong, and Germany was sixth, behind Switzerland.[30] With the American economy more tied than ever before to the world economy,[31] the report suggested that the openness of our system of systems was working as it should.

But subjective ratings of a country's *competitiveness* miss the point. As Paul Krugman points out, "Productivity is not everything but in the long run it is almost everything.[32] The only way to raise wages and continue to sell globally is to increase productivity. The very actions that have created middle-class anxiety about the future—reductions in workforces and the rate of wage increases through reengineering of processes and a focus on total quality—have produced the enormous gains in productivity and lower unit labor costs that are making it more difficult for other countries to compete.[33] The average productivity of a Japanese worker was only 83 percent of an American worker in 1994 and German workers were only 79 percent as productive in nine industries surveyed by McKinsey in 1994. These figures represented a dramatic shift over the last fifteen years: in 1980, a steelworker in the United States needed ten hours to make one metric ton of steel, compared to only seven hours for his Japanese counterpart and eight for a worker in Western Europe. Now the American worker produces a ton of steel in only 4.3 hours, one hour less than either Japan or Germany has been able to achieve.[34]

Americans were not celebrating, however. The economic benefits of these gains in productivity had not yet been reflected in their incomes. The problem was clearly not foreign trade or immigration. The same pressures on wages and jobs could be found in sectors that were not subject to intense foreign competition. Instead, as one international competitive analyst pointed out, "a lot of restructuring came about because of technological change and more intense competition within the U.S. economy."[35] America's educational systems needed to improve and the emphasis in the tax system needed to change from income to consumption to spread the economic benefits of this newfound strength among the population.[36] Further, the country needs to fine-tune its chaordic economic system by looking at the relationships among all of its parts. The automotive industry and its conversion to a lean production approach provides the best example of this kind of change.

The old Chrysler did not just build and design cars the wrong way, it also treated its suppliers poorly, maintaining a strictly hands-off relationship. Every supply contract was put out to bid, and the competition was focused almost exclusively on price. The new Chrysler not only mastered all the other elements of lean production, it learned the concepts of lean supply.[37] First it shifted the flow of information. Research and development responsibility, along with the responsibility for engineering the component, was transferred to the supplier, who went from being dependent on Chrysler for the next contract to having Chrysler depend on it to improve quickly enough to meet the demands of the marketplace. Chrysler also disbanded its auditing bureaucracy, designed to see if its suppliers were making a fair profit or charging too much. Now if the price quoted by the supplier meets Chrysler's overall requirements, the contract is awarded without further negotiations. The key, as Chrysler learned from the Japanese, is to first draw the supplier into a relationship where both sides share similar objectives. The organizational boundaries between Chrysler and its suppliers is becoming increasingly blurred as information flows freely between them.[38] As one economist observed, "It was the human relationship that needed to be restructured as much as the technology."[39]

The importance of relationships in improving the performance of chaordic systems was also revealed by one of America's first experiences with industrial policy. When Japan threatened the entire U.S. semiconductor industry in the 1980s with its superior manufacturing efficiencies, Ronald Reagan reluctantly agreed to form a consortium of American manufacturers. Under a special exemption from anti-trust laws, the consortium would be allowed to share information among its members on how to improve manufacturing processes and become more competitive. The government even contributed some money to the effort, known as Sematech.[40] The answer to the problem turned out to be not the technology per se, but how participants in the system shared information.

Sematech surveyed 200 American firms engaged in the semiconductor business and asked them to name their three best suppliers and their three best customers. The answers, in every case, were Japanese firms. When the researchers inquired why Japanese companies were preferred it was clear that more than anything else, the U.S. firms valued the feedback and information flow they received from them. Based on this survey data, Sematech established a new conversation between the U.S. firms that produced an understanding that if the suppliers undertook the desired types of investments in research and new technology, manufacturers would guarantee orders for the products they developed.[41] The results have been spectacular. After being nearly vanquished in worldwide competition in the 1980s, the United States controlled 43 percent of the world market for computer chips in 1993, while the Japanese held only 41 percent.[42] The Sematech experience demonstrated that the economic function of government is to create an information policy rather than an industrial policy.

It is a lesson that needs to be applied at every level of government and business. As David Friedman found in his groundbreaking study of the Los Angeles economy, "the most successful sectors—entertainment, textiles, and environmental equipment and consulting—tended to be both *open* to new entrants, funding, global competition, and new market development, and *integrated* in the region, dependent on rapid, constantly changing project-by-project interaction with other specialist firms. . . . Not only were these sectors better able to compete in the global economy, they also were less sensitive to, and far more reliant on, Los Angeles' urban environment."[43] The recommendations for encouraging this kind of economic success in Los Angeles emphasized the development of more information, increased communication among the participants, and a rapid review of all regulatory policies that interfered with such information acquisition. A study of the relative success of Silicon Valley's high-tech economy over the equally high-tech regional economy along Route 128 outside Boston concluded that "Regional policy serves best as a catalyst—stimulating and coordinating cooperation among firms and between firms and the public sector. Rather than being orchestrated as top-down intervention or bureaucratic guidance, policy initiatives should evolve as interested local parties exchange information, negotiate, and collaborate."[44] The model for an information age economic system must stress both vigorous competition and complete cooperation among all of its members.

This is not the model being pursued by Japan, where government bureaucracy plays an important role in guiding investments into areas that have been strategically targeted for expansion. But as the Japanese economy has matured from one focused on traditional manufacturing sectors to one more

involved in high technology, the practice of guiding investment strategy became less and less effective. Indeed, it was
overrated from the start. The real key to Japan's remarkable
growth was its total concentration by leading businesses on the
acquisition of information and technology. This knowledge
was then jealously guarded within the country to assure the
success of its export economy, even at the expense of the domestic consumer. The practice was neatly captured in the
words of Katsuya Hayashi, secretary general of Japan's Olym-
pic Committee: "There is no negative impact in letting foreigners in, if the intent is to absorb other techniques and to
make Japanese sports stronger. But some sports have accepted
foreigners without any clear philosophy, apart from winning."[45] In the long run, this self-interested attitude toward
knowledge will hurt Japan's economy; in the short run, it requires an American trade policy focused on breaking down
structural barriers to the flow of information and trade.

When Bill Clinton took over as commander in chief, the
Pentagon concluded a complete "bottoms up review" of
America's military requirements in the post–cold war era. A
significant decrease in the size of the military force was possible, but it was necessary to maintain a viable industrial base
capable of producing, for instance, the nuclear submarines
such a smaller force would still require. The Pentagon recommended that those manufacturing capabilities be kept in operation, even if there was no present need for what they
produced.[46] Gingrich countered that "instead of talking about
our industrial base, we ought to be talking about our information base." He argued that the nation needed to begin to rethink how it fights war, collects intelligence, and uses its power
abroad.[47] Andy Marshall could not have agreed more.[48]

These comments could just as easily have been made about
the nation's economy. Military planning was focused on information and the key role it will play in future combat; stealth
technology's entire purpose was to deny information to the
enemy. At the same time, the Pentagon was trying to discover

how to manage, without any top-down control, the information created by an integrated mesh of all components of military weaponry.[49] In the debate over economic policy, on the other hand, almost nothing was said about how to acquire knowledge as quickly as possible. Educating our children, retraining our workforce, and reengineering our government—even in the most creative ways possible—will not, by themselves, enable every American to succeed in the new information age. Success will require a new system of systems that will allow the economy to rapidly absorb new ideas, share them widely, and restructure itself based on the simultaneous but seemingly unconnected decisions of millions of people. For that system to materialize, an entirely new political structure, in which each citizen will have the ability to take control of his or her own economic destiny, must first be created.

THE NEW AMERICAN SOCIAL CONTRACT

mmediately following the Gulf War, 65 percent of
the American population thought that the United
States was generally headed in the right direction.
Within a year, that number had slumped to 35 percent. During most of the 1992 presidential campaign, between 67 and
72 percent of the country felt "things were off on the wrong
track." Voters wanted to switch direction by electing Bill
Clinton, and for a short time they expressed hope in the future again. But by mid-1993, a majority once again concluded
the country was headed in the wrong direction.[1] The election
of a Republican House in 1994 led to another flurry of opti-
mism, followed by a prolonged period of disillusionment and
cynicism. Disappointment with the political process today is
every bit as great as it was in 1992 and 1994. In August 1995,
three out of five Americans felt the country was headed in the
wrong direction. Seventy percent did not trust the government to "do the right thing."[2] Americans were still looking for
the kind of political change politicians keep promising.

Newt Gingrich believed the Republicans' future depended
on Congress's keeping the promises made in its Contract with
America. His pollster, Frank Luntz, highlighted the most popular items in that Contract by placing at the beginning the Fiscal Responsibility Act, which promised a balanced budget

amendment and the line item veto, and at the end, a vote on term limits. Congress failed to deliver on either one. The rest of the promises spoke more to the Republicans' past than to the country's future. The public wanted something as revolutionary as Gingrich's third wave rhetoric; what is got was something so reactionary that even Barry Goldwater thought about switching parties.

In August 1995, 45 percent of the public disapproved of the job the GOP Congress was doing, while only 38 percent approved. Fifty-four percent disapproved of the Speaker himself. Not only did they dislike Gingrich the man, they did not like what he stood for. Sixty-one percent disapproved of his suggested cuts in Medicare, 59 percent opposed cuts in public housing expenditures, and a similar percentage disliked the idea of reducing the budget for the Environmental Protection Agency.[3] This did not mean, however, what many Democrats hoped it meant. The public did want a balanced budget, and they did want a vastly smaller federal government, but they thought these could be accomplished without penalizing the little guy while rewarding only those wealthy enough to hire the most influential lobbyists. And they were right.

After replacing a Republican president with a Democrat and a Democratic Congress with a Republican, all the public had to show for its effort were different sources of disappointment. It was time to look for a third option. Forty-six percent approved of Ross Perot's decision to form a third party, but only 24 percent wanted him to be the party's standard bearer. Instead, 42 percent preferred to see former Chairman of the Joint Chiefs of Staff Colin Powell run as the party's nominee.[4] His approval rating of 62 percent reflected the public's desire for something other than the harsh partisan rhetoric of the two major parties. Ross Perot and Jesse Jackson, each of whose iconoclastic messages made him the wrong third choice, were viewed by more people unfavorably than favorably.[5] Still, most Americans were dissatisfied with the status quo and the American political arena was ripe for change—the only question was in which direction.

The change the country was looking for would not come from within the duopoly of the two existing political parties. Both major parties had become prisoners of their former respective strengths. Republicans' laissez-faire economic message was not particularly compelling to white-collar workers whose jobs were being rapidly eliminated by the downsizing strategies of American corporations. Democratic appeals for middle-income solidarity with their less well-off brethren sounded off-key to blue-collar workers struggling not to fall below poverty themselves. And neither message held any appeal for knowledge workers, who were replacing both of these constituencies in ever larger numbers each year.

Furthermore, those who work in industrial age occupations are nonetheless information age consumers. They shop at Wal-Mart and club warehouse stores. They use 800 numbers to order from catalogues targeted to their needs everything from clothing to electronics. The cars they drive are chosen from an offering of models and brands more diverse than ever before. To them, as to the knowledge worker, the notion of limiting the voters' choice to only two parties seems increasingly anachronistic. And they know, or at least have begun to sense, that American politics will soon offer a variety of candidates and campaigns as rich and diverse as the programming options that are delivered daily on their cable TVs.

Shortly after the 1992 election, the Democratic party was presented with a plan to build a grassroots organization in this crowded marketplace in support of Bill Clinton. The proposal suggested using direct mail, fax, 800 numbers, and other communication media to create a two-way dialogue between the president and members of his party. Establishment of the right kind of electronic bond could have replaced the work done by state and national parties at the precinct level. Everything that was known about each voter was to be combined with the information that would emerge from the dialogue in a database from which customized messages were to be generated and sent directly to that individual. The basic functions of a political party—communication and loyalty-building—could have been accomplished by one expert programmer, a few people who created the material itself, and the communication networks to deliver the information, which already existed. The concept not only would have become self-sustaining from the contributions each person made, it also would have eliminated most of the party's administrative bureaucracy. The chairman of the Democratic National Committee, David Wilhelm, took the proposal to Mrs. Clinton, who gave it her full support. But when he then told his staff about it, the inevitable bureaucratic reaction set in. His chief of staff, Kent Marcus, vigorously opposed the idea, fearing what it would do to his own position. He organized an effective counterattack that not only killed the idea but also led to the firing of its chief proponent on the party's staff.[6]

Ross Perot was not concerned about anyone's political job. His 1992 campaign demonstrated the power of information technology in mobilizing political support. From the start of his candidacy on CNN's *Larry King Live*, Perot spent his personal wealth on infomercials and 800 numbers to spread his ideas through nontraditional communication channels and to build a base to sustain future campaigns. From these activities and the petition drives that were used to place his name on the ballot in all fifty states, Perot created a database of supporters with whom to communicate directly, long after the election was over. The entire post-campaign operation was funded by the supporters themselves, who contributed $15 each to the United We Stand organization. His use of one-to-one or direct marketing techniques allowed him to build a relationship with each individual and create a foundation for the first information age political organization.

Ross Perot was the first; he was not the last. The Republican candidates in the 1996 presidential primary were the next to try their luck at information age campaigning. Former Tennessee Governor Lamar Alexander, seeking some way to differentiate his 1996 presidential campaign from the other Republican candidates, decided to use the Internet to link his campaign to the voters. From his World Wide Web home page, essentially an interactive display ad on the Internet, he could receive inquiries about the campaign's ideas and activities. Alexander predicted 250,000 voters would click on the page during 1995. That would be every political organizer's dream—a solid base of potential activists with whom to talk. Other presidential candidates invested in their own home pages, none, perhaps, with more sophistication than Senator Phil Gramm. His computerized system asked visitors to his home page if they wanted to volunteer and, if so, an E-mail message was sent to the local coordinator for follow-up. Other candidates are using a variety of communication devices, from broadcast faxes to TV ads tailored to each market, to customize their messages to each voter.[7] The voter thus has a feeling of being linked intimately to the candidate; the campaign gains the chance to learn which messages work and which do not. The private sector has in essence been doing this for some time with remarkable success.

Retailers dream about the day each purchase will be scanned into a database that will also identify the shopper, thereby producing a record of who you are by what you buy. While that technology is not here yet, it is coming, and what it will be able to do can already be observed in the marketing strategies of the nation's leading retailers. For instance, Target, a chain of over 700 discount stores, uses a process called "micromarketing" designed to ensure that each store, even those in the same city, displays merchandise uniquely tailored to the buying preferences of that store's clientele. With a heavy investment in the computer equipment necessary to maintain a database on buying preferences throughout the country, Target has created a mix of merchandise that reflects the races, ethnicities, and ages of its shoppers. Local store managers buy only what they will sell without having to first obtain approval from a central merchandising staff. With a profile of each store's typical customer and the ability to provide precisely what customers want when they want it, in 1994 Target achieved a double-digit growth in profits over those of 1993.[8]

The next stage in information age marketing moves beyond, to a world customized to the *individual.* Levi Strauss and Co. began offering custom-made blue jeans in selected markets in 1994: a clerk enters a customer's measurements on a PC, which transmits the file to a robot tailor at the factory. The finished pair, which sells with about a $10 premium, is shipped to the store within three weeks. Sales of jeans in one store offering the service jumped 300 percent in one year. Levi Strauss is not the only firm that has begun to experiment with customization. Sales representatives of Motorola take customized orders for pagers that are instantly manufactured to their specifications. Andersen Windows offers to customize its product through a computer that permits the customer in a retail store to design the product before it is delivered to the home site.[9] Whether blue jeans or windows, with enough information every individual can be given what was once available only to a wealthy few—products customized to one's own particular requirements.

▪ ▪ ▪

The American public is looking for the same kind of choices from their government and the people who run it. They will not get it, however, from the leadership of either of the two major political parties, which have within them entrenched interest groups as much an obstacle to change as any bureaucracy threatened with loss of its power. Even though only 23 percent of Americans hold a positive view of the religious right, its chief spokesman, Ralph Reed, claimed that 72 percent of the voters in Republican presidential primaries and caucuses were in favor of his Christian Coalition's position on abortion. He bragged that 42 percent of these activists considered themselves born-again Christians.[10] Indeed, the Republicans' determined effort to cultivate this constituency accounted for the single largest demographic gain in the 1994 congressional vote for their candidates.[11] But while religion plays a strong role in most Americans' lives, only about 10 percent of the public can be classified as white religious conservatives—a dangerously thin plank on which to build a political party's platform.[12] Democrats make the same mistake with their continued reliance on labor as the source of electoral strength. Even though unions are the major contributor to the national Democratic party, they are no longer able to deliver the labor vote for the party's nominees. The number of union households has shrunk to less than 20 percent of the population, and, if anything, these blue-collar workers preferred Perot slightly more than the Democratic candidate. The only way to overcome the focus on the past these interest groups cultivate in America's major political parties and accelerate the development of an information age political system is to change the method by which we elect each party's leader and the country's president.

In the last twenty years, unknown candidates with messages that the voters wanted to hear—candidates such as Jimmy Carter or Bill Clinton, or even Ronald Reagan in his first challenge to Gerald Ford—were catapulted to the center of debate because public funding gave them the money they needed, and the electronic media gave them the exposure their candidacies required. The growth in communication choices offered by the new technology will create the opportunity for even more exposure to an even greater number of candidates in the future. As circulation levels stagnate among traditional newspapers and magazines, readership for print publications that more narrowly target their appeal has soared. Almost half of America listens to talk radio on any given day, which has combined this *narrowcasting* approach with a feeling of interaction and involvement. Television now offers six major networks instead of three, and specialized news, sports, and entertainment programming are available on dozens more. Thirty-five percent of Americans find reason to tune in to C-Span, which provides nothing but straight, unedited news.[13] And while only 5 percent of the country was on line during the last election, that number will increase exponentially through at least the next three presidential campaigns. Any attempt to limit the choices voters have to make in the political arena will be undermined by this astonishing new variety of information sources.

For this very reason, the current method of presidential selection is doomed. The 1996 presidential primary rules, adopted by each party and implemented by the various state legislatures, shortened the campaign season and made it more difficult for everyone—except the residents of New Hampshire and Iowa—to acquire the information they needed before voting. The first convention delegates were selected on February 20, and the overwhelming majority of convention delegates were pledged to one of the candidates by the end of March.[14] The two parties knew who their nominees for the November general election would be, appropriately enough, by April Fools' Day. During the next seven months, the public would be exposed to at least two new rounds of fashion, a brand-new network television schedule, and, in all probability, an appeal from at least two other independent candidates for president.

In 1992, with Ross Perot running as a third-party candidate, Bill Clinton became president with just 43 percent of the vote. In 1996, with a third—if not a fourth or even a fifth— candidate in the race, there is every reason to believe that for the second straight time Bill Clinton—or someone else— could become president with the support of less than half of the American electorate. A president without majority support is in danger of losing the moral authority to govern, and a president who cannot govern cannot bring about the fundamental changes in public policy required to complete the transition from the industrial to the information age.

The present arrangement of scattered state-run primaries and caucuses must be replaced by a single national primary, in which every party and every candidate will compete for support. Those who wish to run for the presidency without the official endorsement of an organized political party will use a home page on the Internet, appearances on talk radio shows, or infomercials on TV to generate interest and enthusiasm. These candidates will accumulate the expressions of support they receive through these media and, when they have reached a required minimum, will file them electronically with the Federal Election Commission to be certified for placement on the ballot. Political parties, meanwhile, will continue to nominate candidates in conventions, but the nomination will be for a place not on the November ballot but on the ballot of a national primary. Whichever method is used, all candidates in the national primary will be able to compete on an equal basis.

The two candidates who receive the highest vote totals will qualify for the general election, thus guaranteeing that the winning candidate will have found a way to attract broad majority support. The election will still be decided by the present electoral college system, where the candidate with the largest number of votes in a state receives all of that state's electoral votes, allowing this fundamental change in presidential selection to take place without an amendment to the Constitution.

Campaigning for president will be completely different from today's focus on fund-raising to pay for expensive ads on network television. The end of broadcast distribution monopolies will lead to less expensive communication alternatives, which candidates will quickly take advantage of. Even more effective will be the introduction of interactive campaigning. The combination of computer and communication technologies that is the Internet will provide this capability, making it the most important source of campaign information in the future.

The "Net" is a classic chaord, in Dee Hock's words, a "self-organizing, adaptive, nonlinear, complex community or system, whether physical, biological, or social, the behavior of which exhibits characteristics of both order and chaos."[15] No central computer controls its operations and only a simple set of rules and a voluntary membership organization provide a common mechanism for standards setting, operational administration, and coordination of research and global activities.[16] The result is a spiderweb of connections without obvious design, but one that nevertheless works with exceeding efficiency and effectiveness.[17]

In the space of a single year, from March 1993 to March 1994, the quantity of information carried over the Internet tripled; some estimates place the number of computer hosts on the network by the year 2000 at over 500 million. That increase coincides roughly with the introduction of the World Wide Web, a more user-friendly way to establish a presence on the net. Home pages on the Web allow users to produce information about themselves in voice, video, or text format, which is then linked to other home pages. The ability to both see and share more information created an 1,800 percent growth in Web servers in just one year, 1994.[18] It costs no more to post 10,000 words on the Internet than it does 100, and access is open to anyone who knows how to go on line. Citizens in the twenty-first century will learn about candidates from thirty megabytes of information on their home pages rather than from thirty-second sound bites of paid TV commercials.

Campaigning in the twenty-first century will not only be more efficient, it will be more effective. A small experiment in this future world has already been done. In 1994, the California Center for Governmental Studies established an interactive multimedia system that contained information on all of that state's congressional candidates. Video and text information submitted by the candidates was accessed by voters through a cable television set, video phone, or computer. The reactions were radically different from those exposed to negative ads on television. The news media itself only "covers candidates when they say something nasty about their opponents," but, as on the Internet, any message in this interactive format that is too inflammatory violates the sensibility of the users.[19] Since the voters initiate the communication exchange, the only way to hold their attention is to present "specific and direct information-oriented messages, and to avoid generalities and bromides." In addition, since the information is available when the voter wishes to review it and can be organized to suit the viewer's taste, a more complete and leisurely comparison of all the candidates and their positions on a variety of issues can be made by the voter.[20] Just as the burning intensity of progressives, populists, and socialists became the pragmatic government activism of the New Deal, communicated over the radio by FDR's fireside chats, the new campaign medium will force the current moralistic and angry tone of our political debate to give way to reasoned arguments about the most effective and efficient public policy to pursue. In a curious way, the future will bring us closer to the nation's very beginnings.

■ ■ ■

The American government was designed to work even if the people who held office were sometimes ignorant or incompetent or worse. By first dividing government between the national and state governments, and then dividing it again among the legislative, executive, and judicial branches, "ambition [would] be made to counteract ambition," as Madison wrote in the Federalist Papers.[21] Each branch would be filled with ambitious men who, unable to dominate the others, would do everything they could to be sure no one dominated them. Government would act—when it acted at all—only if what it did had so much to commend it no one would have a reason to withhold support. The American government, designed to protect not so much "life, liberty, and the pursuit of happiness," as Thomas Jefferson wrote in the Declaration of Independence, but the "life, liberty, and property" John Locke emphasized in his Second Treatise on Government, would be incapable of doing anything else. With an extended territory and a limited government, Americans could live securely, dependent only on themselves for survival.

The industrial revolution destroyed the economic assumptions on which the country was founded. The independent yeoman farmer Jefferson had celebrated quickly disappeared. Giant trusts and new corporate organizations made possible by the technologies of the industrial age limited the economic independence of the individual. FDR's New Deal offered greater protection from these economic forces, but in return placed new limits on individual freedom. Those who were most in need were offered the greatest assistance. Half of all Americans were considered poor in 1920, but by 1962 only 20 percent of American families fell below the poverty line, and by 1989 the number had fallen to less than 13 percent.[22] The New Deal, the social contract of the industrial age, was successful. It is now time to replace it with a social contract that recognizes the economic imperatives of the information age.

Computer and communication technology will provide each individual with the ability to acquire all the information necessary to be economically self-sufficient and politically independent. The cost of obtaining additional information from networked databases or faster personal computers in the interest of becoming even more economically productive, while not insignificant, declines rapidly every year. In this new age, the individual will once again have the opportunity to become as self-sufficient as the yeoman farmer of Jefferson's American Dream. This "information question" has replaced the "industrial question," and for the third time in their history Americans must agree to a new social contract if the country is to remain one community.

Economic opportunity can be increased by creating a new spirit of reciprocal responsibility between the governed and the government. Clinton's national service program, which provides educational opportunity not as a right but as an earned reward for those who do community service, most clearly embodies this principle. Liberals do not like it because it asks each person to be accountable for the choices he or she makes, rather then relying on his or her economic status to claim an entitlement to government benefits.[23] Conservatives do not like it because it permits government to play a role in advancing the economic well-being of society, instead of relying solely on the workings of the marketplace. When the new conservatives eliminated funding for the national service program, Newt Gingrich said, "The President has a good idea, but we disagree. . . . It's a question of philosophy and priorities.[24] Liberals' traditional insistence on promoting individual and even group rights without demanding any responsibility in the exercise of those rights angers conservatives, who believe individual rights flow not from government but from God. Their emphasis on personal responsibility, to the exclusion of all group rights, makes them doubly suspect a program that promotes reciprocal responsibility. Neither side in the debate has yet broken free of the assumptions of the industrial age. The combination of responsibility and rights to increase economic opportunity is—rather than a contradiction—an essential part of an information age social contract.

The new social contract must also combine increased freedom with stronger communities. For Gingrich, nothing is more important than personal liberty. His argument that the constitutional right to bear arms is based on the necessity of arming the citizenry to protect themselves from their own government is the starkest expression of the priority he places on individual freedom over the needs of society.[25] Clinton, on the other hand, believes issues of personal liberty sometimes must yield to the needs of the community. There is no longer a need to choose between the two; there are ways to provide each individual with more freedom and a better community in which to live.

In our major cities, local neighborhoods with a common purpose and culture are thriving, even while the city's core may be deteriorating. In Los Angeles County, Pasadena and Santa Monica have flourishing shopping and entertainment centers, Glendale and Burbank have nearly run out of commercial office space, and the ethnic communities in the San Gabriel Valley bustle with burgeoning entrepreneurial activity. Despite this, most Americans think of LA as slowly sliding into an urban cauldron of racial unrest, high unemployment, declining social services, incompetent schools, and intolerable social tension. The network of neighborhoods in which people live and work bears no resemblance to this picture. But the picture shows what people think cities look like—central cities governed from on high by a bureaucratic city hall. It is a paradigm from our industrial past that prevents us from seeing the future that is emerging.

It is not just in our neighborhoods that new bonds of community are being formed. In public housing projects, in our major cities, tenants, given the authority to govern themselves, have produced remarkable changes in the worlds in which they live. The Hunter's View Resident Management Corporation was granted authority to run its own community by a skeptical San Francisco Housing Authority, believing as one bureaucrat said of the residents of the city's most impoverished housing development, "These people will never be able to take care of themselves." Once they were given the opportunity, however, the tenants proved remarkably able to do so. As with any successful chaord, they first adopted some simple principles to guide their self-regulating enterprise. Individuals as building blocks, the importance of community, social capital, and governance and authority were the boundary conditions within which this community came together. As respect, responsibility, reciprocity, and adherence to rules they created became the norms of behavior for this team, the residents were able to create jobs, cut crime, and save money in the administration of the project. Landscaping is done by a group of residents who eventually became skillful enough to set up their own private business. The resident substance abuse recovery facility is led by those who have successfully transformed their own lives. The project was a success because it required all of the residents to make a personal commitment to devoting their energies, their talent, and their time to the venture. Most government programs have begun by removing that choice, dooming all that follows to failure.[26]

The new social contract for America will capture this desire to build more and better communities through individual choice by eliminating bureaucratic regulation and establishing boundary conditions for participation that preserve the common good. Today, a "surfer" on the Net joins any chat group he or she wants. Over 30 million users engage in more than 20 million conversations a day in at least 14,000 on-line conference forums. This new freedom can be used for the wrong purpose, such as instructing others how to blow up government buildings, or it can be used to unite previously divided cultures around the world. The choice lies outside the technology. It is not enough to use marketplace mechanisms to assure the most efficient use of public services; values that reinforce the American instinct for community must also be added to the indifferent workings of the system to make it more effective.

The capacity to form communities and use them as a method to achieve some common purpose has been an American characteristic since this country's founding. Even the determinedly individualistic pioneer culture celebrated the barn-building gathering as an example of how to unite to establish and strengthen a better community. The key to the American community Alexis de Tocqueville celebrated was the voluntary nature of its formation, based on what he termed "enlightened self-interest."[27] This kind of community arises from the concerted, self-interested actions of individuals bound together by a common concern for a particular outcome. As information technology makes each individual less connected to a particular place, the need to find alternative outlets for this desire for community increases. Participation is now organized around civic institutions, such as school and church activities, rather than abstract governmental entities, such as cities or states, which are increasingly unimportant in daily life. Knowledge workers in particular long for the experience of community in their civic life, just as they enjoy the success of working with a team. This new constituency brings a new sense of the value of interdependence to its political judgments. A political strategy that focuses on winning the support of the new majority is most likely to offer a social contract whose values help ensure the success of the new system.

By taking decisions away from government at the national and state levels and instead placing authority with each citizen, an information age public policy will offer new possibilities of personal and economic freedom. There will be a temptation by all to implement these new freedoms without establishing any new responsibilities, but it must be resisted. The preservation of the American ideal requires a new understanding of the role of government. Public policy must not only be designed to help people to help themselves, it must be based on the values that have long preserved our democratic traditions. Citizens now have more authority over their own lives than ever before, but that does not mean they can avoid their obligations to the communities in which they live and work. The new freedom means a new responsibility to use it in ways that enhance not only our own lives but the future well-being of the country.

The new technology of the information age will change the American economy and the American government. Knowledge workers will become the new majority in American politics. Whoever first offers them a new social contract for the information age will become the dominant political force in America in the twenty-first century.

· ACKNOWLEDGMENTS ·

This book could not have been written without the cooperation of several key people in government and politics. While most of them are quoted in the text or identified in the endnotes, others have wished to retain their anonymity—a desire we have respected in these pages. Nevertheless, there are several individuals who require special mention: it was Peter Block who suggested that it was time to define a social contract for government in the information age; Joel Kotkin and David Friedman shared their research and contributed data that greatly enriched our understanding of the issues involved. Drexel Sprecher, Jr., senior fellow at the American Renaissance Foundation, spent many hours discussing the reasons behind the paradigm shift we attempt to describe. Bruce Miller and Mary Ryan Taras provided space and sources for writing this book, even as they disagreed with its conclusions.

As valuable as those contributions were, they pale in comparison to the support we received from our families. In particular, the indefatigable efforts of Bobbie Winograd saved us both from more mistakes than we wish to admit.

M.W. & D.B.

· NOTES ·

Introduction: Politics in the Information Age

1. Price Pritchett, *New Work Habits for a Radically Changing World* (Dallas: Pritchett and Associates, 1994).

2. Peter Drucker, *Post-Capitalist Society* (New York: Harper Collins, 1993), 64.

3. See Kevin Kelly, *Out of Control: The Rise of Neo-Biological Civilization* (Reading, Mass.: Addison-Wesley, 1994), 8–10, and Nicholas Negroponte, *Being Digital* (New York: Knopf, 1995), 157.

4. John W. Verity, "The Information Revolution: How Digital Technology Is Changing the Way We Work and Live," *Business Week Special Annual Edition,* 1994, 10.

5. John Huey, "Waking Up to the New Economy," *Fortune,* 27 June 1994, 36.

6. Ian Morrison and Greg Schmid, *Future Tense: The Business Realities of the Next Ten Years* (New York: Morrow, 1994), 171.

7. Verity, 10.

8. John Naisbitt, *Global Paradox* (New York: Morrow, 1994), 81.

9. Rich Tetzeli, "Surviving Information Overload," *Fortune,* 11 July 1994, 60.

10. "E-lectioneering," *The Economist,* 17 June 1995, 22.

11. *Connections: AT&T's Vision of the Future* (Basking Ridge, N.J.: AT&T, 1993), 5, 9–10.

12. Kevin P. Phillips, *The Boiling Point: Republicans, Democrats, and the Decline of Middle-Class Prosperity* (New York: Random House, 1993), 128.

13. Keith Bradsher, "Americans' Real Wages Fell 2.3% in 12-Month Period," *New York Times,* 23 June 1995, C4.

14. Pritchett, 45.

15. Phillips, 149.

16. "Democrats Lead Assault on Crime," *Mainstream Democrat,* September-October 1989, 7.

17. Phillips, 141.

18. Newt Gingrich, *To Renew America* (New York: HarperCollins, 1995), 132–35.

1. The Death of Industrial Age Politics

1. Harry G. Summers, Jr., *A Critical Analysis of the Gulf War* (New York: Dell, 1992), 195.

2. Dennis Farney, "Strong Anti-politician Sentiment Is Displayed in Poll Showing Deep Pessimism by Electorate," *Wall Street Journal*, 26 October 1990, A16.

3. Bob Woodward, *The Agenda* (New York: Simon and Schuster, 1994), 22.

4. The speakers were Bill Galston, Elaine Kamarck, Doug Ross, and Morley Winograd.

5. Farney, A16.

6. Peter F. Drucker, *The New Realities: In Government and Politics, in Economics and Business, in Society and World View* (New York: Harper Business, 1994), 25–26.

7. Drucker, 111.

8. Peter F. Drucker, "The Age of Social Transformation," *Atlantic Monthly*, November 1994, 64.

9. Bill Clinton, "The New Covenant: Responsibility and Rebuilding the American Community," presented at Georgetown University, 23 October 1991.

10. Clinton, "New Covenant."

11. George J. Church, "Is Bill Clinton for Real?" *Time*, 27 January 1992, 15.

12. Church, 16.

13. Ronald Brownstein, "The Times Poll Spotlight Finds Clinton Locked in Three-Way Tie," *Los Angeles Times*, 12 July 1992, A1.

14. Richard Morin, "Clinton's Ratings Rise as Bush, Perot Battle," *Washington Post*, 28 June 1992, A13.

15. Sam Fulwood, "Clinton Chides Rap Singer, Stuns Jackson," *Los Angeles Times*, 14 June 1992, A1.

16. Terry Hitchins Nicolosi and Jose L. Ceballos, eds., *Official Proceedings of the 1992 Democratic National Convention* (Washington D.C.: Democratic National Convention Committee, 1992), 245.

17. Nicolosi and Ceballos, 316.

18. Stanley B. Greenberg, *Middle Class Dreams: The Politics and Power of the New American Majority* (New York: Times Books, 1995), 122.

19. Mary Matalin and James Carville, *All's Fair: Love, War, and Running for President* (New York: Random House, 1994), 241.

20. Richard Berke, "Unhumbled, Buchanan Backs Bush," *New York Times*, 18 August 1992, A8.

21. " '92 Republican Convention: Quayle Text," *Los Angeles Times*, 21 August 1992, A8.

22. "Choose or Lose: The Home Stretch," interview of George Bush by Tabitha Soren, *Rock the Vote*, MTV, 1 November 1992.

23. "The Poll Findings Converge," *New York Times*, 18 August 1992, A13.

24. Ruy A. Teixeira, *The Politics of the High-Wage Path: The Challenge Facing the Democrats*, working paper 110 (Washington, D.C.: Economic Policy Institute, October 1994).

25. Woodward, 54.

26. This story was related to Elizabeth Drew, Winograd, and others.

27. Peter Hart and Robert Teeter, *NBC/WSJ Study 4039* (Washington, D.C.: Hart-Teeter, June 1993).

28. Al From, "On a Roll: Clinton Cannot Afford to Squander His Momentum from 1993," *The New Democrat*, February 1994, 19.

29. Peter Hart and Robert Teeter, *NBC/WSJ Study 4045* (Washington, D.C.: Hart-Teeter, 15–18 January 1994).

30. Hart and Teeter, *Study 4045*.

31. Peter Hart and Robert Teeter, *NBC/WSJ Study 4036, 4039, 4045, 4049* (Washington, D.C.: Hart-Teeter, 26 January 1993–26 July 1994).

32. Hart and Teeter, *Study 4049*.

33. Times Mirror Center for the People and the Press, *The People, the Press & Politics: The New Political Landscape* (Washington, D.C.: Times Mirror Center for the People and the Press, 1994), 60–74.

34. Mike Mills, "Convergence on the Data Highway," *Washington Post*, 11 January 1995, D2.

35. Greenberg, 280–85.

2. The Birth of a New Constituency

1. Katharine Q. Seelye, "Voters Disgusted with Politicians as Election Nears," *New York Times*, 3 November 1994, A28.

2. Haley Barbour, address, "Town Hall Meeting," Los Angeles, 28 February 1995.

3. Greenberg Research, Inc., for the Democratic Leadership Council, *Survey of Voters, with Figures and Tables*, 8–9 November 1994, 24–25.

4. Greenberg Research, 24.

5. Drucker, "Transformation," 56.

6. Hedrick Smith, *Rethinking America* (New York: Random House, 1995), xvii–xix.

7. Michael Rothschild, *Bionomics: Economy as Ecosystem* (New York: Henry Holt & Co., 1990), 101.

8. Stanley M. Davis, *Future Perfect* (Reading, Mass.: Addison-Wesley, 1987).

9. David Ritchie, *The Computer Pioneers: The Making of the Modern Computer* (New York: Simon and Schuster, 1986), 45.

10. Richard Thomas DeLamarter, *Big Blue: IBM's Use and Abuse of Power* (New York: Dodd, Mead, 1986), 69–70, 88–91.

11. Marilyn A. Harris, "IBM: Trying to Put All the Pieces Together," *Business Week*, 21 April 1986, 62–63.

12. Smith, 83–84.

13. T. Nicholson and J. C. Jones, "Going Like 60," *Newsweek*, 15 January 1979, 71. Sixty was the target for the stock price as well as the market share GM hoped to reach before the chairman's sixtieth birthday.

14. Maryann Keller, *Rude Awakening: The Rise, Fall, and Struggle for Recovery of General Motors* (New York: Morrow, 1989), 56–57.

15. Tetsuo Sakiya, *Honda Motor: The Men, the Management, the Machines*, trans. Kyoshi Ikemi (Tokyo: Kodansha, 1982), 203–4.

16. Sakiya, 170–73.

17. Arno Penzias, *Harmony: Business, Technology & Life After Paperwork* (New York: Harper Business, 1995), 40–41.

18. Christina Duff and Bob Ortega, "Loss Leader: How Wal-Mart Outdid a Once-Touted K-mart in Discount-Store Race," *Wall Street Journal*, 24 March 1995, A1, A6.

19. Times Wire Service, "Panel Urges Loosening of Union Ties," *Los Angeles Times*, 10 January 1995, D3.

20. Joel Kotkin and Morley Winograd, "The New Constituency: California Democrats Are Looking for Votes in All the Wrong Places," *The New Democrat*, November 1994, 16.

21. Kotkin and Winograd, 15.

22. Bill Stall, "The Times Poll; Brown Leads Democrats as Troubles Plague Wilson," *Los Angeles Times*, 27 May 1994, A1.

23. George Skelton, "Fairness Is Pete Wilson's New Mantra," *Los Angeles Times*, 9 January 1995, A3.

24. Kathleen Brown, "Sowing the Ground for a Better California," *Los Angeles Times*, 24 October 1994, B9.

25. Exit polling data from Voters, Research and Surveys (VRS) polling service, 9 November 1994.

26. Dave Lesher, "TV Blitz Fueled by a Fortune," *Los Angeles Times*, 12 September 1994, A1.

27. Greg Krikorian and Dave Lesher, "L.A. Leaders Back Feinstein; Huffington Assails Desert Act," *Los Angeles Times*, 2 November 1994, A3.

28. AnnaLee Saxenian, *Regional Advantage: Culture and Competition in Silicon Valley and Route 128* (Cambridge: Harvard University Press, 1994), 3.

29. Elections Division, State of California, *Statement of Vote: November 8, 1994, General Election* (Sacramento: Elections Division, 1994).

30. VRS.

31. Exit polling data from Mitofsky International polling service, 9 November 1994.

32. VRS.

33. Greenberg, 13.

3. Reinventing American Government

1. From notes taken by Morley Winograd after the meeting concluded. Also in attendance were senior members of the vice president's staff, Doug

Ross, and Allan J. Lichtman, author of *Thirteen Keys to Winning the Presidency.*

2. Theodore Roosevelt, "Acceptance Speech," Progressive Party Convention, 6 August 1912, in Thomas B. Reed, *Modern Eloquence* (New York: Modern Eloquence Corp., 1923), 164.

3. Reed, 165.

4. Woodrow Wilson, "The New Freedom," 1912, in Richard Hofstadter, *Great Issues in American History,* vol. 2 (New York: Vintage Books, 1958), 294.

5. Hofstadter, 297.

6. Basil Rauch, ed., *The Roosevelt Reader: Selected Speeches, Messages, Press Conferences, and Letters of Franklin D. Roosevelt* (New York: Holt, Reinhart, and Winston, 1957), 82.

7. Rauch, 83.

8. Rauch, 85.

9. Allen Nevins, *Ford: The Times, the Man, the Company* (New York: Charles Scribner's Sons, 1954), 452.

10. Democratic Leadership Council, focus group transcripts, Warren, Mich., 9 November 1994.

11. Matalin and Carville, 243.

12. David Osborne, interview by Morley Winograd, 5 December 1994.

13. He also named as one of the first members of the task force David Osborne, whose book *Laboratories of Democracy* had described innovative programs being developed by state governors. One of the governors profiled in Osborne's book had been then–Arkansas governor Clinton. After Clinton was named chairman of the Democratic Leadership Council, the ideas from Osborne's new book, *Reinventing Government,* were featured in the DLC's magazine, *The New Democrat;* one of the DLC's five leading principles, the belief in an "entrepreneurial, nonbureaucratic government," was borrowed directly from that book.

14. Osborne interview.

15. Vice President Al Gore, *From Red Tape to Results: Creating a Government That Works Better and Costs Less: Report of the National Performance Review* (Washington, D.C.: GPO, 7 September 1993).

16. Congressman Dave McCurdy, discussion with DLC leaders, 5 December 1994.

17. President Clinton, quoted in "Hunt On for Government Waste," *New York Times,* 3 March 1993, A23.

4. Preserving the American Commons

1. U.S. Department of Labor, *Bureau of Labor Statistics, Bulletin 2340* (Washington, D.C.: GPO, August 1989), 348–54. Employment statistics from the Bureau of Labor; output measurements based on dividing industrial production by manufacturing employment, standard methodology for measuring productivity in this sector. For the government productivity measure-

ment, real government expenditures were divided by government employment.

2. Seelye, A28.

3. "The American Dream—What It Means Today," *Roper Reports,* May 1994. The same polling data indicated that achieving the American dream seemed harder than it was a generation ago to 64 percent of the people polled.

4. Richard Morin, "What the Public Really Wants," *Washington Post National Weekly Edition,* 9–15 January 1995, 37. From the General Social Survey of the University of Chicago's National Opinion Research Center's annual poll taken in the spring of 1993.

5. Alexis de Tocqueville, *Democracy in America,* trans. George Lawrence, ed. J. P. Mayer (Garden City, N.Y.: Doubleday, 1993). Tocqueville regarded this as a uniquely American characteristic. See especially pp. 520–24 on the relationship between civic and political associations.

6. Morin, 37.

7. Haley Barbour, address, "Town Hall Meeting," Los Angeles, 17 July 1995.

8. Teixeira, 9.

9. Nicolosi and Ceballos, 316.

10. David Osborne and Ted Gaebler, *Reinventing Government: How the Entrepreneurial Spirit Is Transforming the Public Sector* (New York: Penguin Books, 1992), 348.

11. Al From and Will Marshall, *The Road to Realignment: The Democrats and the Perot Voters* (Washington, D.C.: Democratic Leadership Council, July 1993), 8.

12. From and Marshall, 6.

13. Elizabeth Kolbert, "The Vocabulary of Votes: Frank Luntz," *New York Times Magazine,* 26 March 1995, 46.

14. "Laszlo and Associates: Brown Bag Discussion with Stanley Greenberg and Frank Luntz," C-Span, Los Angeles, 10 April 1995.

15. Kolbert, 48.

16. Stanley B. Greenberg, "The Revolt Against Politics," *Third Force,* November 1994, 11. The exact margin in Greenberg's postelection polling was 59 percent to 33 percent.

17. Stephen Barr, "Republicans Promise Bills to Kill Four Cabinet Agencies: Commerce, Energy, HUD, Education Are Targeted," *Washington Post,* 19 May 1995, A23.

18. "Summary of the Unfunded Mandate Reform Act," *Congressional Digest* 74 (March 1995): 74.

19. David Helvarg, "Legal Assault on the Environment," *The Nation,* 30 January 1995, 126.

20. Christopher John Farley, "The West Is Wild Again," *Time,* 20 March 1995, 46.

21. Charles McCoy, "Private Matter: The Push to Expand Property Rights Stirs Both Hopes and Fears," *Wall Street Journal,* 4 April 1995, A1.

22. Helvarg, 128.

23. Elaine Kamarck, interview by Morley Winograd, 19 March 1995.

24. Garret Hardin, "Tragedy of the Commons," *Science*, 1 December 1968, 1243. (For further discussion, see Rothschild, 109).

25. Ed Gillespie and Bob Schellhas, eds., *Contract with America: The Bold Plan by Rep. Newt Gingrich, Rep. Dick Armey and the House Republicans to Change the Nation* (New York: Random House, 1994), 4–5.

26. L. T. Hobhouse, *Liberalism*, Home University Library of Modern Knowledge, no. 16 (New York: Henry Holt & Co., 1911).

27. J. L. Sullivan, "Nutrilite: $1 Billion in Pills," *Orange County Business Journal*, 6–12 February 1995, 1.

28. Jill Abramson and David Rogers, "Shifting Fortunes: As GOP Tries to Shrink Government, Coffers Swell with New Money," *Wall Street Journal*, 9 February 1995, A1.

29. Robert J. Samuelson, "The Rise of 'Ecorealism,' " *Newsweek*, 10 April 1995, 46.

30. William Shireman, "The Wealth of Notions," *Global Futures* 1994, unpublished manuscript, 6–7.

31. Shireman, 6.

32. Samuelson, 21–22.

33. Samuelson, 46.

34. Shireman, 6.

35. William Shireman, "The Reinvention of American Politics After November 8," *Global Futures*, 1 December 1994, unpublished manuscript.

36. Shireman, "Reinvention."

37. Christina Rose, interview by Morley Winograd, 4 November 1995.

38. "The Bottle Bill," *Detroit News*, 28 November 1988, B1.

39. Richard A. Lovett, "Proposition 65 Comes of Age," *California Journal*, November 1994, 26.

40. Frank Clifford, "State Curb on Household Chemicals Under Attack," *Los Angeles Times*, 22 February 1995, 1.

41. Shireman, "Wealth," 95–97.

5. Reengineering American Government

1. Vice President Al Gore, *From Red Tape to Results: Creating a Government That Works Better and Costs Less: Report of the National Performance Review* (Washington, D.C.: GPO, 7 September 1993), 1.

2. Michael Hammer and James Champy, *Reengineering the Corporation: A Manifesto for Business Revolution* (New York: Harper Business, 1992).

3. Elaine Kamarck, address, California DLC Annual Conference, San Diego, 11 December 1994.

4. Barr, A23.

5. Gillespie and Schellhas, 86–87.

6. The proposal had originally been made by Gore in 1991 when he was

a senator. He announced it to the Washington press corps on the day that Clinton was delivering his keynote speech to the DLC convention in Cleveland in the hopes, says Al From, of stealing some of Clinton's news coverage that day.

7. John M. Broder and James Risen, "Clinton Offers Tax Cut Plan for Middle Class," *Los Angeles Times,* 16 December 1994, A1.

8. Gillespie and Schellhas, 5.

9. Irving Kristol, "Times of Transformation," *Wall Street Journal,* 13 June 1995, A18.

10. Lucinda Harper, "GOP Pushing Big Corporate Tax Break in the Form of Depreciation Changes," *Wall Street Journal,* 5 December 1994, A2.

11. Jackie Calmes, "House GOP Clears the Way for Passage of Ambitious Tax-Reduction Package," *Wall Street Journal,* 6 April 1995, A3.

12. Newt Gingrich, "The Contract's Crown Jewel," *Wall Street Journal,* 21 March 1995, A14.

13. Robert J. Shapiro, "Cut-and-Invest: A Budget Strategy for the New Economy," Progressive Policy Institute Policy Report 23, March 1995, 1.

14. Shapiro, 4.

15. Bob Greenstein, Stephen Moore, and David Frum, address, Progressive Policy Institute Conference, Washington, D.C., 6 March 1995.

16. David Wessel and Jackie Calmes, "Clinton's Game Plan for the Budget: Let GOP Carry the Ball on Cutbacks," *Wall Street Journal,* 6 February 1995, A2.

17. Christopher Georges, "House Republicans Draft Plans to Cut Billions in Subsidies for Large Firms," *Wall Street Journal,* 30 March 1995, A2.

18. Paul T. Whyte, " 'We're Not Going to Raise Any Taxes,' " *USA Today,* 7 February 1995, 9A.

19. Rothschild, 77.

20. Rothschild, 213–25.

21. David Wessel, "Nunn-Domenici 'USA Tax' Puts Levy on Consumption to Encourage Saving," *Wall Street Journal,* 26 April 1995, A2.

22. The simplified income tax proposal introduced by Dick Gephardt did tax such investments, for which it was duly criticized. However, by retaining the mortgage interest deduction and creating multiple graduated tax rates, it not only failed to qualify as a flat tax, but lost the advantages of simplicity and efficiency. Other than shifting the tax burden to wealthier Americans, it is difficult to say just what his proposal would accomplish.

23. Toyotas also had one third the quality defects of GM cars. James P. Womack, Daniel T. Jones, and Daniel Roos, *The Machine That Changed the World: The Story of Lean Production* (New York: Harper Perennial, 1991), 82.

24. "When GM's Robots Ran Amok," *The Economist,* 10 August 1991, 64.

25. Womack, Jones, and Roos, 56–57.

26. "1987 Man of the Year: Ford Motor Company Chairman Donald E. Petersen," *Motor Trend,* February 1987, 43.

27. Womack, Jones, and Roos, 79–80.

28. Womack, Jones, and Roos, 99.

29. Womack, Jones, and Roos, 119–22.

30. The rate of any such sales tax depends on the exemptions established and the assumptions made about the rate of economic growth that will occur as a result of this change. In order to be revenue-neutral in today's terms, the exclusion of rents and investments in residential housing, coupled with a requirement that each state government pay for its purchases, requires a sales tax of about 17.5 percent. Adding the rebate for basic necessities and other possible exemptions can raise the tax rate to as high as 20 percent. See analysis by John H. Qualls, president of Micro Economics, Ltd., and consultant to Citizens for an Alternative Tax System, "The Impact of a National Sales Tax on the United States Economy," 16 August 1991, 6.

31. Steven L. Hayes, "Revitalize the American Economy: Replace the Income Tax with a National Retail Sales Tax," testimony before the House Ways and Means Committee, 8 June 1995, 7.

32. Bill Archer, address to the Bionomics Institute Conference, Washington, D.C., 18 May 1995.

33. "Testimony of Senator Richard Lugar, House Ways and Means Committee Hearings on Tax Reform," 8 June 1995. 2.

34. Kelley Holland and Amy B. Cortese, "The Future," *Business Week,* 12 June 1995, 68.

35. "Statement of Dr. Richard W. Rahn on Behalf of the Business Leadership Council on Replacing the Income Tax," testimony before the House Ways and Means Committee, 8 June 1995, 1–3.

6. Rethinking Entitlements

1. Bob Kerrey attempted to do that in the New Hampshire primary.

2. "Announcement Speech: Old State House, Little Rock, Ark." (Little Rock: Clinton for President Committee, 3 October 1991), 6.

3. Robert Shogan, "Five Candidates Debate, Focus on Economy," *Los Angeles Times,* 1 February 1992, A18.

4. The upset victory made Wofford's campaign manager, James Carville, a national star. Clinton had been searching for the right campaign manager and considered it a major coup when he was able to persuade Carville to sign on shortly after this victory.

5. Jack W. Germond and Jules Witcover, *Mad As Hell: Revolt at the Ballot Box* (New York: Warner Books, 1993), 69.

6. William Schneider, "Why Health Care Reform May Be Beyond Saving," *Los Angeles Times,* 14 August 1994, M6.

7. California Elections Division, ix.

8. Schneider, M6.

9. The tax rate would have been about 9 percent to start. Jeremy D. Rosner, "A Progressive Perspective on Health Care Reform," Progressive Foundation, 26 March 1992, 27.

10. Michael Rothschild discusses this point in even more trenchant detail

in an editorial, "Why Health Reform Died," *Wall Street Journal*, 22 September 1994, A14.

11. "Transcript of President's Address to Congress on Health Care," *New York Times*, 23 September 1993, A24.

12. Alain C. Enthoven, "A Cure for Health Costs," *World Monitor*, April 1992, 36.

13. Larry Rohter, "Employers in Orlando Create an Envied Model," *New York Times*, 30 June 1994, B10.

14. Enthoven, 39.

15. Grace-Marie Arnett, "Physician, Bail Thyself Out!" *Journal of the Medical Association of Georgia*, August 1994, 467–68.

16. Clinton's six principles as outlined in his address to Congress were: security, simplicity, savings, choice, quality, and responsibility.

17. Dee Hock, "Institutions in the Age of Mindcrafting," Bionomics Institute Annual Conference, San Francisco, 22 October 1994.

18. John Cleveland, JoAnn Neuroth, and Peter Plastrik, *The Chaordic Handbook: Living, Learning and Organizing at the Edge of Chaos, Or, How Do Messy, Swarming Things Stay Alive?* (s.1 On Purpose Associates, Inc. Circ. Draft, April 1995), 8.

19. Cleveland, Neuroth, and Plastrik, 20.

20. David Vine, "Bending Space and Time: The Virtual Organization," *Internet World*, May 1995, 100.

21. AP Wire Service, "Medicare Cost Woes Date Back," AP Wire Service, 18 June 1995 (Prodigy file, AP-NY-06-18-95 1318 EDT).

22. Grace-Marie Arnett, "Health Care: The Time Bomb Is Ticking," *Common Sense*, Spring 1995, 128.

23. Arnett, 132.

24. Michael Sherraden, "Stakeholding: A New Direction in Social Policy," Progressive Policy Institute Policy Reports no. 2 (January 1990), 5.

25. Rand Corporation study cited by Michael Rothschild in a Bionomics Institute pamphlet entitled "Pre-Existing Condition," reprinted from *Upside* magazine in 1993.

26. For a fuller discussion of incentive alignments, see Michael E. Porter, Elizabeth Olmsted Teisberg, and Gregory B. Brown, "Making Competition in Health Care Work," *Harvard Business Review*, July-August 1994, 131.

27. Gloria Lau, "Bringing Hospitals into the Information Age," *Investor's Business Daily*, 30 March 1995, A6.

28. "Tomorrow's Doctoring: Patient, Heal Thyself," *The Economist*, 4 February 1995, 19.

29. A possible role for government in creating this kind of health insurance instrument would be to *underwrite* the potentially higher risk of the insurance company receiving all of its promised payments. By using its credit standing to create a market for the underlying stream of payments as it has done with FHA mortgages (Fannie Maes), student loans (Sallie Maes), and other government-sponsored enterprises, the federal government could nurture this embryonic instrument until it was fully mature and accepted.

30. Porter, Teisberg, and Brown, 141.

31. Jackie Calmes, "Gingrich Urges Replacing Medicare, But Gives No Specifics or Timetable," *Wall Street Journal,* 6 January 1995, 3.

32. Clinton/Gingrich New Hampshire Debate, CNN Special Transcript #520, 11 June 1995, 17.

7. Reforming More Than Welfare

1. Germond and Witcover, 443.

2. Joe Davidson, "Welfare Mothers Stress Importance of Building Self-Esteem if Aid System Is to Be Restructured," *Wall Street Journal,* 12 May 1995, A14.

3. Barbara Vobejda, "GOP Welfare Plan Would Shrink the System," *Washington Post,* 7 December 1994, A23.

4. Hilary Stout, "GOP's Welfare Stance Owes a Lot to Prodding From Robert Rector," *Wall Street Journal,* 23 January 1995, A1.

5. Elizabeth Shogren and Ronald Brownstein, "GAO Says JOBS Plan Not Working," *Los Angeles Times,* 19 December 1994, A24.

6. A. Lawrence Chickering, *Beyond Left and Right: Breaking the Political Stalemate* (San Francisco: ICS Press, 1992), 21–57. The division among Republicans between what Chickering calls "order right" and "freedom right," is analogous to the problem Democrats had when the "order left," for whom government was an instrument with which to enforce economic egalitarianism, found itself in unexpected conflict with the "freedom left" commonly known as "hippies," over the Vietnam War. Chickering traces the history of these two analogous developments and suggests the use of self-governance solutions to overcome the inherent contradictions of both positions.

7. The claim was more campaign hype than substance. A consulting firm evaluated the first year of Engler's program, which permitted AFDC recipients to receive income from working, and found only minimal changes in the number of welfare recipients who were also working or who used the work incentives to move off the rolls. Carl Horowitz, "Understanding Welfare Reform," *Investor's Business Daily,* 31 January 1995, A1.

8. Horowitz, A1.

9. Horowitz, A1.

10. Anonymous "Dear Colleague" letter dated June 15, 1995, and circulated to Senate staff.

11. Five principles of the DLC are listed in its membership solicitation brochure. In addition to the one quoted, they include statements on behalf of the private sector—as opposed to government—being "the primary engine for economic growth," the need for a "renewed ethic of civic responsibility" based on the idea of reciprocity between the government and those helped by it, a foreign policy emphasis on America leading "other nations toward democracy and market economics," and a call for reinventing government "so that it is both more responsive to those it serves and more

accountable to taxpayers who pay for it." DLC membership application, "Americans at Work: Turning Ideas into Action," printed by the DLC in early 1994.

12. Bill Clinton, press conference, 10 August 1995.

13. U.S. Department of Labor, Bureau of Labor Statistics, Bulletin 2352. *Outlook 2000,* April 1990, 42.

14. Michael J. Mandel, "The Job Market Isn't Really in the Dumps," *Business Week,* 19 June 1995, 42.

15. Marshall Ingwerson, "Moynihan Casts a Long Shadow on Health Plans," *Christian Science Monitor,* 3 February 1994, 1.

16. See Chapter 3, note 1.

17. Will Marshall, "Replacing Welfare with Work," Progressive Policy Institute *Policy Briefing,* July 1994, 11.

18. Marshall, 11–12.

19. Remarks by Larry Townsend to the California DLC's legislative conference in Sacramento, January 18, 1995.

20. Data supplied by Larry Townsend from an audit of all GAIN programs in California done by the Manpower Demonstration Research Corporation.

21. Marshal, 5.

22. Will Marshall, Ed Kilgore, and Lyn A. Hogan, "Work First: A Proposal to Replace Work with an Employment System," Progressive Policy Institute *Policy Briefing,* 2 March 1995.

23. Robin Toner, "Senate Kills Plan to Limit Welfare and Size of Family," *New York Times,* 14 September 1995, A1.

24. The DLC Fax, "Senate Welfare Bill: An Important Step Toward Reform," Democratic Leadership Council, 20 September 1995.

25. "A Slap in the Face for the Working Poor," *The Economist,* 8 July 1995, 23.

26. Jackie Calmes, "House GOP Pushes Through Package That Ends Some Business Tax Breaks," *Wall Street Journal,* 20 September 1995, A3.

27. Marshall, 9.

28. National Center for Health Statistics, "Advance Report of Final Statistics, 1991," *Monthly Vital Statistics Report,* 42.3, supp. 9 (9 September 1993), 25.

29. Marshall, 9.

30. Kristen A. Moore and Nancy O. Snyder, "Facts at a Glance" (Washington, D.C.: Child Trends, January 1994).

31. Robert B. Carleson, "There They Go Again," *Wall Street Journal,* 13 July 1995, A14.

32. Tamar Lewin, "The Decay of Families Is Global, Study Says," *New York Times,* 30 May 1995, A5.

33. The rate of increase in teenage pregnancy is in fact greater among whites than blacks. Kathleen Sylvester, "Preventable Calamity: Rolling Back Teenage Pregnancy," Progressive Policy Institute *Policy Report No. 22,* November 1994, 4.

34. Judith Havemann, "Abortion Rate Increased under NJ 'Family Cap,'" *Washington Post,* 17 May 1995, A15.

35. Charles P. Wallace, "Welfare Is No Longer on a Roll in New Zealand," *Los Angeles Times,* 21 April 1995, A5.

36. Shireman, "Reinvention." Fifty-six percent of all Americans believe learning is the principal objective of their lives.

37. For a more detailed list of tasks and the relative effectiveness of public, private, and civic sector efforts to accomplish them, see Osborne and Gaebler, Appendix A, 347.

38. Steven Rattner, "GOP Ignores Income Inequality," *Wall Street Journal,* 23 May 1995, A22.

8. Replacing Crime with Community

1. Adam Walinsky, "The Crisis of Public Order," *Atlantic Monthly,* July 1995, 48.

2. Sylvester, 11.

3. Douglas A. Smith and G. Roger Jarjoura, "Social Structure and Criminal Victimization," *Journal of Research in Crime and Delinquency* 25.1 (February 1988), 27–52.

4. "Marriage Trends Studied," *Facts On File* 52.2713, 19 November 1992, 879.

5. The last attempt at welfare reform, the Family Support Act, was passed in 1988, leading many analysts to conclude that there is a causal link between its provision of federal assistance to unwed mothers who are engaged in job-training activities and this renewal in birth trends. Correlation, however, does not prove causation.

6. Moore and Snyder.

7. Sylvester, 2, 38.

8. Walinsky, 41.

9. Walinsky, 46.

10. Walinsky, 52–54.

11. Hart and Teeter, *Study 4039.*

12. "The Police Corps and Community Policing: A Progressive Response to Crime," Progressive Policy Institute *Policy Report No. 4,* March 1990, 9.

13. Walinsky, 1.

14. "Crime as a Cause of Poverty: From a Speech by Congressman John Lewis, Democrat of Georgia," *Atlanta Monthly,* July 1995, 49.

15. D'Jamila Salem, " '94 Crime Bill Is First in Five Years," *Los Angeles Times,* 22 August 1994, 3.

16. Al From, interview by Morley Winograd, 5 September 1994.

17. From a discussion between Morley Winograd and Bill Clinton on Sunday, May 18, 1991, just before the DLC convention began.

18. Ronald Brownstein, "Clinton Must Still Search for Ways to Break Gridlock," *Los Angeles Times,* 22 August 1994, A3.

19. Janet Hook, "Voters Tell GOP Moderates They Share Doubts on Agenda," *Los Angeles Times,* 16 April 1995, A1.

20. Gillespie and Schellhas, 50.

21. John J. Fialka, "NRA Support for House GOP Freshmen Pays Off, But Lawmakers Worry About Reformer Image," *Wall Street Journal,* 20 June 1995, A20.

22. Joe Davidson, "Bill to Broaden Criminal Evidence Passes in House," *Wall Street Journal,* 9 February 1995, A8.

23. Gingrich, *Renew,* 202. For a summary of the arguments of the "Standard Model" see "Second Amendment Symposium" issue of the *Tennessee Law Review,* Spring 1995 (University of Tennessee, Knoxville College of Law). The five people whose arguments in favor of this constitutional interpretation are most often cited are Robert J. Cottrel, Stephen P. Halbrook, Don B. Kates, Joyce Lee Malcolm, and Robert E. Shalhope.

24. Gerald F. Seib, "Terrorism Fear Running Deep, U.S. Poll Finds," *Wall Street Journal,* 27 April 1995, 14.

25. Joe Davidson and Christopher Georges, "Crime-Legislation Revision Threatens to Create a Split Among Republicans," *Wall Street Journal,* 14 February 1995, A22.

26. Michael Ross, "House Pushes Revision of Omnibus Crime Bill," *Los Angeles Times,* 10 February 1995, A21.

27. Joe Davidson, "Pataki, New York GOP Stalwart, May Lead Way to Ending Some Mandated Minimum Sentences," *Wall Street Journal,* 2 May 1995, A26.

28. Charles Oliver, "The Trade-offs in the Drug War," *Investor's Business Daily,* 4 May 1995, A1.

29. Oliver, A2.

30. Joseph A. Califano, "It's Drugs, Stupid," *New York Times Magazine,* 29 January 1995, 40.

31. William Dunn, "When Dealing Drugs Is a Second Job," *American Demographics,* January 1992, 17.

32. Oliver, A2.

33. James Q. Wilson, *Crime and Human Nature* (New York: Simon and Schuster, 1985), 44. In 1975 Wilson published a major treatise that attempted to use all the known research on the causes and nature of crime to support a general theory of criminal behavior, suggesting it was developed through a choice individuals make based on the consequences of committing a crime: "The consequences of committing the crime consist of rewards and punishments; the consequences of not committing the crime also entail gains and losses. The larger the ratio of the net rewards of crime to the net rewards of noncrime, the greater the tendency to commit the crime." The theory, however, fails to take into account the impact of the community in which he is raised or lives on the individual's calculations.

34. Kolbert, 48.

35. Michael Ross, "Democrats Unite Against GOP Crime Bill," *Los Angeles Times,* 14 February 1995, A16.

36. Fox Butterfield, "Policy Leaders Are Disturbed by GOP Crime Bill," *New York Times,* 16 February 1995, A16.

37. Joe Davidson, "President Clinton Threatens Veto as House Prepares to Vote on Crime Bill," *Wall Street Journal,* 13 February 1995, A16.

38. John Hoerr, "The Payoff from Teamwork," *Business Week,* 10 July 1989, 56.

39. John Burgess, "The Happy Union of People and Machines: Survey Finds Increasing Acceptance of Technology," *Washington Post,* 30 May 1994, WB 13.

40. Amanda Bennett, "Economists Demonstrate that Neighbors, Not Wardens, Hold Keys to Cutting Crime," *Wall Street Journal,* 7 December 1994, B1.

41. "Making Cities Safer, Good Fences . . . ," *The Economist,* 25 March 1995, 30–31.

42. Courtland Milloy, "A Little Slice of Paradise in Washington," *Washington Post,* 17 May 1995, B1.

43. Natalie S. Glance and Bernardo A. Huberman, "Dynamics of Social Dilemmas," *Scientific American,* March 1994, 76.

44. John DiIulio, Jr., "Why Violent Crime Rates Have Dropped," *Wall Street Journal,* 6 September 1995, A17.

45. Haynes Johnson, *Divided We Fall* (New York: Norton, 1994), 214–16.

46. William D. Eggers and John O'Leary, "No Easy Answers," *Reason,* February 1995, 51.

47. Hoerr, 57.

48. Ed Kilgore, interview by Morley Winograd, 31 May 1995.

49. Summers, 13.

50. Summers, 144–45.

9. Rethinking Race Relations

1. Al From, "The New Politics," *Mainstream Democrat,* March 1991, 4.

2. From, interview.

3. Peter A. Brown, "The Democratic Dilemma," *Campaigns and Elections,* May–June 1989, 36.

4. William A. Galston, "Rebuilding a Presidential Majority," *Mainstream Democrat* 1.1 (September–October 1989), 11.

5. William Galston and Elaine Ciulla Kamarck, *The Politics of Evasion: Democrats and the Presidency* (Washington, D.C.: Progressive Policy Institute, September 1989), 7.

6. David Eugene Price, *Bringing Back the Parties* (Washington, D.C.: Congressional Quarterly, 1984), 145.

7. From notes taken by Morley Winograd, who participated in the meeting as Michigan Democratic party chairman.

8. Morley Winograd attended the meeting in the latter capacity; quotations from personal notes taken.

9. Because Michigan election laws at the time permitted members of either party to vote in each other's primary in violation of the national party's rules, the state Democratic party held a separate primary that year in which

only party members were allowed to vote. The national media treated Jackson's win as a major endorsement of his policies when it was, in fact, a tribute to the greater organizational skills of his campaign in making sure this limited set of voters went to the voting locations established by the party.

10. Jesse L. Jackson, testimony before the Democratic party's Fairness Commission, New Orleans, 24 August 1985.

11. Democratic Leadership Council, *The New American Choice: Opportunity, Responsibility, Community: Resolutions Adopted at the 1991 DLC Convention, Cleveland, Ohio* (Washington, D.C.: DLC, 1991), 8. The altered wording quoted here is from the records of the convention parliamentarian.

12. Al From and Will Marshall, "New Democrats and the 1994 Elections," *Third Force*, November 1994, 2.

13. Hugh Davis Graham, *The Civil Rights Era: Origins and Development of National Policy, 1960–1972* (New York: Oxford University Press, 1990), 331.

14. "Congress and the Nation," *Congressional Quarterly* 3 (1973), 711.

15. California Civil Rights Initiative pamphlet. Berkeley, Section (a).

16. Arnold Rothstein, personal interviews by Morley Winograd, January–April 1995.

17. Excerpted from President Clinton's speech at the National Archives on federal affirmative action programs, as recorded by the Federal News Service, July 18, 1995.

18. Paul Richter, "Consultant Dick Morris' Low-Profile Influence on the President Confounds Both Democrats and his GOP Clients," *Los Angeles Times*, 17 June 1995 (Prodigy file).

19. Paul Richter, "Democrats Listen for Tick of Jesse Jackson Time Bomb," *Los Angeles Times*, 18 July 1995, A1.

20. Steven Roberts, "Affirmative Action on the Edge," *U.S. News & World Report*, 13 February 1995, 35.

21. Drucker, "Transformation," 62.

22. Seymour Martin Lipset, *American Exceptionalism: A Double-Edged Sword*, unpublished manuscript.

23. William P. O'Hare, Kelvin M. Pollard, Tania L. Mann, and Mary M. Kent, "African Americans in the 1990s," *Population Review*, June 1991, 8, 28.

24. Henry Aaron, "Symposium on the Economic Status of African Americans," *Journal of Economic Perspectives* 4 (Fall 1990), 5.

25. Joel Kotkin, "The Hot Zone: Why Did the Affirmative Action Debate Erupt in California?" *New Democrat* 7.3 (May–June 1995), 16.

26. Shireman, "Wealth," 39–40.

27. University of California, "The UC System's Student Body," *Los Angeles Times*, 20 January 1995: A24. African Americans comprised 6.2 percent of the UCLA student body and 5.6 percent of Berkeley's compared to only 4.3 percent in the system as a whole, with less than 4.5 percent at any other campus.

28. Alan Chute, interview by Morley Winograd, 5 September 1995.

29. See Paul M. Barrett, "Birmingham's Plan to Help Black Owned Firms May Be Alternative to Racial Set-Aside Programs," *Wall Street Journal*, 27 February 1995, A14.

10. Empowering America's Schools

1. Lawrence Mishel and Jared Bernstein, *The State of Working America* (New York: M. E. Sharpe, 1994), 331.

2. Drucker, "Transformation," 54, 56.

3. Robert B. Westbrook, *John Dewey and American Democracy* (Ithaca: Cornell University Press, 1991), 180–82.

4. Westbrook, 170–72.

5. Westbrook, 182.

6. Richard G. Lefauve and Arnoldo C. Hax, "Managerial and Technological Innovations at Saturn Corporation," *MIT Management,* Spring 1992, 9.

7. Michelle Krebs, "Smith's Legacy," *Automotive News,* 16 July 1990, 43.

8. Lefauve and Hax, 9.

9. James Gleick, *Chaos: Making a New Science* (New York: Penguin, 1987), 121–53.

10. James C. Collins and Jerry I. Porras, *Built to Last: Successful Habits of Visionary Companies* (New York: Harper Business, 1994), 5–6.

11. Lefauve and Hax, 11.

12. Lefauve and Hax, 10.

13. Cleveland, Neuroth, and Plastrik, 23.

14. Ron Wolk, "Lessons from Saturn," unpublished manuscript (prepared for *Education Week*), March 1994, 4.

15. Beverly Geber, "Saturn's Grand Experiment," *Training,* June 1992, 31.

16. Wolk, 4.

17. Geber, 29.

18. Geber, 32.

19. Geber, 28.

20. Lefauve and Hax, 18.

21. Geber, 28.

22. Virginia Kemball, interview by Morley Winograd, 5 August 1995.

23. Deborah Meier, *The Power of Their Ideas* (Boston: Beacon Press, 1995), 4.

24. H. Smith, 153–56.

25. H. Smith, 154.

26. H. Smith, 165.

27. Ted Kolderie, "Beyond Choice to New Public Schools: Withdrawing the Exclusive Franchise in Public Education," Progressive Policy Institute *Policy Report No. 8,* November 1990, 10.

28. Jon Pepper, "It's Time for Schools to Learn a Business Rule: Competition Means Improvement," *Detroit News,* 25 June 1995, 1D.

29. Dennis Kelly, "Easing Rules but Requiring Hard Results," *USA Today,* 7 June 1995, 1D.

30. Claudia Wallis, "A Class of Their Own," *Time,* 31 October 1994, 54–55.

31. Wallis, 54.

32. Jean Merl, "Rethinking Schools: Charter Puts Fenton on Fast Track to Success," *Los Angeles Times,* 23 October 1994, B3.

33. Nanette Asimov, " 'Dream' School Prepares to Open in S.F.," *San Francisco Chronicle*, 8 September 1994, A15.

34. Wallis, 58.

35. Peter Applebome, "Some Educators See Experimental Hybrids as Country's Best Hope for Public Schools," *New York Times*, 12 October 1994, B7.

36. Alan Katz, "Charter School Proposed: Fundamental Academy Surprises Cherry Creek," *Denver Post*, 12 June 1995, 1B.

37. Editorial, "Denver School Board Flunks Charter School Test—Again," *Denver Post*, 24 April 1995, B7.

38. Gabriella Stern, "Saturn's Mystique Is Endangered as GM Changes the Car and the Organization," *Wall Street Journal*, 27 July 1995, B1.

39. Smith, 170.

40. Chester Finn, Jr., and Diane Ravitch, "Charter Schools—Beware Imitations," *Wall Street Journal*, 7 September 1995, A14.

41. Kenneth G. Wilson and Bennett Daviss, *Redesigning Education* (New York: Henry Holt & Co., 1994), 22.

42. Lewis J. Perelman, *School's Out* (New York: Avon Books, 1992), 141.

43. Perelman, 218–19, 222.

44. Wilson and Daviss, 204.

45. Wilson and Daviss, 72–75.

46. Drucker, *Post-Capitalist Society*, 66.

11. Retraining America's Workforce

1. Doug Ross, interview by Morley Winograd, 4 December 1994.

2. Drucker, "Transformation," 71.

3. Peter Plastrik, "Reinventing the Federal Unemployment and Training System: Helping Millions of American Workers Secure New Jobs," Progressive Policy Institute *Policy Report No. 19*, March 1994, 6.

4. "Government Doesn't Work," *Focus Group Discussions Among Unemployed Workers*, videotape prepared for the U.S. Department of Labor by Yankelovich Partners, 15 February 1994.

5. Plastrik, 4.

6. Fred R. Bleakley, "Job Searches Still Last Months, or Years, for Many Middle-Aged Middle Managers," *Wall Street Journal*, 18 September 1995, B1.

7. Doug Ross, interview by Morley Winograd, 4 December 1994.

8. Rothschild, 213–25. In his presentations the author uses a graph of the different types of grocery stores, vividly illustrating the point Ross coincidentally was trying to make.

9. Peter Plastrik, "A GI Bill for American Workers," *New Democrat*, January-February 1995, 24.

10. Plastrik, "Reinventing," 3.

11. Doug Ross, interview by Morley Winograd, 5 December 1994.

12. David Stoesz, "Social Service Vouchers: Bringing Choice and Compe-

tition to Social Services," Progressive Policy Institute *Policy Report No. 16,* July 1992, 2.

13. Stoesz, 3–4.

14. William Ford, interview by Morley Winograd, 15 July 1992.

15. Statement by Doug Ross before the Subcommittee on Labor, HHS, and Education Appropriations, U.S. House of Representatives, 22 February 1995, 3.

16. Office of the American Workplace, U.S. Department of Labor, *Integrating Technology with Workers in the American Workplace,* internal document (Washington, D.C.: U.S. Department of Labor, 1993).

17. Thomas Roberts, "Who Are the High-Tech Home Workers?" *Inc. Annual,* 1994, 31.

18. Christopher Georges, "Most Americans See Their Income Slip Even Though the Economy Is Booming," *Wall Street Journal,* 26 October 1994, A2.

19. Georges, A14.

20. VRS.

21. Doug Ross, interview by Morley Winograd, 6 November 1995.

22. Plastrik, "GI Bill," 25.

23. Morton Kondracke, "Neo-Politics: The Left-Right Smooch In," *New Republic,* 25 November 1991, 20. This very informal group, which existed in Washington during the Bush administration, included Jim Pinkerton, of Bush's domestic policy staff, William Bennett, Elaine Kamarck, HUD Secretary Jack Kemp, Governor Lamar Alexander, PPI Fellow Bill Galston, Representatives Newt Gingrich and Vin Weber, Senators Bill Bradley and Joe Leiberman, and David Osborne. Its most substantive accomplishment was a day-long symposium entitled, "Left and Right: The Emergence of a New Politics in the 1990's?" (30 October 1991), which first explored the possibilities of an information age politics not based on those ideological divisions.

24. Al From and Jack Kemp, "GI Bill for Workers' Empowerment: Job Training," *Los Angeles Times,* 20 June 1995, B9.

25. Doug Ross, interview by Morley Winograd, 22 July 1995.

26. Asra Q. Nomani, "Common Ground: Overhaul of Job Training Seems a Bipartisan Pushover," *Wall Street Journal,* 6 June 1995, A1.

27. Governor James Blanchard, interview by Morley Winograd, 9 July 1995.

28. Dennis Mulqueen, "Tuition Plan Swamped by 82,495 Applicants," *Detroit News,* 12 August 1988, 1A.

29. "MET, The Nation's First Prepaid College Tuition Program," *Q&A* (Lansing, 1995), 5.

30. Mulqueen, 8A.

31. Chris Christoff, "State May Dust Off MET Tuition Plan," *Detroit Free Press,* 3 July 1995, 1A.

32. Eric Koeplin, interview by Morley Winograd, 4 August 1995.

33. Christoff, 2A.

34. Pete Waldmeir, "Engler Has Enough Sense Not to Sink the MET Fund, No Matter How Badly He Wants to End It," *Detroit News,* 19 August 1991, B1.

35. Christoff, 2A.

36. Steven Waldman, *The Bill* (New York: Viking Press, 1995), 121.

37. Waldman, 62–67.

38. Waldman, 131–40.

39. Waldman, 235–45.

12. Creating a Learning Economy

1. Jim Roche (Marshall's confidante), interview by Morley Winograd, 4 September 1994.

2. William E. DePuy, "FM 100-5 Revisited," *Army*, November 1980, 17.

3. Thomas E. Ricks, "How Wars Are Fought Will Change Radically, Pentagon Planner Says," *Wall Street Journal*, 15 July 1994, A1.

4. Bradley Graham, "Revolutionary Warfare: New Technologies Are Transforming the U.S. Military," *Washington Post National Weekly Edition*, 6–12 March 1995, 6.

5. "The Information Advantage," *The Economist*, 10 June 1995, survey 5.

6. Graham, 6. Admiral William Owens, vice chairman of the Joint Chiefs of Staff and in charge of the military's effort in this area, states that the trick is to manage all the pieces to gain "dominant battlefield awareness. . . . It is a challenge for us to realize the vision of the system of systems."

7. Womack, *Machine*, 109–20.

8. William M. Bulkeley, "Pushing the Pace: The Latest Big Thing at Many Companies is Speed, Speed, Speed," *Wall Street Journal*, 23 December 1994, A1.

9. Michael Selz, "Small Manufacturers Display the Nimbleness the Times Require," *Wall Street Journal*, 29 December 1993, A1.

10. Office of the Press Secretary, "Remarks by President Clinton, President Bush, President Carter, President Ford, and Vice President Gore in Signing of NAFTA Side Agreements," (Washington, D.C.: The White House, 14 September 1993), 11.

11. Greenberg, *Dreams*, 33.

12. Paul Krugman, "Does Third World Growth Hurt First World Prosperity?" *Harvard Business Review*, July–August 1994, 113–20. He also presents the clearest case for how economic growth in less-developed countries can lead to increased living standards for citizens of more-industrialized countries, even where wage rates are as disparate as between the United States and Mexico. His analysis does suggest, however, that this kind of increased competition between different types of economies might account for some of the current inequalities of income in the United States.

13. Cleveland, 30.

14. Cleveland, 34.

15. Helene Cooper and John Harwood. "World Trade Pact Limps Toward a Showdown, Bruised by Talk Radio, Sovereignty Issue, Politics," *Wall Street Journal*, 23 November 1994, A16.

16. Helene Cooper and John Harwood, "The Rules Change: Major Shifts in Global Trade Are Ensured as Senate Gives GATT Final Approval," *Wall Street Journal*, 2 December 1994, A1.

17. Michael Clough, "The Global Connection," *Los Angeles Times*, 5 February 1995, M1.

18. David Friedman, *The New Economy Project, Final Report* (Los Angeles: New Vision Business Council of Southern California, 5 August 1994), I–4. As Friedman has pointed out, the actual job losses in California were concentrated almost entirely in Los Angeles and occurred for the most part because of cutbacks in defense industry spending and a cyclical decline in construction spending. The new economy was growing so rapidly it overrode all other factors.

19. Ronald Brownstein, "Immigration Debate Roils GOP Presidential Contest," *Los Angeles Times*, 14 May 1995, A18.

20. Brownstein, "Debate," A19.

21. Hilary Stout, "House GOP Won't Revise Plan to Deny Aid to Teenage Mothers, Legal Aliens," *Wall Street Journal*, 13 January 1995, A16.

22. Rich Thomas, "America: Still a Melting Pot?" *Newsweek*, 9 August 1993, 18.

23. Brownstein, "Debate," A19.

24. Joel Kotkin, "Nativists on the Left," *Wall Street Journal*, 25 July 1995, A12.

25. Friedman, *Project*, I–12.

26. Kotkin, "Nativists," A12. Kotkin points out that the "order left" is as interested in restricting immigration as their supposedly sworn enemies on the "order right," but for different reasons. Once again, both groups unite in opposition to creating a more dynamic society.

27. James A. Johnson, "What Immigrants Want," *Wall Street Journal*, 20 June 1995, A18.

28. Friedman, *Project*, I–15.

29. Terence Roth, "Global Report Finds U.S. Has Replaced Japan as the Most Competitive Economy," *Wall Street Journal*, 7 September 1994, A3. The 16,500 business leaders surveyed considered economic strength, international activity, government policy, financial markets, infrastructure, management, science and technology, and the skills of the populace in reaching their judgments.

30. Terence Roth, "U.S. Is Ranked Most Competitive Economy in the World," *Wall Street Journal*, 6 September 1995, A2.

31. Michael Clough, "The Global Connection," *Los Angeles Times*, 5 February 1995, M1. Clough estimates that 23 percent of the United States manufacturing output is exported and 28 percent of the goods Americans buy are imported.

32. "American Business: Back on Top?" *The Economist*, 16 September 1995, S4.

33. Roth, "Global," A3.

34. James Gerstenzang, "Three U.S. Industries Leading the Way in Global Economy," *Los Angeles Times*, 27 January 1995, A1.

35. Roth, "Global," A3.

36. Gerstenzang, A12.

37. Womack, 146–48.

38, David Friedman, interview by Morley Winograd, 25 May 1995.

39. Gerstenzang, A12.

40. Larry D. Browning, Janice M. Beyer, and Judy C. Shetler, "Building Cooperation in a Competitive Industry: Sematech and the Semiconductor Industry," *Academy of Management Journal*, February 1995, 113.

41. David Friedman, interview by Morley Winograd, 25 May 1995.

42. Gerstenzang, A12.

43. Friedman, *Project*, ES 5–6.

44. Saxenian, 166–67.

45. David Friedman, "Nomo," *Los Angeles Times*, 16 February 1995, B6.

46. Briefing on the "Bottoms Up Review" conducted by Deputy Secretary of Defense John Deutsch at the Pentagon, 9 September 1993.

47. Thomas E. Ricks, "Gingrich Blasts Clinton's Plans for Pentagon," *Wall Street Journal*, 9 February 1995, A3.

48. Ricks, "Wars," A1.

49. "Defense Technology," *The Economist*, 10 June 1995, survey 11–16.

Conclusion: The New American Social Contract

1. Hart and Teeter, *Study 4039*.

2. John Harwood, "Sluggish 'Revolution' Has Voters Thinking Politicians Are All Alike," *Wall Street Journal*, 28 August 1995, A1.

3. Robert L. Jackson, "Poll Finds Support for Independent Race," *Los Angeles Times*, 24 August 1995, A16.

4. Richard Benedetto, "Some Second Thoughts About a Third Party," *USA Today*, 29 September 1995, 5A.

5. Robert Jackson, A16.

6. Simon Rosenberg, interview by Morley Winograd, 6 October 1995.

7. Gerald F. Seib, "Presidential Races Are Being Changed by Latest Technology," *Wall Street Journal*, 4 August 1995, A1.

8. Gregory A. Patterson, "Target 'Micromarkets' Its Way to Success: No Two Stores Are Alike," *Wall Street Journal*, 31 May 1995, A1.

9. Glenn Rifkin, " 'Digital' Jeans Pour Data and Legs into Customized Fit," *New York Times*, November 8, 1994, A1.

10. *This Week with David Brinkley*, ABC, KABC, Los Angeles, 24 September 1995.

11. Fred Steeper, "This Swing Is Different: Analysis of 1994 Election Exit Polls," *Cook Political Report*, 8 February 1995, 8.

12. Hart and Teeter, *Study 4045, 4049*.

13. Paul Sperry, "A Changing Information Market," *Investor's Business Daily*, 27 March 1995, 1.

14. Gerald Seib, "Republican Hopefuls Jockey for Position as Race for Presidential Nomination Gets Early Start," *Wall Street Journal*, 29 December 1994, A12.

15. Hock, "Institutions."

16. Membership in the Internet Society or ISOC (International Society for Open Computing) is drawn from commercial, government, and nonprofit institutions on a voluntary basis.

17. "The Accidental Superhighway," *The Economist*, 1 July 1995, survey 6.

18. "Accidental Superhighway," survey 7.

19. "E-lectioneering," 21.

20. Tracey Westen, "Can Technology Save Democracy?" Electronic Democracy Conference, Washington, D.C., 6 June 1994.

21. Henry Cabot Lodge, ed., *The Federalist* (New York: Modern Library, 1941), 337.

22. Chickering, 92.

23. Al From commenting on Congressman Bill Ford's reaction to the DLC's proposal.

24. New Hampshire debate.

25. Gingrich, *Renew*, 202.

26. Robert B. Hawkins, Jr., and Flagg Taylor, *From "Projects" to Communities* (ICS Press: San Francisco, 1995).

27. Tocqueville, *Democracy in America*.

· SELECTED BIBLIOGRAPHY ·

Chickering, A. Lawrence. *Beyond Left and Right: Breaking the Political Stalemate.* San Francisco: ICS Press, 1992.

Collins, James C., and Jerry I. Porras. *Built to Last: Successful Habits of Visionary Companies.* New York: Harper Business, 1994.

Davis, Stanley M. *Future Perfect.* Reading, Mass.: Addison-Wesley, 1987.

DeLamarter, Richard Thomas. *Big Blue: IBM's Use and Abuse of Power.* New York: Dodd, Mead, 1986.

Drucker, Peter F. *The New Realities: In Government and Politics, in Economics and Business, in Society and World View.* New York: Harper Business, 1994.

———. *Post-Capitalist Society.* New York: HarperCollins, 1993.

Germond, Jack W., and Jules Witcover. *Mad As Hell: Revolt at the Ballot Box.* New York: Warner Books, 1993.

Gingrich, Newt. *To Renew America.* New York: HarperCollins, 1995.

Gleick, James. *Chaos: Making a New Science.* New York: Penguin, 1987.

Greenberg, Stanley B. *Middle Class Dreams: The Politics and Power of the New American Majority.* New York: Times Books, 1995.

Hammer, Michael, and James Champy. *Reengineering the Corporation: A Manifesto for Business Revolution.* New York: Harper Business, 1992.

Johnson, Haynes. *Divided We Fall.* New York: Norton, 1994.

Keller, Maryann. *Rude Awakening: The Rise, Fall, and Struggle for Recovery of General Motors.* New York: Morrow, 1989.

Kelly, Kevin. *Out of Control: The Rise of Neo-Biological Civilization.* Reading, Mass.: Addison-Wesley, 1994.

Matalin, Mary, and James Carville. *All's Fair: Love, War, and Running for President.* New York: Random House, 1994.

Meier, Deborah. *The Power of Their Ideas.* Boston: Beacon Press, 1995.

Morrison, Ian, and Greg Schmid. *Future Tense: The Business Realities of the Next Ten Years.* New York: Morrow, 1994.

Naisbitt, John. *Global Paradox.* New York: Morrow, 1994.

Negroponte, Nicholas. *Being Digital.* New York: Knopf, 1995.

Osborne, David, and Ted Gaebler. *Reinventing Government: How the Entrepreneurial Spirit Is Transforming the Public Sector.* Reading, Mass.: Addison-Wesley, 1992.

Phillips, Kevin P. *The Boiling Point: Republicans, Democrats, and the Decline of Middle-Class Prosperity.* New York: Random House, 1993.

Rothschild, Michael. *Bionomics: Economy as Ecosystem.* New York: Henry Holt & Co., 1990.

Saxenian, AnnaLee. *Regional Advantage: Culture and Competition in Silicon Valley and Route 128.* Cambridge: Harvard University Press, 1994.

Smith, Hedrick. *Rethinking America.* New York: Random House, 1995.

Summers, Harry G. *A Critical Analysis of the Gulf War.* New York: Dell, 1992.

Waldman, Steven. *The Bill.* New York: Viking Press, 1995.

Westbrook, Robert B. *John Dewey and American Democracy.* Ithaca: Cornell University Press, 1991.

Wilson, James Q. *Crime and Human Nature.* New York: Simon and Schuster, 1985.

Womack, James P., Daniel T. Jones, and Daniel Roos. *The Machine That Changed the World: The Story of Lean Production.* New York: Harper Perennial, 1991.

Woodward, Bob. *The Agenda.* New York: Simon and Schuster, 1994.

· INDEX ·